Christine Hogan is a Sydney-based writer and journalist who has worked as an editor in newspapers and magazines, as a network executive, and as a news, current affairs and documentary producer in television. *Men: A User's Guide* is her first book. She is currently writing her first screenplay.

men
A User's Guide

Christine Hogan

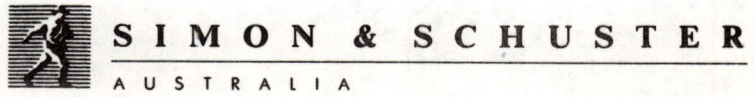

MEN: A USER's GUIDE
First published in Australia in 2003 by
Simon & Schuster (Australia) Pty Limited
20 Barcoo Street, East Roseville NSW 2069

A Viacom Company
Sydney New York London Toronto Singapore

Visit our website at www.simonsaysaustralia.com.au

© Christine Hogan, 2003

All rights reserved. No part of this publication may be reproduced, stored in a retrieval system, or transmitted, in any form or by any means, electronic, mechanical, photocopying, recording or otherwise, without the prior permission of the publisher in writing.

National Library of Australia
Cataloguing-in-Publication data

Hogan, Christine (Christine Anne).
Men : a user's guide

ISBN 0 7318 1025 2.

1. Man-woman relationships. 2. Mate selection.
3. Men - Psychology I. Title.

646.77

Cover design by treehouse creative
Internal design by Avril Makula GRAVITY ADD
Typesetting by Letter Spaced
Typeset in Sabon 11 pt on 16 pt
Printed in Australia by Griffin Press

10 9 8 7 6 5 4 3 2 1

Contents

Acknowledgements ix
Introduction xi

The facts of modern life
1 User or loser? You choose 3

The big questions
2 What's love got to do with it? 11
3 Does a woman need a man? 24
4 What do men really want? 28

Preparation is everything
5 Spit and polish … hers 33
6 The sweet smell of sexual success 45

Comes the moment, comes the man
7 Where do you get one? 55
8 The dating game 66
9 Love out-sourced 78

Natural selection
10 Different, not equal 91
11 Mummy dearest 99
12 Pick me! Pick me! 105
13 Stereotypes and other clichés 114

Putting the man under man-agement
14 The 'F' word 131
15 Unified Theory 144
16 Let's talk about sex, baby 150

Basic history for Users
- 17 Some great Users in history   163
- 18 And some great losers...   178

Comes the man, comes the makeover
- 19 Manners maketh the man   191
- 20 Once were cockscombs   201
- 21 God is in the detail   218
- 22 Care and maintenance (on-going)   228
- 23 Tattoo, you?   233

Troubleshooting
- 24 Time out   241
- 25 Love gone wrong   245
- 26 The other woman   252

Strategies
- 27 Say a little prayer for him?   263
- 28 The smart User's rules   269

Dedication

For my parents, John and Mary Hogan, who gave me many things, including an example of what a partnership between a man and a woman could be, if it were based, as theirs was, on love, admiration, respect, shared values — and a keen sense of the ridiculous.

Acknowledgments

Where to start to acknowledge my debts for the enormous efforts of so many people who have helped me with this project? Perhaps with my agent, Harry M. Miller, who encouraged the idea of *Men: A User's Guide* from its earliest moments and through the years bullied, cajoled, wheedled then finally embarrassed this book out of me. To Harry, my thanks for showing me that not only did I have a book in me and what to do about it, but also for keeping the faith.

To all the staff at the Harry M. Miller Group, past and present, my thanks also go, particularly to Linda McClelland, Suzanne Hannema and Wendy Cohen. They held my hand at various stages of the process and said exactly the right thing at the right time.

My unending gratitude belongs to former publisher at Simon & Schuster Angelo Loukakis, who understood the idea based on the title, and his associate, Jody Lee, who was patient and never gave up hope while she waited to see what would emerge. Thanks, too, to Simon & Schuster's managing director, Jon Attenborough, and all his staff, for supporting and maintaining the project.

Julia Collingwood, managing editor at Simon & Schuster, did me a personal, as well as professional, favour when she handed the draft of *Men: A User's Guide* to writer and editor Suzanne Falkiner for assessment and then structural edit. During the process, which might otherwise have been tiresome and quarrelsome, Suzanne guided me in the right direction with clarity, kindness, and understanding. As a coach, she propped me up when I looked feeble, and gently insisted on a couple of additional elements — for one of which I am greatly in her debt. This book owes much to her skills and patience.

Line editor, Joanne MacKay, saved me from further disasters. Any errors that remain, I'm afraid, are mine alone.

Several other people nurtured me during the time I was writing this book: principal among them are my family and friends. As well, there was a special support squad — Jean Salvadore at the Grand Hotel Villa d'Este on Lake Como (which is not a bad place to go to contemplate love and romance); Italia Giagu, who gave me space and a desk to write on in Sardinia and welcomed me into her family at the same time; and Sue Woolfe, my writing teacher. Sue taught me during a Sydney University writers' retreat late one spring in Tuscany, and became my mentor, and more importantly, my friend. Words really cannot express my thanks to and admiration for them all.

Some men are standout examples of their sex and provided inspiration while I was writing this book. They include my brother, Peter; my friend Sam; *mon professeur* Monsieur Jacques; and my occasional correspondent George the navigator, who helped me find my bearings just when I needed them most.

Many women, particularly Jane, Gail, Jacki and Mandy, have contributed to this book also by their support, frankness and openness about their lies, feelings and relationships. I am so grateful for their trust in me and for their confidence that these stories would be handled sensitively.

And as for any man from my past who suspects he sees traces of himself in these pages, you're wrong. It wasn't you. It was one of those other guys.

Introduction

I began writing this book for a couple of reasons. The first was completely selfish. For some time I had been wondering about men and my relationships with them.

For a woman who loves men, I wasn't doing so well in the romance stakes. (Understatement. Serious understatement.) In fact, I was doing so badly I had almost decided to pull up stumps and give up any thoughts of a steady, loving and supportive relationship with a man.

It couldn't be them, it must be me, my lack of confidence told me. After some spectacularly bad choices and the accompanying emotional train wrecks, I was just about ready to take the veil, figuratively speaking, and resign myself literally to life as a born-again nun. Like many women, I had kissed a lot of frogs and just couldn't face any more.

But it was startlingly clear that I was not the only woman to find herself in this situation. There is a growing number of women in their thirties and forties, well-educated women with good jobs, interesting and otherwise happy women, who have given up on the mating and dating game and resigned themselves to singlehood.

And there are women in the same age-group who, depressed by the prospect of having to date, will stay in patently problematic relationships, or pick complete duds as partners, just so they won't have to be single.

About this time, I began to turn my 'it's not them, it's me' thinking around, and consider the shocking prospect — what if it were them, that my problem was just picking the wrong blokes, and not that there was something deeply awry with me? I wanted to try again — but this time, I wanted to be prepared.

Now preparation is something that isn't frequently associated with going into a relationship. Quite often, these ignite in the heat of the moment, when judgement is obscured, and chemistry takes over.

But like many uncontrolled experiments by amateurs with chemistry sets and a nameless packet of crystals, these things can tend to blow up in your face. Sometimes that can happen explosively in just a short time, and sometimes it can be a slow fiasco over decades and involve children and even grandchildren.

Choosing a mate is one of the most important decisions anyone can make in a lifetime, or in the lives of their children, so why wouldn't someone want to be ready for that, I thought.

It was a watershed moment, and I wondered where the manual was to help me discover what I might have been doing wrong, and what I might do right to improve a future relationship. What I needed was a handbook to figuring out men and how to manage them. I haunted bookshops looking for one, which would cover the question but deliver the answer in a way that was fun at the same time.

I looked and I looked but found nothing that helped. Here was the second reason to write this book myself — it might have some value to other women who find themselves in the same position.

So I started the field research, and was amazed by the people I met, the frankness with which women discussed relationships with men in the early twenty-first century, and the openness with which men discussed the situation with me. In fact, I became so addicted to doing the research, I didn't want to stop it.

When I told people the title of my book, there were two fairly typical reactions. One was a slow delight, to think that women might finally be able to own up to managing men, after millennia of doing it by stealth. And the second was shock from some people — what on earth was I doing writing this, after a career of writing about contemporary social issues for major newspapers and magazines, as well as having worked on the feminist bible, *Ms.* magazine, in New York?

To me, there is no difference between what these publications did and what this book is designed to do — help women live their lives better. The focus of much of my writing was, among other things, about managing your stocks,

Introduction

building a better CV, asking for a raise — all the things that women needed in the 1980s as they climbed the corporate ladder.

This book is about looking at the last great frontier for women — how they can live and work in the modern world and still manage to create and maintain loving and enriching relationships with men.

In doing this, I have discovered a number of things which women today might have forgotten, and could do well to remember, as well as some new twists for the modern relationship.

If you are a woman who has ended up on the debit side of love and want to discover something of how to meet and manage men for fun and possibly something more, this might well be the place to start figuring out what you want. Friend or fling? Boyfriend or long-term lover? The choice is yours — just make sure it is rational and informed.

Has it worked for me? Well, I'm not going to say too much about my private life just now, but I can tell you I have had a grin on my face a lot more often of late.

I'd love to hear how you go with your own male-meet-and-manage endeavours. If you like, drop me an email on usersguideprimer@yahoo.com.au. Good luck — and whatever you do, don't forget to enjoy yourself!

Christine Hogan
Sydney
June 2003

the facts of modern life

1
User or loser? You choose

The front page of the morning newspaper can, on occasion, ruin your day. Things start well: you get up, have a shower, a cup of tea, fight the early morning peak-hour traffic. So far, so good. You grab a cappuccino and the newspaper on the way in to work. You are glancing through it then suddenly, disaster in black and white in your newspaper. The article's conclusion is familiar and goes something like this: if you are a single woman and close to 40, you have more chance of being hijacked by terrorists, kidnapped by pirates or even hit by lightning than getting married.

As you read the paper, you recognise this as one of those frequent stories about marriage rates in Australia. For many women in their late twenties and thirties who think they have all the time in the world to form a relationship with a significant other and possibly have a family, it's like an arrow straight through their hearts.

'Australians have never been so lonely,' was the declaration that opened a recent story in Sydney's *Daily Telegraph*. 'Census figures released yesterday show Bridget Jones and her male counterparts make up an increasing proportion of the Australian population, living solitary lives and eschewing the institution of marriage,' wrote journalist Anna Cock. The figures drawn from the 2001 census, indicated that some 1.56 million of us live in a one-person dwelling.

This bulletin about the lonely generation was bad news for those not in stable relationships who were hoping for an eventual dignified retirement from the mating and dating mega-meat market. The prospect of being single, alone and lonely until the grave might have made them gloomy enough to order a pineapple Danish or two to go with the skinny cap.

According to our national headcount, there are more 'available' women (never married, or separated, divorced or widowed) aged twenty-five to forty-four than men in every capital city, except Darwin. It also shows that nationally there *should* be 9000 more available men in that age group than women. The men are there in theory, but the Australian Bureau of Statistics (ABS) can't find them. (One demographer speculated that these available men are probably out being availed upon, rather than staying home on a chilly winter night to fill in a form for the stocktake.)

For conservatives, traditionalists and other advocates of family values, for hopeful singles, and mothers longing to be grandmothers before Hell freezes over, the figures don't look good. They're enough to depress anyone who ever thought that somewhere, sometime, a stable relationship might be not only a desirable but a realisable option. And then they tell us there are 9000 eligible men missing!

According to the ABS, the marriage rate has fallen to a 100 year low; some forty-two per cent of Australian women (and forty-four per cent of men) will never marry. Twenty odd years ago, that figure was twenty-five per cent and twenty-six per cent. The median age now for a trip down the aisle is around twenty-seven for women and thirty for men. Somehow, people have neglected to get married. *But why?*

The reasons more and more of us are avoiding marriage are obviously many and varied, but equally obviously those reasons include the threat of divorce. According to the Bureau's figures, the number of Australian marriages that end in divorce is around one in two — an unhappy record. And the average duration of a marriage is around eleven years. (This, interestingly, is about the same length of time that marriages lasted in England around the time of Henry VIII. But then it was death, not divorce, which turned men and women into serial marriers.)

All that pressure in the paper and you have just got to the office and the real work is yet to commence.

For some people, being single in an increasingly single world is a fine option. If that's what you want, then that's terrific. But many women don't. They want a modern version of the happy, stable, couple-based relationship, but can find themselves trapped in an increasingly unhappy search for a soulmate as well as a mate. So what can we do about it? Turn into a User, that's what. That's what this book is all about. But first we need to take a look at that word 'user'. For our purposes, 'user' means a woman who wants to be smarter about love and to manage her romantic life more effectively.

Men need Users more than Users need men

That's an encouraging thought, isn't it, and one that is not often appreciated by women. Give it a bit of consideration before you start your research to find Mr Right, or even Mr Okay He'll Do At A Pinch.

For those of you near fainting with horror at the idea of using another human being, just refer to a piece of constantly quoted research about the happiest group in Western society. For more than thirty years, the received wisdom was that single women were happier than married women. According to the same study, based on mental health data by the American researcher Jessie Barnard, the happiest people in society were married men. (The order was married men, single women, and then married women.) The unhappiest group? You guessed it, single men.

But recently, an Australian survey has turned this wisdom on its head. In this study, married women appear happier than their single sisters. Dr David de Vaus, senior research adviser at the Australian Institute of Family Studies, tested this theory on a sample of more than 10,000 Australian men and women — and found it to be untrue.

According to Dr de Vaus's study (published in *Family Matters* in 2002), if you are a single woman, you are more vulnerable to mental health problems than a married woman. The same goes for single men. Almost twenty-five per cent of never-married, divorced or separated men and women had experienced problems in the previous twelve months.

His figures show that of those surveyed thirteen per cent of married men and women had suffered a mental health problem in the same period. What was different for women was *what* they suffered. Women were more prone to depression and mood disorders than men, who were more likely to suffer from drug and alcohol related disorders.

So being married or in a relationship seems to be better for your mental health. But there's another reason *why having a relationship seems a good idea*: it's in our nature. No matter what advances feminism has made for women in terms of social, political and economic policy, some things remain the same: most of us look for partners to nurture and be cared for by. Since coupling is a biological and social urge, which for most of us is going to happen anyway, you owe it to yourself — and any children you might have — to do your utmost to get the best man and the best possible relationship you can.

> *Perhaps the greatest social service that can be rendered by anybody to the country and to mankind is to bring up a family. But here again, because there is nothing to sell, there is a very general disposition to regard a married woman's work as no work at all, and to take it as a matter of course that she should not be paid for it.*
> GEORGE BERNARD SHAW, 1856–1950

So how do you go about finding the right man? Ovid, in his *Ars Amatoria*, written 2000 years ago, gave advice to young women about where to find eligible young Romans — shops, art galleries and public parks were good, as were the public games, where young men could be cuddled up to on cramped seats. Ovid also advised on the right level of confidence to demonstrate when such a young man was found (not excessive). According to Ovid, love is a tricky god — you have to prove yourself worthy of it: something that requires mind and character, class and brains. Fortunately, these are the smart User's strong suits.

In the end, the choice to become a clever User is simple and it has nothing to do with turning yourself into a hard-hearted gold-digger, intent only on duping some poor innocent bloke out of his hard-earned money or his happily single state.

On the contrary, you can comfort yourself that using a man is for his own good. Men need to be used — it keeps them out of trouble and it brings out the best in them. (Any examination of prison figures in Australia will show you that the most represented people are single men.) It's symbiotic — if a man is well used and treats his woman well in return so that he gets more of the same, that's a fair exchange. By using a man properly, you are investing in his own long-term happiness — as well as your own.

So how do you do it? That's where *Men: A User's Guide* comes in. Think of it as your handbook for managing the most complicated and potentially most rewarding relationships of your life — the ones you have with those wonderful creatures, men.

the
big
questions

2
What's love got to do with it?

The French call it *le coup de foudre* — literally, the lightning strike. It's the moment when an individual is zapped by a bolt out of the blue and falls instantly, rapturously, and — almost always — dangerously in love. The *coup de foudre* has proved the undoing of many.

It happens all the time in literature. Jane Austen's supporting heroines spot a parson or a second son across a crowded ballroom and suddenly their destinies are incarnate. They set sail on a course of sin-free seduction from which none can dissuade them, and matrimony is the safe port at the end of it all. (Though perversely *Pride and Prejudice*'s Elizabeth Bennett takes one look at Mr Darcy and it's loathe-at-first-sight. She then spends the better part of three hundred pages overcoming a distaste for him before finally hurling herself heartily against his broad, broad-cloth clad chest.)

> *It is a truth universally acknowledged, that a single man in possession of a good fortune, must be in want of a wife.*
> JANE AUSTEN, 1775–1817

Elizabeth Bennett could have done with a copy of a contemporary version of *Men: A User's Guide*. It might have helped her abandon her prejudices earlier and to have seen the solid virtue which lay beneath Mr Darcy's glamorous surface and obdurate pride. Equally, any number of romantic heroines could have benefited from User strategies to help them choose and then secure the objects of their affections. Tragic Cathy from Emily Brontë's *Wuthering Heights* really needed to rethink how she picked a man. If she had paid attention, she would have recognised 'rough as a saw edge and hard as whinstone' Heathcliff was a toxic boyfriend from the very off.

It's one of Life's paradoxes: almost all of us want to fall in love and make a match which will endure and enrich us spiritually but hardly any of us have the faintest idea about how to make that happen and then how to make it last. You wouldn't step into an exam without having studied for it, would you? You wouldn't undertake a presentation at work without having prepared for it? So why would you start on an undertaking like falling in love — something which could affect you personally, your family, your future children — without preparing yourself for the eventualities?

And why would you continue to try to muddle through without a game plan if you have already settled upon your mate? There are things you can do to help make him a better man — and yourself a happier woman. That's where *Men: A User's Guide* comes in!

This is the basic premise of *Men: A User's Guide*: men are at once terrifically complicated and terribly simple creatures. Their mechanisms can be delicate: their egos certainly are. How much easier it would be for women, then, to manage them, and our relationships with them, if we had a manual! A handbook which would help women — the primary Users of men — manage them better: from love at first sight to strategies to managing love gone wrong, to man maintenance and how to deal with the other woman.

I know some of you might be feeling a little uneasy at the idea of loving an individual and using that person for your own ends. Be clear: using men for sex, for love, for companionship, as providers and as fathers is not a disgraceful idea. Nor is it a new one. It's human nature. First things first, though. Time to rid yourself of any negative ideas about users. (NB: in not one of the dictionaries I consulted did I find a pejorative definition of the word.)

User, n. A person who uses (esp. a particular commodity or service).
The Concise Oxford Dictionary

There is no prejudice attached to user's guides for computers, vacuum cleaners, washing machines, toasters, electric blankets. The term is used as a complete neutral to describe the people operating the equipment. Well, you will never in your life find a more delicate mechanism than a man, so when you fall in love with one, why shouldn't you have of an instruction booklet to help you get the most out of him? And even before you fall in love with one, and want the best for him (and yourself) why should you be deprived of information and strategies which might help you both to come out ahead of the game?

Let's start at the very beginning

Without a handbook and a game plan, things don't always work out so well. And love at first sight can be particularly problematic. The buxom starlet Pamela Anderson was love-struck when she first clapped eyes on Motley Crüe member Tommy Lee and married him quick (but not so) smart. After (in rapid succession) two children, a divorce and a case of Hepatitis C that she blamed on her tattooed husband, Pamela came to understand the meaning of 'marry in haste, repent at leisure'.

Can you remember the first time you fell in love at first sight? The leap of the heart, the sudden change of breathing, the fixed gaze — it's as though the whole world fades to black around the object of desire. Now, *that*'s a feeling!

I am still to recover properly from my earliest case of the *coup de foudre*. He was not so much a man in uniform as a boy in the cadet corps: to my eyes, the epitome of style and glamour. He was an older man, all of fifteen, and the closest thing to a sex god I had ever seen apart from David Cassidy (which should give you some idea of where I was coming from). When he pulled rank and blew his whistle to bring his little troop of medical orderlies into line, it pierced me to the heart. I felt as though I had been felled with an axe.

> *❦ This sex attraction, though it is so useful for keeping the world peopled, has nothing to do with beauty; it blinds us to ugliness instead of opening our eyes to beauty. ❦*
> GEORGE BERNARD SHAW, 1856–1950

For three years I thought of no one else (well, hardly anyone else. Okay, quite a few others, but I never forgot him — or the feeling) and when I was seventeen, I finally saw this vision again at university. Whenever the smoke of a Black Russian (I know, I know, but I was young!) curled over his lips, I was a study in sweaty palms and stammering, inchoate longing. Clearly, the fit of adolescent passion had not passed. You could dress this up, this rush of blood, as love at first sight, but it was a more basic reaction. I might have had an innocent idea of what love in general was about, a slightly hazier idea of what romantic love would be (all those Georgette Heyer novels, but this was lust, something those practical life education classes had forgotten to mention. Since we are generally unprepared for lust, no wonder many people are reduced to emotional rubble by the first manifestation of shattering, physical chemistry.

> *Men, when they lust, can many fancies feign.*
> ROBERT GREENE, C. 1560–1592

Love is an incredibly hit-and-miss affair. According to yet another group of scientists, the whole question of love (or lust) at first sight for women depends on which stage of the menstrual cycle they find themselves in. At the time of ovulation, we are apparently more likely to find the rugged good looks of a hunter/provider attractive — someone along the lines of Sean Connery or Arnold Schwarzenegger. (Hands up those who would prefer to pass on Arnie.)

Closer to menstruation, we find a caring, more nurturing sort of man — in the softer Leonardo di Caprio style, say — rather more our cup of tea. The kind of man who would fetch us a cup of tea while we're tucked up under the doona, watching re-runs of *Sense and Sensibility* (with, sigh, Alan Rickman, sigh, Hugh Grant) on a long, rainy Sunday afternoon.

When it comes to where and who you love, you might think that you have choices, but grumpy old Arthur Schopenhauer, argues otherwise. He reckons love is a biological trick, designed to bond men and women for the propagation of the species. If love wears off over a period of time (the old 'familiarity breeds contempt' theory), then what does that matter to the biological imperative? Man and woman *do* breed, their offspring *are* born, the species is safe and there is one more generational stepping stone to the future. If a couple is unhappy, that doesn't matter a bit in the grand plan, because the future of Mankind is assured for another generation.

The German philosopher calls this the will-to-life — the drive which sets our feet on the path of the dating and mating game from puberty. Birds do it, bees do it, even ninety-five-year olds with mail order, twenty-something brides do it.

Schopenhauer himself doesn't seem to have done it much. He was a man who, rebuffed by women throughout his life, eventually devoted his love and affection to his dogs. Poodles, they were, and while poodles are fine, intelligent animals, they can look a teeny bit queeny. Which might have been what did it for Arthur's romantic intentions — the objects of desire couldn't take him seriously.

> *Life is so short, questionable and evanescent that (meeting members of the opposite sex) is not worth the trouble of major effort.*
> ARTHUR SCHOPENHAUER, 1788–1860

Schopenhauer understood the fundamentals of the drive to procreate, propagate, pick up members of the opposite sex in bars and take them home and shag them silly. That's what he boiled human nature down to. However, we have acquired a few refinements over the years.

And here is the sticky centre of the problem. If we are going to be used by our natures in this way, what can we do to improve the situation? The very least is that as individuals — not a species — we make sure that while we might be linked to another human being by the will-to-life, we make it the best experience possible. And since you and I both know that men are not going to be sitting around pondering on this (Nature has programmed them in other ways), it's left to women to be the smartest Users.

So what's love got to do with it? The square root of nothing much at all for some of us. But if you are very clever, you will be a User who will manage her man/men with skill, success and aplomb. For the most part, they won't even know that it's happened to them. And if they ever work out what's going on, they should be very grateful you have gone to all this trouble to make them happy and keep them that way. They should then invest in you, to make sure you keep on doing it. That's what's known in nature as symbiosis.

So, after all that, have you decided that you want to be happy in a relationship or to have a better relationship? Then you have to become a User, out and proud!

What's it all about, love?

But what *exactly* causes love? British scientists now think they are getting closer to the sweet mystery of it all. According to research, within the first ten seconds of meeting someone, we decide whether that person is attractive or not. (That long?) First, there's physical appearance, then comes the voice, loaded with clues to identity. The first time we open our mouths accent reveals place of origin and educational levels, and tone tells the listener something about personality.

We're pre-programmed in the 'lust (let's be truly honest about what this feeling boils up to) at first sight' department. According to those same British scientists, we're equipped from infancy with a colour-by-numbers map of our ideal partner. We first find love with our parents and we try to replicate that relationship again and again. Studies show we are more likely to marry a person with the same colour eyes as our opposite sex parent, which makes it difficult for those with hazel-eyed fathers — it's a huge pool to choose from.

> *No thorns go as deep as a rose's.*
> *And love is more cruel than lust.*
> ALGERNON CHARLES SWINBURNE, 1837–1909

Familiar patterns?

Though love at first sight might not be the beginning of your particular story, it seems that most love stories have quite a lot in common. Marcia Millman, professor of psychology at the University of California, Santa Cruz, in her book, *The Seven Stories of Love and How to Choose a Happy Ending*, argues (after studying thousands of films) that there are only so many ways we can be in love.

'When people choose a sexual partner,' she writes, 'they are making an unconscious attempt to relive a past conflict or loss, to deal with something that happened in childhood or in the past. By finding the right partner, they are seeking to resolve this problem and master it.'

In terms of improving real life unions, Millman argues we can learn from art. 'I wanted to write a book that would illuminate romantic love, and help readers have more gratifying relationships,' she says. She wants people to identify the stories of their relationships so they can write their own happy endings: 'By understanding why a particular story appeals to us, we can learn better to control its course in real life.'

> ❝ *We are what we repeatedly do. Excellence, then, is not an act, but a habit.* ❞
> ARISTOTLE, 384–322 BC

The real-life versions of the love stories she identifies are: first love (*Romeo and Juliet* and *Westside Story*); the transformation (*Pygmalion*, *My Fair Lady*); obsessive love (*Fatal Attraction*, *Othello*); love between unequals (*Jane Eyre*, *Pretty Woman*); the sacrifice of self for the other (*Casablanca*, *The Bridges of Madison County*); the rescue (*Beauty and the Beast* and *Shadowlands*); and the story of courageous love (*An Affair to Remember* and its offspring, *Sleepless in Seattle*.)

So which one best describes your love story? (Lose points immediately if you said *Addams Family Values*.) And which scenario would you most like to subscribe to?

First love

Idealised, hyper-romantic love puts us in the arms of people our parents might otherwise have thought quite wrong for us. The most enduring version of this story scenario is *Romeo and Juliet*, which turned into the musical *Westside Story* in 1957.

The problem with this love story is that it can't turn out happily. You never see the fourteen-year-old Juliet setting up house with her sixteen-year-old husband and if anyone tried that these days they'd either be living in a Third World backwater or some survivalist enclave in the United States. People get locked up for this. Now it's called child abuse.

> *The magic of first love is our ignorance that it will ever end.*
> BENJAMIN DISRAELI, 1804–1881

Romeo and Juliet have no future. Their lives are all in the present. The poignancy of their story lies in its intensity and the loss we all know that they must face. Romeo and Juliet have no way out — they have to go through with the daft plan of the sleeping draught or risk being ground into dust by the mundanity of life.

Still, there are true stories of childhood sweethearts who remain in love sixty or seventy years later. These long-term marriages must be rather interesting places to live. As one old woman memorably told a survey by *The Australian Women's Weekly*: 'I don't know anything about sex. I've been married all my life.'

The transforming power of love

The power of the *Pygmalion* plotline revolves around a creeping attachment between the creator and the created, the teacher and the taught. In the original Greek myth, Pygmalion, having given up on real women, carves Galatea, his own paragon of beauty, out of ivory. He falls totally in love with her, and the power of his love induces the goddess Aphrodite to make the statue human.

The theme is continued in *My Fair Lady*, where the determined bachelor Henry Higgins bets his friend, Colonel Pickering, that he can take any urchin from the gutter (cue Eliza Doolittle) and make a lady out of her. Henry, despite his crusty mien, falls in love with the Cockney flower-seller. Her transformation to a lady is completed without her losing her soul, while his transformation from teacher to lover is also accomplished.

Shakespeare had gone the transformation route in *The Taming of the Shrew*. His Katherina was all fuss and trouble, until the adventuring Petruchio began to court her in his own way. 'Thou must be married to no man but me;/ For I am born to tame you, Kate;/ And bring you from a wild Kate to a Kate/ Conformable as other household Kates,' he tells her. But what he has seen in her, beneath the hissing and the spitting, is a woman of passion and fire who could return his admiration and affection in full measure.

In Jane Austen's *Emma*, Mr Knightley reads the headstrong heroine such a blistering lecture about behaving badly that she takes his scolding to heart. At the same time, Knightley is instantly transformed in Emma's eyes from eccentric bachelor into romantic hero and potential mate.

Tears signal the transformation at the end of the film, *Cinema Paradiso*. Salvatore (Toto), now a famous film director, goes back to the town of his boyhood for the funeral of his friend and mentor, Alfredo, the movie projectionist. In a series of flashbacks, we see the transmission of his passion for film from the older man to his protégé, then the boy growing up, falling in love for the first time with Elena — and then losing her. He finds her again after years apart when he comes back for Alfredo's requiem mass — and finally makes love to her.

The adult Salvatore had become something of an automaton, a man who had schooled himself to live without love. But Alfredo left him a legacy — all the screen kisses excised from the films over the years by decree of the priest. At the end of the director's cut of the film, the grown-up Toto sits in a darkened theatre. He is watching those missing love scenes and comes to understand the passion missing from his life. And he finally discovers the gift of love that Elena has given him, before sending him back to his own life.

> *If love were what the rose is,*
> *And I were like the leaf,*
> *Our lives would grow together*
> *In sad or singing weather,*
> *Blown fields or flowerful closes,*
> *Green pleasure or grey grief.*
> ALGERNON CHARLES SWINBURNE, 1837–1909

In real life women, for the most part, transform men by the power of love, rather than vice versa. But what no one tells you at the outset is that the transformation process is not going to be a short-term project. This improvement of a partner can go on for decades. It also requires a lot of patience, and you really can't do it outside the home or in front of anyone else. Such behaviour can look very controlling — best do it in private.

Obsessive love

Othello or *Fatal Attraction*? In both stories, lovers become obsessed with their partners — and the result is untimely death. Othello is an easy mark for Iago's plot to convince him of Desdemona's infidelity because of his own insecurities. In *Fatal Attraction*, the Michael Douglas character demonstrates extreme carelessness when he picks Glenn Close's character for an extra-marital fling. You would have thought her tragic perm would have been warning enough. Tough luck for him when the casual lover turns into a complete psycho, pops the bunny into the pot, and then, only half-dead, surfaces from the bottom of the bathtub for more.

In George du Maurier's late nineteenth century novel *Trilby*, the failed musician Svengali hypnotises his victim, Trilby, and makes her into one of the great singers of her time. (If this sounds familiar, it should. It's very close to the relationship of Christine and her mysterious singer teacher in *The Phantom of the Opera*.) In the end, Svengali's obsessive love proves the end of him, and his creature Trilby dies soon after because she cannot live without her puppet-master.

Do these plots remind you of your relationship? Then get out while you're still breathing! Do you have girlfriends involved with either a Moor-type figure or a husband who comes with his own bunny-boiler? Get her counselling, help her to pack and then hide her at your house until you can get an apprehended violence order.

Love between unequals

'I need someone, older and wiser, telling me what to do,' that's how the song goes in *The Sound of Music*. It's a prime example of love across the social divide as the aristocratic autocrat, Captain von Trapp, falls for the novice-nanny-siren Maria. In *Jane Eyre*, the plain governess falls in love with her employer, Mr Rochester — such a pity about the mad wife locked upstairs.

Pretty Woman, in which the hooker with the heart of gold, Julia Roberts, wins over Richard Gere's millionaire, is a modern take on the theme. Gere even gets to save her honour (pretty well in tatters after a career as a prostitute on a Hollywood boulevard, you would have thought) when she is almost raped by a churlish business colleague of his.

Increasingly, it's the men who live downstairs and have to marry up — the idea in Billy Joel's *Uptown Girl*, his hymn to his former wife, the tall, blonde, beautiful model Christie Brinkley. (This is a huge challenge for women who are still programmed to marry up and wonder where all the eligible blokes have gone. One maths professor I know of married 'down' when she fell in love with a tradesman who came to lay her carpets and hung around to help hang the curtains. She was well-off, cultivated, didn't need someone to provide for her and so could afford to choose whoever suited her best, regardless of social conventions.)

The sacrifice of self

You can see this concept of the renunciation of selfish pleasure in *Casablanca*, when Humphrey Bogart sends Ingrid Bergman off at the end on that plane with her husband, played by Paul Henreid. Bogey sacrifices their happiness together so he can save Europe, which has to be his reward. Ingrid dawdles towards that plane with Paul. She knows what's ahead for her — the lukewarm comfort of her marriage bed.

Renunciation is the result in *The Bridges of Madison County*. Ultimately, the Clint Eastwood character fades into the distance, leaving Meryl Streep, his housewife/lover alone to await the return of her husband and family. Their personal happiness is jettisoned for the continuing happiness of her family.

There's not quite so much sacrifice of self going around these days. The idea of giving up something for a greater good suffered a deathblow in the free-love era of the 1960s and then was finally wrapped in a shroud during the 'Me' decade of the 1980s.

Most of us think Ingrid should have gone off with Humphrey and that's pretty much what audiences thought in 1942 when they first saw it — but then it was about personalities. Bogey had more charisma than poor, stolid Paul.

Rescue me

Take me in your arms, rescue me! Another favourite love fantasy for women. It's been popular since time began and reaches its apotheosis in the 'One day my prince will come' scenario (white charger optional) of the *Snow White* fairytale. There are dozens of variations on the theme, including *Beauty and the Beast*, where only Beauty can see the inner beauty of the trapped Beast, and only the power of love can set him free (which makes it a combination rescue/transformation story).

A lot of women invest in rescue scenarios — *Snow White*, *Cinderella*, *Sleeping Beauty* — and dream that they too will at some stage be rescued by the man of their dreams. Sometimes, those dreams do come true by themselves. Smart Users will strategise *how* to make the dreams come true — which is where *Men: A User's Guide* will come in handy.

> *Whoso loves believes the impossible.*
> ELIZABETH BARRETT BROWNING, 1809–1861

Courageous love

Here is the romance story that the commitment-wary twenty-first century needs to pay special attention to. Films such as *An Affair to Remember* and its tribute movie, *Sleepless in Seattle*, deal with people who were wary of love and had to find the courage in their own hearts to take a risk. If you want to live out a love story like *Sleepless*, you would be well served to find a child who will interfere in your life and use your credit card to make an airline booking across a continent for you. That's what the child of the Tom Hanks character did to help out the hopeless dad in Nora Ephron's film. (Actually, you might be in two minds about what to do about a child like this — ground him in an attempt to really crack down on that juvenile truanting fraudster, or give him your everlasting thanks.)

Another pattern?

Marcia Millman might have missed an important variation on the transformation pattern. It's the story of redemptive love, the love that changes everything, the love that challenges the soul to remain unchanged in the face of passion itself.

It's the theme of the main love story in *As Good As It Gets*, where Jack Nicholson's character, Melvin, finds his carefully controlled and neurosis-ruled world is penetrated by a small dog and the misfortunes of his neighbour. Melvin's egocentric need for order in the chaos of life sends him out of his usual orbit, and into disorder via the life of Helen Hunt's waitress character. Every time the outside world steps into his cloistered fortress of an apartment, his carapace is chipped away. In the end, he is overwhelmed and redeemed by the force of his love for her. It's reciprocal: in return, she understands with absolute clarity that he is telling her his heart's truth when he says he loves the fact that he alone understands that she is the most amazing woman in the world.

This is what most romantics yearn for. In the last frames of a film, in the last few pages of a book, the hero/heroine is altered and becomes a better person because their heart has opened to love.

3
Does a woman need a man?

When it comes to choosing their mates, men might as well drag out a board, stick up a few snaps of vaguely marriageable women in their acquaintance and start hurling darts. For many hopeful bachelors, Lady Luck will provide a better choice than what they come up with themselves. Occasionally in the past, they've had a bit of a go at getting hold of the right woman for the task. Take for instance this well-known and almost certainly apocryphal example:

> Wanted: Woman able to cook, clean and provide companionship. Must have own boat. Contact Mick at Bayside Bait and Tackle. PS: Please include photo of boat.

That's a variation on a theme which has been around forever. You can find a similar, heart-felt plea for a mate in the early nineteenth century from a man who placed this personal ad in a newspaper:

> Any gal what got a bed, calico dress, coffee pot and skillet, knows how to cut out britches, can make a hunting shirt, and knows how to take care of children, can have my services until death parts both of us.

You will note that this Arkansas farmer did not ask for a photograph of the bed and an example of the dressmaking skills, but that was probably only because the art of photography had not developed sufficiently to make it easy to preview a bed or britches, and no single gal in her right mind was going to make a hunting shirt and send it off to some unknown yokel in the country, no matter how genuine his ad made him sound.

This second advertisement outlines perfectly the requisite assets and skills in a wife of the time. The first does the same, but in a rather more flippant way. In neither does the man outline any of his own charms or benefits. In truth, he seems not to have needed to. It is simply sufficient that he is male and the subtext is that any woman would be glad of him.

But what does a User really need a man for these days, when things are rather more complex than his want of a boat or a hunting shirt? Thanks to the immense social changes of the last fifty years, unmarried women find themselves no longer servants to fathers and brothers, or economic slaves unable to get a home loan on the strength of their own signature. (For the record, it has only been about thirty-five years in Australia since a woman was able to borrow money for a home without a man's signature backing hers. And now, interestingly, women are the ones who are mainly doing the research into finding the loan for the marital home. At the same time, there are more and more women bank managers and mortgage lenders.

Women are now better educated and so they are able to earn better money. They are no longer dependent on a man to provide them with food and shelter in return for bearing and raising his children.

How would such an advertisement for a woman read today?

> Wanted, woman to share life with twenty-first century man. Must have well-paid job, be able to do ninety per cent of housework unaided, bear children, then accept primary responsibility for raising them. Should at same time be sex machine and psychotherapist, and able to finish the Business Activity Statement on time. Email jpeg image and bank statements.

It doesn't sound like much of a deal for women.

The problem for men these days is that all these women with well-paid jobs and high levels of education don't really leave much room for them to be in charge. If a man isn't the primary breadwinner and isn't the best educated one of the pair, what on earth is he there for? Men cast their eyes around, see independent women earning their own livings, buying their own drinks and jewellery, and begin to feel very afraid.

> *Throughout history, females have picked providers for mates. Males pick anything.*
> MARGARET MEAD, 1901–1978

So why does a modern woman actually want a man at all?

To go out with. You can look a little lonely if you keep turning up at parties by yourself — or, more interestingly, with your girlfriends in an Ellen de Generes sort of way. It can give rise to some rather unhelpful speculation about your sexual orientation.

To take you home. Nothing is drearier than having to wait for a cab at the end of a big night out. It's so much easier to have him, the designated driver, bring the car around.

To change a flat tyre. You could go to the local community college and learn how to do this, but it is such a messy procedure and is so hard on the hands. Better to join the local auto club or get a man to do it for you. Also, people who are capable are extremely reassuring to be around — if only those men who call for an electrician to change a fuse knew that competence is such a turn-on.

To take the top off the nail polish when it's stuck. Equally, for putting things on top of the cupboards when you can't be bothered to get the ladder out.

To program your VCR. If you don't have access to children under the age of twelve, you will probably need a man to program your VCR. You could learn to do this yourself, but there is just so much useless information you will be able to put in your brain in one lifetime, and VCR skills are just clutter.

To sort out the Options menu on your computer. Still in the VCR line, testosterone seems to be linked with the ability to do things with computers. A man can be very useful to you when it comes to sorting out the Options. (If he is useless with the PC, try not to look at him condescendingly — that is very bad for his self-esteem.)

To keep you warm in winter. If you pick a cuddly one, he will come in very handy for snuggles in winter. (The ones who drag the doona over to their side of the bed and then hurl it on the floor need to be sent to the spare room or made to sleep on the floor next to the bed until they promise to reform.)

To go downstairs to see what those odd noises are about.

To introduce his male friends to your girlfriends. This sometimes works, unless the man in question has a terrifically unappealing group of friends with names such as Dustbin Lids, Lardy or Spike.

To carry the luggage. If you've got one that tells you 'if you pack it, you carry it', find another one.

What does a smart User actually need a man for?

Not much, really. You can choose to be independent. You can get someone from Hire a Hubby to do the chores around the house. You can borrow sperm from a friend and have a baby as a single mother. You can even raise your child alone. You don't *need* a man for any of those things — but in the end, human beings are social animals and we are programmed to procreate.

And if you are going to do that, you will need to know something about men so that you can choose the best one possible. And the first thing to know about men is this: What do *they* need?

What a woman doesn't need a man for

Upkeep. These days women can keep themselves and, quite often, their families as well.

Motherhood. The customary fashion in which women become pregnant has much to recommend it, but as single, radical lesbian mothers across the country keep proving, there are other methods.

Completion. The smart User knows that unless she can provide her own happiness, she will be locked in a dependent relationship with a loser.

Validation. Smart Users stamp their own tickets!

Sanitation. We were forced to learn to take the rubbish out ourselves a long time ago. We also know where the dump is — if your man is a hoarder, that should be enough to make him very nervy.

But... The User can use a man for fun. There is nothing wrong with this at all, so long as no one gets hurt. She can also use a man for more serious ends — his happiness, her happiness and the future of the human race (Arthur Schopenhauer would be pleased!).

What you don't want to do is fall into the same trap as some men do and let Fate control the outcomes. You need to choose smartly. And this is how you start to make the right choices for you and him.

4
What do men really want?

The correct answer to this question for the woman who is serious about being a User is not, 'Who cares?'. The proper answer is Sex. Steamy sex that curls the toes, flattens the insteps, melts the bones. Sex reflected in the sheen of sunlight on damp skin. Love on a deserted, white sand beach beside a crystal blue lagoon in Tahiti, with the volcanic mountains towering above you. Sweaty sex in a bungalow in a tropical thunderstorm in Bali. The feel of flesh melting in the inky shadows of midnight. Urgent, driven sex in the warmth of a long summer afternoon, hidden in the shade of *Magnolia grandiflora*. The smell of a body sated. The taste of an arm crooked around you. Hours of consciousness-stealing sex, of twined limbs and souls, then finally the intimate comfort of post-coital exhaustion.

Do I have your attention? Okay ... sorry ... fooled you. This is not really what men want. It's obvious that they don't want this sort of collision of mind and matter. If they did want it, they'd be having it because there are very few women on earth who would say 'no' to the above. This is exactly the sort of sex a lot of women want, too. Men might do very well to listen and understand that women would like more to their sexual relationships than just the meat — even *with* three veg. Fillet steak is marvellous, but who wants it every time you pull up a chair to the dinner table? Sometimes, it's all about the side dishes.

A lot of men, of course, would object to that description of what goes on between men and women, saying it never happens that way with them. It happens often enough, though, to have made the joke about an Australian man's idea of foreplay ('You awake?') completely recognisable to both men and women. (Incidentally, the Irishman's idea of foreplay is: 'Brace yourself, Brigid!'.)

If men wanted the sort of sex women do, peace would break out and end the battle of the sexes for all time. There would be no misunderstanding about what either side required from the engagement, and the rules would be clear. But sex is not a precise activity, and while a man might see the destination of his own orgasm as the Holy Grail, many women take a rather more Zen approach. To them, it's about the process and that can take a little time.

That's enough about sex for a moment. Let's think about men in theory rather than practice. And here is the problem: before a woman can become a User, she must understand men. And to do this, you have to answer that elemental question: What do they really, really want? This question, of course, has absolutely no relevance if you are (1) planning to enter a nunnery (not nearly enough of those around these days to provide any sort of career path) or (2) are considering an alternative lifestyle and sexual orientation.

But presupposing you are not planning to dedicate your life to God or become a lesbian (fine choices, both of these paths), you will need to consider this question since it is, as far as men are concerned, The Big One. The answer is at once extremely complex and very simple.

Bear in mind that men are unevolved organisms. How else can you explain the fact that they never seem to grasp the fact that if you leave sweaty shoes and socks in the bottom of a sealed gym bag, something really nasty happens to them? Or their complete lack of understanding of the garbage collection system, which is why they look surprised every time you tell them that it's time to put the bins out.

And while they might be very acute in almost every other aspect of life, they are reduced to hopeless rubble when it comes to actually going into a shop and buying you a present which you like and actually fits?

> *Woman wants to live her own life; and the man wants to live his; and each tries to drag the other to the wrong track. One wants to go north and the other south; and the result is that they both have to go east, though they both hate the east wind.*
> PYGMALION, GEORGE BERNARD SHAW, 1856–1950

There is a biological answer: Man (capital M) wants to dominate genetically as much of the planet (or their home, office or general environs) as they can. This is called, in some quarters, the genetic imperative and means, reduced to the most basic level, that they want to have as much sex as possible to improve their chances of doing exactly that — and it doesn't seem to matter whether the sex is good, bad, indifferent or, in some of the more extreme examples, even consensual.

At a more materialistic level, it means that they want to acquire as many trophies in life as possible. You remember the adage: 'He who dies with the most toys wins'. This is such an '80s idea, but there are quite a number of dinosaurs left over from those 'greed is good' times, and you might have to navigate your way around one or two. If you're lucky, you will escape the worst of them. If you're not, you'll end up like Catherine Zeta Jones, stuck with one of these old boys. She might have negotiated a pre-marriage contract which in the event of a divorce reportedly earns her a cool US$5 million a year for her pains — but that hardly seems enough when you think about Michael Douglas and his lifted face.

The toys in question include a powerful job which generates the funds to fill the toy box, the right wife or wives (generations of them in some cases, each blonder and younger and more glittery than the last), a stock portfolio with clout, the phallic symbol car with go-faster everything, and a powerful boat. There are even some plutocrats who want, as an expression of their own psyches, the latest, sharpest, edgiest and shiniest little Gulfstream jet.

However, men are still aware that he who dies with the most toys is still dead. And they also know that there is no boat or car in existence that will come and visit them in the hospital, nor will a stock portfolio send flowers. Sometimes, not even the gilt-edged wife will make an appearance at the bedside.

In the end, men want the same things as women. We all want to be loved and accepted for who we are. We might have different names for what we want — men want sex, women want romance. Men will romance women to get sex, women give sex to get romance. (It's lucky we all have the same goal, even if we go about things quite differently.) So now you know what a man really wants, it's time to get ready and help him find it … and you!

preparation
is
everything

5
Spit and polish ... hers

Men are not interested only in breasts, and it's unfair to say so. If they were, all a woman who wanted to attract a man's attention would have to do would be to stand around with her breasts on a tray, just like a wannabe starlet at the Academy Awards or a prostitute hoping to boost trade.

No, they're not all breast-obsessed. Some are quite interested in legs, as well, and a good bottom will do at a pinch. Still others are interested in minds — though not as many as women might like. Others also go for faces, as one of the most beautiful faces in Australia, Maggie Tabberer, has remarked.

There is no doubt that most men like their women with a little flesh on their bones. The lollipop look works in Hollywood, where the camera is said to add five kilos to everyone, but not among chaps looking for something to hang onto in their loved ones. The famously beautiful French actor Catherine Deneuve, said that as a woman gets older, she has to make a choice between her *derrière* and her *visage*. Deneuve picked the face, which was a great idea for her, since at the same time she kept the focus on her *décolletage* and her breasts. (The French have a sweet expression to describe a woman who is thus endowed: *beaucoup de gens sur le balcon* — lots of people on the balcony. Madame Deneuve has a more than modest crowd on hers.)

> *A fine woman shows her charms to most advantage when she seems to most conceal them. The finest bosom in nature is not so fine as imagination forms.*
> A FATHER'S LEGACY TO HIS DAUGHTERS BY DR GREGORY, WRITING IN 1774

Breasts are a secondary sex characteristic and as such clearly draw a lot of attention. The attention is not just male — just look at the number of women who are either choosing to pump up the volume of their modest mammary glands, or turn down the noise of breasts which sometimes seem to have a life of their own. Some women — those women who seem to live out their lives in the pages of weekly women's magazines — are blowing them up and letting them down at a fantastic rate. See blonde American starlets Pamela Anderson and Anna Nicole Smith in particular. Their bosoms seem to go in and out with the tide.

Depending on the market you are aiming for, you should either show a little cleavage, or a lot. Say, for instance, you are pining for a gangsta rapper in the style of Sean 'Puff Daddy P. Diddy Bo Jangles' Combs ... no subtlety required for these boys. To attract their attention, you'd need to show almost all your secondary sex characteristics, as well as give a fair indication of your primaries. Their women dress to reveal in the style of Puffy's former squeeze, Jennifer Lopez, who favoured flash-trash couture from the house most loved by gangsta hookers — Versace. (The fact that Prince Charles dressed his mistress, Camilla Parker Bowles, in a Barbara Cartland-pink frock from Versace for their first official dinner together in the first half of 2000 was a little startling. The dress was even more remarkable for its dowdy modesty. Gianni Versace would never have gone so soft on Camilla.)

Before you try to slip into one of those tarty frocks, you should really establish if your body is up to the task. The spirit might be willing, but the flesh could be just a little too fleshy. If it is too, too much, go to the gym immediately and stay there until you are a perfect size eight, or you decide you love yourself just the way you are, whichever comes first. However, you can be sneaky and hide the excess while you have your bosoms out on parade. You will probably need to conscript a dressmaker for this project, but it will be worth it in the end.

(Attention: do not go too far with the voluptuous woman within. Being slightly overweight by film-star standards is fine, but being obese is not healthy. You will run the risk of anything from heart attacks to diabetes to stroke. You might get your man, but you might not be around to enjoy him. Go for curvy, not Michelin woman. And be careful — some women need therapy to work out why they have weight problems. They use their bodies as shields against intimacy. If you think this sounds like you, talk to your doctor about it.)

> *All women's dresses are merely variations on the eternal struggle between the admitted desire to dress and the unadmitted desire to undress.*
> LIN YUTANG, BORN 1895

The smart User has a wardrobe with a day/night split personality — and in the vampy one, there are lots of splits, slashes, see-throughs and generally temptressy garments. These are the clothes that attract attention in a bar or a club, but they should not necessarily open to the waist from the neck as well as the knee. It's easy to attract attention dressed like a lady of the night trying to find a new pimp, but you might really regret the quality of the man you pick up.

When it comes to grooming, less is certainly more. Users want to manage men who want to be managed by women, not by female impersonators. That would be death to the wallet — all those cosmetics cost a fortune. And it would be too punishing to lose a bloke to an ersatz woman with bigger hands, bigger feet and a deeper voice than yours.

The User's basics

Dress for success at work

At work, dress for your next job, not as though you are ready for your next headjob. A certain restraint is called for if you seriously want to climb the corporate ladder. The potential for wardrobe conflict, of course, lies in the fact that most people meet their future mates in the workplace. So you will need to dress to attract, but not attract unwanted attention.

To find the balance to express your personality appropriately, try these suggestions.

Wear solid colours. Floral prints are fine for your granny or at a garden party, but nothing suits work more than navy or black. For extra oomph, try red. Stay away from lolly colours and fiddly details.

Do not show your cleavage, or bare your arms — unless you are planning on a career as a hostess in the hospitality industry. Cover up for work, but make sure you can unbutton the shirt, take off the jacket for after working hours.

Careful with the shoes. Follow-me-home-and-fuck-me shoes belong in a bar, a club, a disco, but not in the office. Medium-heeled pumps are perfect. Keep a change of shoes in your drawer at work if you are going out for lunch or drinks.

Jewellery should be discreet. Gypsy earrings belong in a gypsy encampment, not the CBD. Keep jewellery down to a dull roar — simple and classic.

Don't be a bag lady. How many women do you see in the office district at lunchtime who are weighed down with a tote that could cope with five kilos of essentials — and invariably does? If you have a lot to cart, take a smaller bag within the larger one and use it whenever you don't need to refer to the contents of the portable filing cabinet.

Make-up — restraint, please. Leave the super paint jobs until you are heading away from the office fluorescents and towards the more forgiving lights of the night.

Perfume should be understated, not overpowering. Plenty of time for the big fragrances to bloom at night. Wear an *eau de toilette* version of your favourite for day, and pump up the volume with perfume in the same style for night.

Lingerie should never be seen. Keep the bra straps out of sight and make sure the Visible Panty Line is not.

Dress for sex-cess after work

After hours, change the emphasis from strictly business to totally pleasure.

The little black dress (LBD). The vamp's uniform! Have at least one, maybe more. You can wear them under a jacket during the day, then bare after dark. These dresses go from work to the theatre and never miss a beat. In linen, wool or silk or a wool/silk blend. No patterns, synthetics or tricky shapes — clever Users like their dresses like their men and that means smart and simple and very adaptable. Men never notice detail, so they won't remember if you have one little black dress, three or thirty-three.

Follow-me-home shoes. There's a time and place for everything, and this is when sexy shoes come into their own. There should be nothing plain and simple about the User's feet at night. (You'll have plenty of time to wear comfortable shoes when you're in the old people's home.) The best of these have killer stiletto heels and winkle-picker toes to show off extremity cleavage. The women who wear these shoes are the women mothers used to warn their sons about. The mantra for sexy feet is 'Man-o-lo Blah-nik.' It's rumoured that *Sex and the City*'s Sarah Jessica Parker can actually run in hers. (She's obviously been practising — these shoes are designed to help women fall over, not run. They tip the hips back, thrust the pubic bone forward along with the breasts, and elongate the shape of the leg.) Or you could try another chant, perhaps: 'Ter-ry Bi-vi-a-no.' These shoes are made to snog in.

But there are more rules about shoes. For instance, never wear white shoes at night. Or during winter. No brown shoes with a black dress. (Actually, brown shoes are so boring they should be banned for all time. Men can still only get away with them in the country. Which, by the way, is where suede shoes also belong.) You do not need to be told that your shoes, no matter what their function, should always be clean, properly heeled and not scuffed.

A black suit. See LBD, above. This one comes with a silk camisole underneath and the promise that once he pulls off your glasses and lets down your bun, he will reveal your inner siren: 'My goodness, Miss Prim, you're beautiful!'.

A small handbag. Black of course. What do you need to carry in it, anyway, besides the emergency kit — your phone, a lipstick and the car keys, a small wallet and clean white cotton hankie with hand-rolled edges? (No tissues on a date, thanks. You risk sneezing it to bits if you actually use one.) Large handbags and briefcases are for people who are slaves to their jobs, not sex goddesses like you.

> *She looked as though she had been poured into her clothes and forgot to say 'when'.*
> P. G. WODEHOUSE, 1881–1975

Black underwear. When it comes down to it, this is where the action is. So make sure it's up to the action — clean and pretty. (You never know when you might fall under an attractive man!) Choose La Perla, Yves Saint Laurent, Collette Dinnigan, perhaps Elle Macpherson. A little silk, a little lace, a little under-wire. The object of your affections won't have a chance.

Black fishnet stockings. The finer these are, the more contradictory they appear as a garment. Hooray, they're wholesomely sexy and slutty at the same time! Try them and see how *Irma la Douce* you can get.

Black eye make-up. Just kidding. That Lily Munster look is not for the woman planning to be a good User. Keep the look vampy and smoky, and the lipstick crimson. (You'll find any anthropologist worth his/her salt — Desmond Morris among them — ready to tell you this is because reddened lips echo aroused genitals. This seems like a bit of a stretch really, unless the species memory goes back to the time when naked human creatures scraped their knuckles around the ground and presented their bare haunches for the appreciation of the jungle toughs, and somehow blokes today still have that image hardwired into their brains.)

Black nail polish. Just say no. There are two — count them, two — colours for nails: scarlet and nude. That's quite some choice. Let women who are downtrodden go for colours you should only find in a Smarties box. Keep the polish unchipped, the nail length reasonable. You don't want a man to be scared that you might accidentally slash his throat in the throes of passion. Particularly just after you've had a fresh manicure — you might break a nail.

Your hair. It should never frighten anyone, particularly not small and impressionable children. Big hair always threatens to make a comeback, which should make fans of Fran Drescher in *The Nanny* very happy. But generally, successful Users have more conservative heads — neat, glossy, well cut and not too much hairspray. It's such a passion killer when some guy tries to run his fingers through your hair and he gets trapped in the teasing, the knots, the mousse and the spray. You could be caught like that for hours and eventually have to cut him free.

But what if you are unexpectedly asked out for a drink after work? You've got hair good enough for day, but not for night, and there's not a hairdresser in sight?

Don't worry, either learn to be a tease or get with the gel. If you can put your hair up into a French roll, do it fast. Or pull it back into a barrette.

At a pinch, use a hair band (but these really don't work on women older than Alice in Wonderland.) If you have short hair, spike and gel it up.

Jewellery. Bring out the big guns and the sparkly stuff at night. (The correct response to anyone giving you jewellery is generally 'Thank you'. The jewels should be both real and substantial — as should the thanks. Users never give the stuff back, either. Let the giver beware.)

Remember what your granny said (or would have if she thought of it), no diamonds (except the engagement ring) before lunch ever, and only before five on really special occasions. Wear pearls wherever and whenever you please.

And do what Coco Chanel used to do when she dressed to go out: she'd look at herself in the mirror and take at least one piece of jewellery off before she went out the door.

How should you dress on other social occasions?

That takes care of work and after-work. What about weekends and tricky social situations? What, for instance, would the smart User wear to meet her new loved one's family for the first time? Not the Manolo's, that's for sure, unless you want your footwear to telegraph your intentions to his mother. It's far better to go the slightly conservative and very covered route, until you have at least seen where his parents are coming from. The tiny hipster jeans might be just the go, but save them until at least the second encounter.

At the beach
Your first romantic weekend is at the beach? The successful User will go simple and light. You don't want to alert him to your inability to let go of things with your over-abundance of equipment (or your make-up bag). Wear a pair of jeans and a sweater; take shorts, t-shirts, swimmers, and a cover-up that can double for the beach or the night. Leave all the heels at home, along with the jewels (unless you are going to the Gold Coast, where lots of clanking gold is compulsory).

In the mountains
The mountains require heavier weights and multiple layers, walking shoes (still no heels) and flannelette jammies. (It is generally better to be thought of

as eccentric than die of hypothermia.) If you can't quite come at the jammies, though, pick a pretty nightdress and a warm dressing gown. No jewellery needed here, either.

On the boat

He's got a boat, you say? Congrats! What about the cruise wear then? Look, co-ordinated wardrobes of French navy stripes (fantastic on *matelots* and too camp on almost everyone else) are okay if you are a fading television star and have the time to change five times a day, but not for more sane individuals. Resist the impulse to get matching anything. White is perfectly acceptable in almost any context afloat (and it makes you easier to spot if you fall overboard). Do not take your heels with you — the decks will not thank you if you do. Soft, flat shoes — topsiders or made from canvas — with good traction are essential to give you some purchase and keep you standing upright in all weathers. Don't forget the hat — you want to be burning with passion, not sunstroke. And speaking of weather, try to waterproof your hair. Slick it down, tie it back and don't whinge about getting it wet. That comes with the territory.

At the races

He asks you to the picnic races. Don't, whatever you do, just hear the word 'races'; otherwise you might dress for the Spring Carnival at Flemington, all flying feathers and frilly frocks. You will end up looking like an overdressed out-of-towner at the more relaxed race meeting he's proposing. Dress down. Pack those flats again. Try not to scare the horses with your hat or your hair.

Picture perfect

Everything's fine if everything matches. Some Users have really got the wardrobe thing down pat. They're clean, tidy, sexy and glamorous before they step into the world. Others don't find they need the same level of eternal vigilance regarding their appearance. Before you choose high maintenance or complete dagginess, think very carefully. Here are some Users who have got it all worked out.

Sophia Loren. Apparently she refuses to leave home until she looks absolutely flawless. Some of us would never get out at all if we applied that rule to ourselves. She's a bit like a more real version of Joan Collins in that her face wouldn't crack if she laughed.

Princess Caroline. She got her grooming gene from her mother, Princess Grace of Monaco. Her sister, Princess Stephanie, wasn't as fortunate and ran off to the circus, where her lapses were not as noticeable as they might be on the Corniche in Monte Carlo.

Elle Macpherson. She's almost forty and she has the leggy grace of an ageless thoroughbred. Elle is the first to admit she is no classical beauty, but she has always made the most of her good points and never looks anything apart from bandbox perfect.

Happy hooker lookalikes

Men love this stuff. Can't imagine why.

Kylie Minogue might consider popping her proper knickers back on by the time she turns thirty-five, which is just a minute away. Actually, she *has* put her tiny little knickers back on — the woman who was formerly known as the Singing Budgie has launched her own underwear range. Perhaps she could flog some to …

Jennifer Lopez, who clearly dispenses with most of hers, most of the time. She is undoubtedly a beauty, but the only way we could see more of J Lo is if she turned herself inside out. Which is what seems to have happened to …

Melanie Griffith, the forty-something wife of Spanish heart-throb Antonio Banderas, was so desperate to keep her husband that she had plastic surgery. Maybe she should try more shock frocks from …

Donatella Versace, the younger sister of the designer Gianni Versace, is the high priestess of the 'hooker on a holiday' cult (adepts include Elizabeth Hurley and others of her ilk) and it seems she won't be happy until the rest of the women in the world look the same.

Sloppy Jo's

These are the clothes the User wears when she's home alone. Even the world's most beautiful women cannot get away with this look outside the house. These girls try, but they need to pay more attention to their wardrobes.

Jennifer Aniston. At awards shows, she has her own bohemian high style. But when she's out of the public eye, Jennifer seems perpetually, radically dressed down. But then maybe she feels that since she is married to Brad Pitt she has done all the work she needs to do.

Courtney Cox Arquette. Maybe it's a *Friends* thing, this relentless grunge away from the spotlight. But at lease Courtney doesn't look as out there as her husband, David Arquette, who appears to dress himself with oddments from charity bins.

Natalie Imbruglia. The singer is vying for the title of boho princess of the world, but she has tough competition from Kate Moss.

Meg Ryan. The girliest forty-plus woman in the world seems to have caught a serious case of daggy dressing from Australia's own *Gladiator* Russell Crowe. How long before she is seen in a flannelette shirt as homage to a lost love?

Madonna. She seems to have two gears: dressed to the nines or looking as though she has just stumbled in from a squat. Whatever, it's a relief for her public that she has moved from the lethal cone-bra stage, but the boyz in the hood gear looks a little awkward when she takes Lourdes to nursery school.

Look smart and be smart

Is there a balance to be had between being smart and looking sexy? Of course there is — and there are even some men who find a woman's brain the biggest turn on of all. So work on the externals but don't forget the engine (the body) needs the driver (the brain). And keep listening to your woman's intuition — if you don't, you will pay. You will become, as Coco Chanel once said, 'a woman who knows all the things that can be taught and none of the things that cannot be taught'.

Looking beautiful naturally

Balance your life. Exercise regularly — it gets the blood moving, which aids in removing toxins from the system, and also has an impact on improving your state of mind. Sleep well. This is the time when your body can heal itself, and your subconscious sort out the day.

Balance your diet. Make sure you are feeding your body properly. You know which foods are healthy choices — and chocolate is not one of them. Nor are chocolate-covered biscuits, Cosmopolitans, cocktail party savouries, fags or glasses of chardy.

Every day you should:
- be sparing with oils, fats and sweets
- have two to three serves of milk, cheese or yoghurt
- have two to three serves of meat, fish, dry beans or eggs
- Have two to four serves of fruit
- Have six to eleven serves of bread, pasta, rice or cereals.

And also make sure you are drinking at least two litres of water a day.

Do you need to lose weight? Do it for the right reasons — your own health and wellbeing. Remember to set yourself realistic goals so that you don't set yourself up for failure and comfort-bingeing.
- Cut down on the calorie intake
- Get moving and increase your physical activity level. Walk for an hour a day if you can
- Shrink your body by shrinking your servings
- Think healthy, not thin
- Don't be hard on yourself. Every so often, give yourself a little treat and really enjoy it
- Love yourself, no matter what.

Balance your mind. Give yourself some quiet time to do whatever you like — read a book, listen to music, go for a walk on a beach in the rain, meditate. Include in that quiet time some space for a facial once a week and a body treatment once a month.

Balance your appearance. Every day, keep yourself in shining, gleaming condition from the tips of your toes to the top of your head. Make sure your clothes are also in good condition — no missing buttons or scuffed heels.

Balance your world. Meet it standing up straight and with a smile. A series of Pilates classes will help with the first — the system works of toning, increasing strength and flexibility. For an accredited Pilates studio near you, contact the Australian Pilates Method Association, telephone 02 9990 3021. If you feel healthy and look good, you'll find you will start to smile naturally.

> *In the factory we make cosmetics. In the store we sell hope.*
> CHARLES REVSON, 1906–1975

The Joan Collins's guide to looking beautiful 'naturally'

At nearly seventy, Joan Collins married her almost forty-year-old lover. From a distance and in dim light, she looks thirty-something — which is probably the age of some of her wigs. Notwithstanding that, in the advice to women stakes, Joan certainly deserves a hearing. Here are some of her pearls of wisdom, gathered during a very busy lifetime.

Romance. Why stop at one husband when you can have five? According to Joan, their ages should be in inverse proportion to yours, for example, you are twenty, he's fifty; you're fifty, he's twenty. Easy, isn't it? This way, you should be assured of never having a partner who needs Viagra.

Fashion. Joan peaked in sexual allure and power in the 1980s, when she played super-bitch Alexis Colby in *Dynasty*. Which means you will never see her out of big shoulder pads and shiny, spangled fabrics. Remember Shirley Bassey's advice — don't change the act, change the audience!

Beauty. The queen of knuckle-deep make-up, Joan insists that high gloss artificiality always works. 'The problem with beauty,' she says, 'is that it is like being born rich and getting poorer.'

Health. Joan says, 'Use it or lose it!' She practises what she preaches with vitamins and exercise, including swimming and Pilates.

Outlook. She's *determinedly* upbeat and says, 'Live for today'. Which is very good advice from a woman going on seventy for women of any age!

6
The sweet smell of sexual success

Here is a secret some women would kill to know — Ysatis is a total man-magnet. My friend Ellen Kate in New York heard about it from a friend who, whenever she is between relationships and looking for an exciting new date, splashes on the Ysatis *eau de parfum* (a white flower, woody-Oriental launched by Givenchy in 1984) and off she goes. According to her numerous field tests, the perfume (in the same family as Valentino's Vendetta, Nino Cerruti and Gale Hayman's Beverly Hills) is a never-fail passion arouser.

So there you have it: perfume has a dual function. It makes you feel great when you put it on, and it can help you pull blokes, too. There are some famous babes who swore/swear by certain smells. Marilyn Monroe believed in Chanel No5 (she wore it to bed). Elle Macpherson and I once had a conversation in a plane going to Lake Mungo about Vetiver by Guerlain — she wears it all the time. It's a men's fragrance, but on her it smells as fresh and green and as sexy as a soft, warm night in the south of France — and I hope it does the same job for me! On the men I know who wear it, Vetiver smells like sex in the afternoon. Highly recommended.

When I'm dressing up and going out, I always splash on the Shalimar. The sexiest French woman I ever met always wore it and among her conquests during her late teens were John F. Kennedy *and* his father, Joe. (Though, to be fair, the deck was stacked in her favour. It was Summer, they were in the south of France and those boys were pretty easy gets.) The vanilla in it is so calming that even if nothing happens you'll feel really relaxed.

Sex and smell have long been linked, and their impact is a lesson best learned early by the smart User. We live in a world soaked in smells — from fabric softeners to deodorants to dish-washing liquid, but the sense of smell is still one of the keenest when it comes to mating and dating. Centuries ago, if a prospective partner smelled good, that probably meant he was healthy and appropriate to mate with. (That's sort of where we got kissing too — from licking someone's skin to judge their state of being.)

> *Kiss me as if you entered gay*
> *My heart at some noonday.*
> ROBERT BROWNING, 1810–1889

Given the importance of smelling good in most courtships these days, the way things were is an absolute revelation. How did people date and mate when things smelled like the pits? The stench of real life in Renaissance Europe would be almost incomprehensible to our corner of twenty-first century society, where two showers a day are closer to the norm than one and personal freshness a public duty.

It must have been Hell. William Manchester in his book *A World Lit Only by Fire: The Medieval Mind and the Renaissance* gives something of what the world would have smelled like in retelling the story of a medieval serf who wanders out of the countryside to find himself in a narrow alley of perfumeries. The smell knocks him out and he is only revived when a shovel of manure is waved under his unconscious nose. Equally, Alain Corbin in his scholarly work *The Foul and the Fragrant: Odour and the Social Imagination* attempts to put the smell back into history — as aromatic disinfectant, proof against plagues and agues, as vehicle of seduction, as inescapable metaphor for the great unwashed.

The perfumers' art had become critically important in the seventeenth century, when regular bathing was thought to decrease the body's resistance to fevers and agues. (This is an attitude that persists in some cultures to this day and means loads of jokes about certain nationalities, their aversion to soap or deodorants and lack of personal hygiene.) 'Plunging into water involved a calculated risk,' writes Corbin. 'Baths were thought to exert a profound effect on the whole organism ... the courtesan owed her infertility to her excessive preoccupation with toilette.'

As a result, the plunge bath was out for a time — hygiene was achieved by dry washing, rubbing perfume soaked linens (*toiles*) on the skin. In the seventeenth-century bedchamber, the little linen squares used for bathing and the larger linens used under clothing, draped a table next to a commode chair and adjacent to a huge curtained bed. The bath was back in fashion during the eighteenth century, with tubs resembling *chaises longue* extremely popular among those with enough money and space to accommodate one.

> *As a perfume doth remain*
> *In the folds where it hath lain,*
> *So the thought of you, remaining*
> *Deeply folded in my brain,*
> *Will not leave me: all things leave me:*
> *You remain.*
>
> MEMORY, ARTHUR WILLIAM SYMONS, 1865–1945

The more appealing and acceptable aromas changed with the passing centuries — from the heavy musk scents of the eighteenth century to the lighter flower waters of the nineteenth. (Corbin cites six permissible floral notes to perfume handkerchiefs from the 1860s — rose, jasmine, orange blossom, acacia, violet and tuberose.)

The choice of scents is wider now, but the purpose is the same — to make one person smell sexually inviting to a potential sex partner. Just think about that the next time your loved one gives you toilet water more suitable for his granny than his lover. In the same way, there are fragrances suitable for male friends, lovers, husbands, brothers and fathers. Take your pick!

Preparation is everything

Eau de bloke

Dirt. Gin and tonic. Angel food. Grass. Tomato. Is that what you'd expect to find down your bib after a particularly well-lubricated summer barbie? Maybe, but the list is also part of a range from the US perfumers Demeter, who clearly have abandonned the more recherché fragrance names such as Vol de Nuit, L'Aimant, Angel and Fragile. These guys are in the anti-name game and are picking very muscular tags for their perfumes. (For the record, Dirt smells mossy and woody, and Gin and Tonic smells like a gin and tonic with a twist of lemon, though why you'd want to smell as though you'd bathed in mother's ruin rather than just swallowed a bathtubful of it is a trifle mystifying.

Now, Cristobal. That's more like it. It's the name for a 'proper' men's fragrance from the house of Balenciaga. He's 'resolutely contemporary ... a gentleman charmer impelled by desire, deep-rooted values. He aspires to the return of a certain lifestyle, a natural elegance. Surprises by his refinement and charisma, charms by complex personality and intense gaze.'

Who wouldn't like to meet a man like that without having to buy a ticket to Barcelona? He's not the sort of chap who favours short-sleeved shirts, organises the tunnel ball comp. at the annual church picnic and enjoys all the sex appeal of a leftover tea bag. Hang on, there's more. 'He evokes discreet, yet obvious, desire,' the press release for the fragrance continues. (If you stop to try to work out what that means, we'll be here for years, so please just accept the notion of a desire which is, at once, both obvious and not obvious and let's move on.)

The main thrust behind men's fragrance ads is to make women — the more active part of the market — decide what sort of man they want. In turn, they respond by paying for the fragrance that promises to turn old Norms and young Jareds into new Cristobals.

Whatever the style, there's a fragrance to conjure him up. Want a strong but sensitive, urbane but creative, a rugged New York architect-type? Allure Pour Homme from Chanel is for you. That is exactly the type Chanel used in their ad campaign. Perhaps you'd prefer a man who can build his own boat? That would be the bloke from Fahrenheit by Christian Dior. (Unfortunately, in the ads, the boat and its builder seem marooned in the middle of the desert, and he looks as though he's waiting for the arrival of the new Great Flood to float him off his Namibian sand hill. Subliminal message? This is a man looking for a navigator in life.)

These days, you can't move for some new fragrance hitting an already crowded market, jostling for position and shelf-space. Life used to be so much easier — fathers were either Old Spice or Blue Stratos. The Old Spice-types were frankincense-oriented, while the Blue Stratos dads seemed to be sailors fixated by either the blue water in the bottle or the thought of getting well away from mum and the kids for a Saturday afternoon.

Recently, Eau de Kenzo, Dolce & Gabbana Masculin, and Giorgio Armani's Emporio Armani, have all produced new fragrances designed as sex-aids. The names say it all — there is Romance for Men from Ralph Lauren, Desire from Alfred Dunhill. Take your pick of what you want from your man — love or lust?

Smells that work

The sexual allure of a fragrance is totally subjective and depends on skin chemistry. Something that smells wonderful on you might smell like room deodoriser on your sister. A fragrance that smells like petro-chemical extract on her could make you seem the sultriest beauty of all time. So are there fragrances which work for everyone? You have to try before you buy, then wear a fragrance for some time before you can know.

Or you can take some advice from an expert. Beauty writer Fiona Stewart named her top three fragrances, sure to work every time on an object of desire. (You'll need a certain proximity to him when you try this. If you use so much that you don't need that closeness, you will have used way too much! You'll be in the bank at lunchtime and men who are complete strangers will either be trying to attach themselves to you or fleeing.)

Stewart started with Jean Patou's Joy, a classic floral fragrance, heady with jasmine, which was first released in 1930. Then she moved on to Shalimar from Guerlain in 1925. It's a classic oriental fragrance, very vanillary. Both are available in Australia. But her third choice was interesting. It was Fracas, by Piguet, a single floral fragrance — in this case, tuberose — which was released in 1948. It smells like a storm at night in a tropical garden and is worn by the sexiest women in the know around the world.

Aromatherapy

The therapeutic properties of smells have been well known for thousands of years. You might find some of them beneficial as you plan your progress to being a successful User. Here are some possibilities:

1. Lavender is a sedative, with antiseptic and antidepressant properties. Put it in the linen press, on your pillowcases, or on your grandmother.
2. Eucalyptus purifies. And clears out the sinuses. Can trigger childhood memories of mother or Matron and Vicks rubbed on a congested little chest.
3. Mandarin raises happiness levels. Other citrus smells such as orange do too. At the same time, they raise energy levels. (Not to be used by pregnant women.)
4. Jasmine and neroli have aphrodisiac qualities. Put them in the parts of the house where you would like to be kissed.
5. Sandalwood is an aid to meditation, an essential aspect to remaining calm.

Just how you get these smells into your life depends on how careful you are. Scented candles are not recommended for clumsy clots with cats that like to jump on the furniture.

Burning essences — from fragrance houses such as Floris, Cath Collins or Diptyque for instance — are safer. They come with their own rings to pop on the top of light bulbs. The best scents for love? Narcissus and hyacinth.

Treat *pot-pourri* with care. You need to keep it well aired and refresh it often with the appropriate oils. If you don't, it can go mouldy and smell stale.

Air freshener in the bathroom is a naff no-no. Subtle, scented candles are a much better idea for the lavatory — all that tiled area is safer for an open flame.

Nothing will make your home smell better than a good clean. Polish the furniture with beeswax, arrange fresh flowers such as freesias, tuberoses, roses, bavadia. Burn gum leaves and pine cones. (Make sure you have a fireplace first.) Put on the fresh coffee, bake some bread and it's welcome to the scented version of *The Little House on the Prairie*. Kiss John-boy good night!

Kiss me, you fool!

Okay, you've passed the smell test. Can you pass the taste test? The smart User is ready to snog at all times, because it wouldn't be smart at all to allow a satisfying pash to pass.

- Every morning, noon and night, brush those teeth. Floss every day. Use mouthwash.
- Got some Tic Tacs? They should be a User's constant companion — in her handbag or her desk drawer at work. The fact that they have hardly any calories at all is a plus. (Unless you eat them by the handful — not recommended.) Want to get rid of that garlic breath? Eat parsley. The herb is good for your kidneys and helps eliminate the garlic odour.
- If you want to taste fresh and lemony, suck a piece of lemon, then chew it and swallow. Too much lemon juice, though, can start to wear the enamel on your teeth — not an ideal outcome.

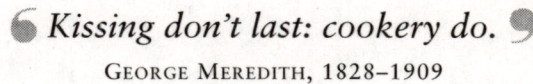

> *Kissing don't last: cookery do.*
> GEORGE MEREDITH, 1828–1909

comes the
moment,
comes the
man

7
Where do you get one?

Before you can use a man, you have to find one, and then work out if he is the sort of man worthy of, and agreeable to, being used. There is no use in trying to use a man who is dead set against it. Things can get ugly really quickly.

It is best to start with the best quality man you can find. (Sometimes, you will have to wait, but it will be worth it.)

Finding the right man is not a theoretical exercise. It is completely hands-on. You actually have to get out there and smell the flowers — and the fellas. It's a primal need that goes right back to when our ancestors had to sniff food to see if it was edible. Kissing and sniffing are in the same atavistic category, but don't try it these days on a total stranger in the fruit and veg section of the supermarket. You'll be on charges before you can say sexual harassment.

We know from Chapter 6 that perfumers have refined their science and thrown all of our prehistoric knowledge into confusion. These days all you have to do to smell like sex on a stick is wear Arden's Beauty or Dior's Diorissimo — just like every one else with the price of a bottle in their pocket. This presents a few problems of its own. How to pick the right one, when every man you meet smells so good?

Field research, that's how. You have to get out there and dig. And there is no reason at all why you can't press the family into action as part of your support team, either. You might think it's too late to get your Dad to make an arranged marriage — particularly since the only single men he knows now are the guys at the service station and a confirmed bachelor who plays the organ every Sunday at the local church.

Location, location, location!

If you are looking for the right man, or even just a new man, get out and scout! Below you will find the best places to meet potential love objects broken down into age groups.

You are fourteen to eighteen. McDonald's queue; behind the McDonald's counter. The bus stop. School. Woodwork classes. Rave parties. Big family gatherings, like christenings and weddings. The inter-school formal. Your brother's mates from school. Your best friend's cousins. Dancing lessons (jazz and tap rather than ballet, perhaps). Remedial coaching classes.(Necessary because you have spent too much time hanging around McDonald's staring at boys.)

Eighteen to twenty-five. University. Dance clubs. Your best friend's boyfriend's best friend. The train. (Not kidding. This is great.) The gym. (At least you'll know what you are going to cop before it happens … and so will they!) The local used car yard. The local cheap and cheerful Vietnamese joint.

Twenty-five to forty-five. Bars. Weddings. House auctions in flash suburbs. The local BMW dealership. Work. (A boss can be so attractive round about Christmas.) Higher education classes. Scuba/abseiling/canyoning/sailing lessons. The Internet. Divorce parties — this is where you can decide if you like the look of your best friend's first husband now that she's finished with him. Ricky Martin concerts. (Perhaps not such a good idea — it could seem a desperate attempt to look hip.)

Forty-five to sixty. Hospital. (You can try out your new breasts on someone who has just had a penile implant.) The Range Rover dealership. Superannuation maximisation seminars. The opera at half time. (Don't take your mother — it looks pathetic. Factor of two if he's with his). Home deliveries. Up-market restaurants on Friday at lunchtime. Group therapy. Meals on Wheels — you go to them.

Sixty plus. Big family gatherings, like funerals. The old people's home. Rolling Stones concerts. The queue at social services while you try to fix a problem with the pension. Meals on Wheels — they come to you.

So what are the other alternatives?

Work

Take a good look around your work station, desk, counter or bench. Does it look like your knight in shining armour is over there by the window on the help desk? If the answer is yes, immediately dismantle your mouse, pretend the PC is down and ask for help. If it's no, you might need to work a bit harder.

Most people meet their mates at work, so you will need to choose your career carefully. Otherwise you could find yourself tied to a career not only for your own life, but also for his.

Information technology. Information technology is promising. So is tourism. These are growth areas in the Australian workplace and it is really neat that between them they divide the population into two groups by personality. The analyticals head for the technology-oriented area, and the warm, fuzzy and friendly head for tourism. (Actually a lot of the latter used to find themselves in sales, but the hospitality industry seems a better place for all those longing to please complete strangers.) There's a downside to the touchy/feely jobs: work in sales and hospitality always brings the chance of a deal not being completed, or the client not being totally happy, and that can be crushing.

Medicine. Fifty years ago, hospitals were fantastic date and mate venues, veritable hotbeds of unrequited love, passion and intrigue. You don't imagine all those young women went into nursing because they had Florence Nightingale complexes, do you? A rare few might have, but many went into the profession with the sub-agenda of securing a future beyond the bedpans. To them, a hospital was a marriage market with autoclaves. A good many of them did succeed in marrying doctors, which explains why there are so many attractive, middle-aged medicos these days with rather possessive receptionists or nurses. The two point three children have left home and the wife needs something to do, so she might as well help out her husband while fending off any possible overtures from female patients.

This is not the case today, because female medical students, all earnestly pursuing their studies, are effectively the primary pool for courtship by medical students and registrars alike. Since studying medicine is no joke, and the attrition rate is high unless you are academically inclined, you might like to consider some other areas in which to establish yourself both professionally and socially.

Veterinary science and engineering. The faculties with the best ratio of men to women in university used to be veterinary science (and it still has a certain craggy appeal) and engineering. (You had to be careful here since there were different social styles among the engineers, and ranged from the civils to the electricals, which varied on the charm scale. There was always a looming danger that you might accidentally find yourself bound for life to a mining engineer.)

Advantage of workplace romance: Propinquity. You'll always know where he is — or should be. You'll always have something to talk about.

Disadvantage: Propinquity. You might still have to sit next to him if the relationship doesn't work out. It could be suffocating to be kept under surveillance.

Dating agencies

A dating agency can be expensive and unreliable and you might end up as part of an undercover exposé on *Today Tonight*. It's difficult to get success rates from these agencies, but certainly many do warn their clients that people outside the 'norms' in terms of looks or size might have trouble finding a match. Well, that would come as no surprise to the applicants, who would have already frequently felt the wretched sting of rejection. Having said this, the only man I know who used a dating agency married one of the women he was introduced to, and their long-term marriage is like many others now — hanging together for the sake of the children.

Friends

What about your girlfriends? It's a tried and true method, and one that worked for Prue, who knew she just needed to find just one person and how hard was that? Prue explained to me how she found her husband: 'I decided to make it a competition among my friends. They're clever and love a bit of fun. I told them I was seriously looking for a relationship and gave four of them three months each to introduce me to some of their most promising, single male friends,' she said.

> *To accomplish great things, we must not only act, but also dream; not only plan, but also believe.*
> ANATOLE FRANCE, 1844–1924

'Every week, they gave me an update. Every other week, I saw a couple of new guys — generally at dinner, with them as chaperones. It was brilliant. A couple of them tried to introduce me to the same person, who ended up being the man I married … I had to keep on their cases, otherwise they might have lost interest. Mostly, I kept telling them that X had introduced me to a great guy, that I was really interested in. Even though there was a prize at the end of it all — a bottle of champagne — they did it for the challenge.' It worked. Prue's been happily married for nearly five years now.

The advantages of Prue's method: you increase your chances by enlisting your friends to your cause. You will meet people liked by people you like. But if you reject a perfectly good candidate without sufficient reason, they might feel aggrieved. Here's the thing: you actually have to get out into the real world and take a few chances. It will be a cold day in Hell when you actually find a new man in your life while you are sitting on the couch in your nightgown under a doona, applying a packet of double-dipped Tim Tams directly to your gums and watching endless chick flicks on the video and wondering why the men you know are more Rupert Everett (too gay) than George Clooney (not gay enough).

However, if the sound of that doona thing appeals just a little, here are some ever-popular chick flicks you might like to settle in with for the season: *An Affair to Remember, Sleepless in Seattle, When Harry Met Sally, Brief Encounter, While You Were Sleeping, My Best Friend's Wedding, Strictly Ballroom, Little Women* and *Runaway Bride*.

A word of caution: do not attempt to watch all of these at once: you will be completely awash and it will take ages to dry out the pillows. Alternatively, if you want a cheerful chick flick, see if you can get hold of *Pillow Talk*, and then try to block out any thought of Rock Hudson not being completely straight with Doris Day.

> *There is nothing a woman hates so much as to see men selfishly enjoying themselves without the benefit of feminine society.*
> KATHARINE TYNAN HINKSON, 1861–1911

Family

Never dismiss out of hand any suggestion from any member of your family that they might have found the right bloke for you. But remember, forced marriages are not generally accepted in Australia. You still have a say. And also bear in mind that your Nanna's idea of a perfect mate for you might be dependent on the fact that he has nice table manners, the right religion and hasn't recently been seen spitting in the street. Ask yourself if anyone who has your best interests at heart is going to introduce you to a sex god. It's just not that likely you could get so lucky.

However, anyone is worth a little look. It could be a story to tell your mutual grandchildren, just about the time you start trying to organise their private lives for them and getting them to marry their own, distant, cousins.
Advantage: You can discuss his kinfolk with authority and impunity — after all, they're yours too. A mad family (and which one isn't?) is a brilliant thing to have in common — its members give you such marvellous talking points.
Disadvantage: Consanguinity. Marriage between first cousins is not recommended for people who like their children complete with chins.

> *Dancing is wonderful training for girls. It's the first way you learn to guess what a man is going to do before he does it.*
> CHRISTOPHER MORLEY, 1890–1957

Parties and bars

It's chancy to take home from a bar a person whose name you barely know and won't remember in the morning. You could find a real-life Mr Goodbar.

Parties can also be extremely hazardous for even the most prudent judges of men. It's amazing how even an ordinary man can look like Clark Gable through the bottom of a wine glass at eleven at night and then, to your horror, like a nerdy loser when viewed through the bottom of a glass of orange juice at eight the following morning.

For those of you who are a little bit reckless, there really are some rules you need to consider before you slip into the sequinned mules and fling on the party frock.

The first is, never drink a brightly colored drink. Anything that is lurid pink, blue, acid yellow or green, probably should be used as a toilet cleaner, not mixed into a cocktail glass and passed around at parties. This goes double if the drink is opaque.

If that drink has a name like Virgin's Ruin, Slow Seduction, Screaming Orgasm or Harvey Wallbanger, just say no prettily and move on. These names are not a hint but a warning of what is to come, and are designed to embarrass ('Would you prefer a Long Slow Screw or a Cock-Sucking Cowboy?'). Truth in advertising should require cocktails to be a little more honestly named — but then who, in her right mind, would willingly wrap her fingers around something labelled Surefire Ice Pick Headache or Total Lunacy After Only One Of Me?

Having one or two of the above tends to inhibit the ability to count, form coherent thoughts and make a proper value judgment about how you want to spend the next few hours. These deadly cocktails make you think you've only had a couple until your feet start to go numb and you find yourself leaning against a stranger (or worse, at the Christmas party, your boss) and that person is starting to look pretty good to you.

This sort of rocket-fuel inspired behaviour tends to land you in the position where the love, or hate, which you otherwise dare not reveal begins to rattle ominously at its cage door. While the ancients Romans declared '*In vino, veritas*', sometimes it's best not to let the truth genie out of the bottle and into your glass.

If you disregard this rule about exotic drinks, you might well find yourself breaking the other big rule for parties. If you start to feel your mouth forming the words 'I've always wanted to tell you this …' don't pass go, don't collect $200, just try to shut up. This phrase is inevitably followed by disaster, or words that can never be taken back — words such as 'I've always fancied you' (poison for your private life, particularly if you are looking at a girlfriend's boyfriend), or 'why are you such a complete moron?' (and there goes that career path, right down the plughole). Just put down the glass, get yourself into a cab immediately and then go home to your own bed as quickly as you can. (But take a telephone number before you go — you might need it some time soon.)

Once you are home, however, disconnect all the telephones and hide the mobile, otherwise you could find yourself in the middle of a drink and dial episode to the far reaches of the world. Or even worse — talking to the person to whom you were about to unburden yourself at the party! Write yourself a little note next to the telephone number you collected earlier and then you can decide — presupposing you can read the scrawl — if you really want to follow up that addled contact in the cold clear light of day.

(One final rule for office Christmas parties: never, ever, photocopy any part of your body on the office copier. Not unless you want to see bits of yourself scanned into the office computer system and used as screen savers until the next Christmas party when some other dill decides doing the same thing seems like a really smart move.)

Best for any knees-up, one alcoholic drink and then stick to the mineral water. You are a woman on a mission — so keep yourself tidy.

Advantage: sober, you'll see what alcohol does to a man. The morning after, you will also be able to find the telephone number he gave you — and remember what he looked like.

Disadvantage: if you drink heavily, a prospective lover will see how alcohol works on you. Can you stand the exposure?

On the move

It *is* possible to find a man on the 8.04 am to Central. It's equally likely you can find one flying in business class to Los Angeles or first class to Rome. You pick.

Advantage: you can eventually get off if his direction doesn't suit.

Disadvantage: sometimes, you can get carried past your stop — particularly if you are lulled into a false sense of security and doze off.

Some other places to meet men

Religious services. At least you should be assured the people you meet are genuine, if a trifle earnest.

At the supermarket. Take a quick glance at the trolley of a man who might interest you and deconstruct it. Muesli? Good — shows he's switched on. Bran Flakes? Not good. Possible indicator of gut problems. Olive oil? Bad — he should be buying this in a proper deli. Bananas? Good. He obviously likes fruit with a sense of humour. Tampax could mean an unnecessary complication, unless he's buying them for his mother — and how likely does that sound?

At a non-threatening, active sporting event. Golf is good. Mini-golf is miles better — there are more giggles and less opportunity to be beaned by a golf ball.

At an evening class run by the stock exchange. Mmm, an interest in money and how to make it work for you. Good relationships have been built on less. But remember, if you marry for money, you'll spend your life earning it. And when he tells you to come, you'd better come quickly.

On a blind date. There is a lot to be said for a pre-arranged meeting. Your friends should know a little about his background. Although their geek-meters are not likely to be as finely tuned as yours — out-of-date experience in the date market can send their judgment a little skewiff on occasion — you can be pretty well assured that the guy they are proposing is unlikely to be a serial killer.

Where not to meet men

Hell's Angels chapter meetings

You will meet men here, of course, but not one you will ever be able to produce in public, let alone introduce to your family and friends. Try to picture the scene: you on the back of the bike, he's in the colours up front, burning up your parents' front drive. Then try to picture yourself taking off the crash hat and revealing a 'do which is not helmet hair. Impossible. Then try to imagine your father enduring the meeting with anything approaching equanimity.

It's more likely he'll have a stroke. Killing your father is not the ideal way to begin any significant relationship.

Night classes

Cooking classes. First of all, you have to decide what sort of cuisine you fancy, before you even think about what sort of fanciable bloke might take that class. Thai green chicken curry? Guacamole and chocolate chicken? (Calm down and think about what mess you are going to get into in the kitchen here.) Since he's going to all the trouble of learning how to cook, can't you just hear the tortilla graduate insisting: 'But you know the rules! I cooked so you have to wash up.' Scraping the seafood off the ceiling after a little vigorous paella making can smother the smallest signs of romance in the amount of time it takes to plaster it up there.

Computer and language classes. You will grow old trying to meet men *you* might find interesting at a computer class. Also, it is almost impossible to find one at all — at least one under the age of 60 — in a language class, unless it's German and then he'll be boning up as a precursor to spending a year in Bonn completing his PhD thesis on the vivisection techniques of Galen. (Galen was the third-century Greek who liked to slice up elephants to see how they worked.)

The same goes for French and Italian classes. The first are filled with retiring and retired chemists, who, drunk on Peter Mayle's A *Year in Provence*, or Frances Mayes's *Under the Tuscan Sun*, are about to pack themselves off to a troglodyte village in the Loire for a little serious Sancerre research, or end up in a Tuscan hill town exploring the relative delights of the local Orvieto. *Bonne chance, mon brave*, and *buona fortuna*.

The Italian classes have more talent because the lecturers tend to be attractive, charming and bright — sigh — and the students more expansive and expressive than their counterparts in the French group. Since these guys are looking forward to spending time with their Sicilian fiancées on the plains near Catania, you need to take care on a couple of levels. The first is purely linguistic — those Sicilians speak dialect, so if you're trying to share study time with them, you won't be learning the language of Dante. And the second is a minor matter — the alternative government is still rife in Sicily. With your luck, your classmate's loved one will turn out to be a Mafia princess.

Go to language class, by all means. Then export the learning when you go on holiday, where you will be able to practise on the locals and have some real fun.

Life-drawing classes. You'll see a naked guy, meet a lot of nice women and some lovely old guys. Is that what you're after?

Funerals

No matter how good you look in black, don't even think about it, unless you are over sixty.

White-water rafting, bungee jumping, anything remotely life-threatening

Very bad for your hair. You'll look like a drowned rat, then you might actually become a drowned rat.

The gym

You'll know what he looks like stripped down. This is a good thing. He will know what you look like with your leotard wedged up your bottom. Not a good thing.

8
The dating game

Dating etiquette

It's Friday night. You are in a bar and while you are not quite as white-hot as Carrie Bradshaw, ordering Manhattans in a trendy nightspot in New York, you're looking pretty good and the Prada shoes aren't pinching, which means you've really got something to smile about. No wonder the solo man on the opposite side of the bar notices you and sends over a drink. What should you do?

Do what Carrie does. If he's attractive and looks interesting and if he's appropriately dressed for his surroundings, by all means *accept* — have a chat. Time to get flirty! If he's none of the above and looks like an accountant or a sex maniac and you still think it might be a good idea to have a drink with him, you should never be allowed out without a chaperone. Report to your mother at once.

When he arrives at your side, what do you say? Keep it light. Admire him — his taste, his eyes, his tan, his fencing scar, his wedding ring (okay, maybe not that). Show an interest in him. Who doesn't like to be appreciated? Make sure, though, that the flattery doesn't tip into falseness. Start with the basics: what do you do or how do you like to spend the weekend? Build up a useful profile of a man who might just turn out to be worth a longer-term investment than five minutes over a drink in a bar.

It would be even better if the lone man on the other side of the bar were not alone but with some of his pals instead. You can tell so much about prospective dates by their mates. There he stands, in the middle of a group of his work colleagues or members of his squash team or soccer squad, giving you enough context for you to read him like a book. (If he's out with his flatmates, you can even get a preview of his wardrobe, since they will undoubtedly have similar tastes, if not actually share the same clothes around.)

So he buys you a drink and after the preliminaries, you can ask him about his friends. Now, if they're the under-forties from a pigeon-fanciers club, or used to all be on day-release together, you really don't have much of a decision to make, unless you, too, are a pigeon-fancier (so unlikely) or have a passion for ex-cons (something for which you should seek clinical help rather than fulfillment).

In this case, after a little further small talk, say (nicely), 'Thanks so much for the drink, but I really must be going,' and then head straight out that door. On the outside, thank your lucky stars that you discovered these skeletons early. However, if he says something like, 'We're all part of a Gregorian chant ensemble' or 'We're the ASX chapter of the Harley Davidson-fanciers tour group', then you might have a little food for thought. Just how much do you fancy Gregorian chant? How attached could you become to a man with a Hog? Could your skin stand up to all that wind damage? Could your hair stand up to the helmet?

Check out his friends

My friend Anastasia met her ill-fated boyfriend, Joe, in his context. 'A group of six of us had taken an apartment on the Gold Coast for the university break. The owner/manager of the apartments was reluctant to let us have the place, because he insisted where there were groups of girls, there were always boys,' she told me. 'We were astounded and said take a look at us, do we look like the sort of girls who would have boys in? Honestly, we were a muddled mix of hormones, pimples, over self-conscious clothes, bad haircuts and puppy fat. The charmlessness of the four of us more than outweighed and totally obscured the two raving beauties who were also part of the party. He had another look and clearly, he didn't think any of us was boy bait. He let us have the flat.'

That was a mistake, as the landlord soon understood. Youth is, in and of itself, beautiful. At the same time, Anastasia and her group learned a lesson too — sometimes, it doesn't matter to boys what girls look like. It just matters that they are girls and that they are there. This explains why quite a lot of people who are, let's say, *challenged* in the looks department, manage to cut a swathe through the opposite sex. They are simply there.

'The first day we were on the beach, a football team appeared and that was that. We had a caravan of admirers for a week. There were fantastic odds — fifteen guys, six girls — and a couple of vet students who were already there with us. They became our guardian angels and self-appointed chaperones, which was for some of us a mixed blessing.

'But it was really incredible to get to know a guy in his own social milieu — notwithstanding that it was a football tour which means a lot of drinking and male bonding. It also meant quite a lot of harmless fooling about with the girls — and some quite tender moments as well. That came as a bit of a surprise to me because I had grown up with three brothers who, when they weren't torturing me, were silently tolerating me. It was easy to understand more about a guy when you could see him with about twenty other people in a small space.' Just like *Big Brother*, really, but without the cameras or the voting.

This image of Joe — particularly his honesty in his interaction with his friends — helped Anastasia fall in love with him. Pity that what she didn't see was that Joe was pathologically incapable of being honest with the opposite sex. 'It didn't work out in the long run, but with his mates, he's still that dependable guy. It's just with women he turned out to be totally unreliable,' she said.

Jennifer, on the other hand, has been married for more than four years to a man she met in context — with his mates at the local surf club. She knew exactly what she was getting into when she started to go out with James. 'He was a lovely guy, the sweetest of his group. Mind you, that wouldn't have been hard. There were guys in that club who were incredibly awful. There was a tight little group of four who hung around, smoked dope and went surfing all day. One of them was called Rubbish, two others were called Ox and Hoss, and then the most outgoing of them all was this character called Tinny, because he was the proud owner of a flashy powerboat the others named, predictably *The Tinny*,' Jennifer remembered.

'When it became obvious James and I were getting closer, they became as jealous as old girlfriends. They tried everything to split us up, always telling James they had seen me with another guy (generally one of my brothers) or that I was running around on him. Then, one of them tried to hit on me, and that was the end. I told James it was over, and why. Loved him, hated his mates.'

> *Love does not consist in gazing at each other, but in looking together in the same direction.*
> ANTOINE DE SAINT-EXUPERY, 1900–1944

It might have ended there, which would have suited the surf-club gang of four right down to the sand. But James didn't want to be forced to choose between the friends he'd had since he was a Nipper and his new girlfriend. So Jennifer and James reached an agreement. His friends were his friends, hers were hers, and they drew a line in the sand between their lives together and the time they spent apart.

'It was perfect. I never had to see Rubbish, Tinny or the others again — except at the wedding. James still sees those guys, but they've grown apart. He's married, a couple of the others are engaged, and they're busy with lives of their own. I just had to say I didn't want to spend any more time with them and wait them out. Though as they have got older, they're less offensive now. Or maybe I'm just more tolerant.'

One of the prime activities for blokes with their mates is watching sport — either in real life or on television. The successful User will recognise both these leisure pursuits as taking the heat off her, and providing him with an interest. How many times have we heard an avid sportsman declare his devotion to anything from three-day eventing to the luge from the depths of a sofa in front of a live broadcast, when you know for a fact that the man in question hasn't been near a horse since he fell off a merry-go-round at the age of six, and couldn't have picked a luge from a pot of rouge two days before the Winter Olympics opened?

Women who are not-so-smart Users tend to resent the amount of time men spend watching sport. It's a waste of effort. If they are out watching sport, then you should make the most of *your* time out. And if they're parked in front of the television watching the ice hockey, at least they are safe and within earshot and you might be able to encourage them to help with the housework during the commercial breaks.

And there can be an unexpected bonus — the excitement of a hard-fought win for the favourite team has sometimes been known to stir even the most dedicated lounge lizard into becoming an unexpectedly passionate lover. Just make sure you're away from the family room (which might contain young and impressionable family members) before this win/win situation occurs.

How his mates can be useful

- While they are all out at the footy, you can have your girlfriends around for a Sunday in front of the VCR and a collection of girly movies. It's also a good opportunity to have and give facials and pedicures at the same time.
- They can also occupy him while you go and visit your mother (that saves everyone's nerves) or have lunch with a male friend (which saves his).
- When he goes fishing, you can go shopping. This is a perfect opportunity to buy and get the stuff home and into the cupboards before he comes round from his day out with the boys and the bait. Don't forget to remove all evidence such as bags, dockets, excess tissue paper, etc. This is not deception, it's simply *good crisis management* — manage it ahead of time, and there will be no crisis!
- It's winter, you love skiing, he prefers hiking. Send him off to the hills with the boys and turn yourself into a snowbunny. Or he's action man on the weekend and you just want to play front row with the couch potatoes. Call his pals, pack them a picnic, wave goodbye fondly. Take the phone off the hook. Grab a book and a block of Cadbury's Dairymilk Chocolate, and climb into bed. Men never understand about the sheer indulgence of these three combined — particularly if they all happen in the afternoon. Make sure you're up and have searched the bed for chocolate bits before he comes back.
- His night out with the guys means you get a night out with the girls.
- His single friends can, on occasion, be a useful resource for your

unmarried girlfriends, either as dates or possible husband material. Just don't help the match along too much, in case it all ends in tears and some of the blame is sheeted home to you.
- They have to listen to the boring golf stories and look interested. Again. And again.

Remedial classes for dating duds

> *A general review of the sex situation*
> *Woman wants monogamy;*
> *Man delights in novelty.*
> *Love is a woman's moon and sun;*
> *Man has other forms of fun.*
> *Woman lives but in her lord;*
> *Count to ten and Man is bored.*
> *With this the gist and sum of it,*
> *What earthly good can come of it?*
> DOROTHY PARKER, 1893–1967

What earthly good indeed? But still we persist with the 'sex situation' and every so often we need, not so much the modern phenomenon of a speed-dating session, but a little remedial dating class to help us along the way. Once again in the name of research, I went to a course on mating and dating. (I hasten to point out, though, that the order of things was in the reverse — dating came first. And there was no discussion of mating at all — what the students did after the dating was apparently their own business.)

Times have changed, and so have courtship rituals for working singles — people so wrapped up in their jobs they seem to have forgotten how to get a date, let alone go on one.

At the time I was very single. Time and experience had taught me that my last loved one was not the right partner for me. So while it was billed as just for fun, I went along to the class with a serious purpose in mind. Perhaps, just perhaps, I might learn the secrets of dating success. Maybe I was doing something wrong and this class might just help. Every Tuesday night, I turned up to the class with six other women and five men to learn the secrets of successful mating and dateing.

The class was varied. Members were aged from twenty-eight to forty-something, mostly professional, all more or less polished, some divorced, one a widow and some never married. It was soon reduced by one when a thirtyish woman, who had joined the class simply because she wanted to get out and about, stopped coming. She would rather, she had confided to her classmates in lesson one, stay home on Saturday and read the paper than go out with a man. As it turned out, she obviously preferred to stay home on Tuesday nights as well.

The rest of the class stuck it out and discovered the top five qualities, according to the moderator, that you should have to attract a partner. (Give yourself a smack if you listed cute butt and dimples — it's not that superficial.) Okay, so here they are:

Good self-esteem. If you think you are pretty terrific, then the chances are that other people will think the same about you, no matter how deluded you might be. On the other hand, if you honestly feel that your attractiveness level is somewhere between the hunchback of Notre Dame and Granny out of the *Beverly Hillbillies*, you will certainly communicate that to others. Think about how healthy the self-esteem of Americans seems to be — but be careful: there is a fine line between a healthy self-esteem and an out-of-control ego.

If you are a trainee User, and your self-esteem is a problem, you can work on it. Take a multi-faceted approach. Try relaxation, including yoga or Pilates; twenty minutes of meditation a day; self-hypnosis; exercise (an hour's walk three times a week can improve outlook); tai chi; and muscle relaxation. If that doesn't work, go to the movies on Saturday afternoon and check out the others in the crowd. If these people can get dates, you will be able to as well.

Confidence. It worked as a mantra for Maria in *The Sound of Music* ('I have confidence in confidence alone ... Can't you see? I have con-fid-ence in meeeee!!'), so it must be okay. People like other people who are confident, who can take charge and be dominant (in the nicest possible way). However, they do not like people who are controlling.

A relaxed approach. It's no surprise to learn that people respond well to others who appear to be calm and at ease. Well, it stands to reason. Who wants to be around someone who is wound tighter than a watch spring? Being relaxed also indicates that the self-esteem and confidence are in pretty good shape as well. It also shows the world that you are not at odds with your environment and haven't worked yourself into a flight or fight response.

Being personable. People who are warm and outgoing attract more people than those who are reserved and withdrawn. The ones who make an effort, who move outside their own comfort zone to increase yours, are appreciated. They generally greet the world with a wide smile, an open heart and an outstretched hand. You'll find their more reserved brothers and sisters huddled in corners at parties, siege mentality engaged.

Good communication skills. This, of course, is a two-way street. Good communicators are good listeners as well as good talkers. People love it when you pay them attention and actually listen while they speak. And if you encourage them with little murmurs, they will rate your communication skills higher. The sweetest sound to anyone is that of his or her own name. If you are speaking to someone, use their name occasionally, to let them know you paid enough attention at the introduction to remember it.

The moderator gave the class some ice-breaking gambits — but use them at your own discretion:

'It's a beautiful/wet/hot/cold day.' Remember, no-one ever said you had to be original with an opening gambit — just ask a chess grandmaster. They use the same opening moves all the time.

'What are you doing on the weekend?' This one feels a little pushy to me — as though the questioner is asking to be included in the plans, but it's actually better than the first. It elicits information, whereas the first opener can be closed right down with a yes or no.

'That's a wonderful Manet.' This obviously really only works if you're standing right in front of one, but you understand the theory.

'Are you waiting for someone special — or will I do?' Although the counsellor seemed to think this was a good opener, it sounds as though the questioner doesn't think he/she is special at all. Unless you are Winona Ryder and it can be interpreted as charming self-deprecation, it's definitely loser-speak. Worse, though: this sounds incredibly twee.

'I'm new around here and need some help. Could you tell me where I can find the train station/the tinned peaches/the spells for beginner's section?'

Be careful if the person you ask does know where those *grimoires* are. Warlocks might be fun to watch on *Buffy the Vampire Slayer* but would you really want to date one?

I was slightly taken aback to hear one of the class ask the facilitator if using one of these lines wouldn't make her appear, well, just a little bit forward. 'Who cares!' chorused the rest of the class, and the woman who didn't wish to appear too fast retreated quickly into her natural reserve.

That class was an odd experience. Our basic personalities, obvious at the beginning of the course, became more pronounced as the weeks passed. For instance, in the first class, one of the men — an engineer — announced very firmly that the problem with women was that they never listened enough. He was divorced and clearly was still suffering from the trauma.

After week three, I went to dinner with the engineer. You cannot imagine what it was like. The dinner was pleasant enough, and certainly there was no problem with him speaking. In fact, that's what he did — about himself, without pausing for breath, the whole night. He didn't ask me a single question about me and my life. Instead, he spent two hours telling me, in detail, how he had rebuilt his vintage sports car from the wheels up.

It was obvious why his wife hadn't listened — the marvel was how she had stood it for so long. He was obsessive and a complete bore. I tuned out after about ninety minutes, which probably just confirmed his opinion about women in general. I couldn't wait to leave and then I had to spend three more Tuesday nights trying to avoid another instalment of his adventures with a shifting spanner.

Things they never teach you at remedial dating

Sometimes, on a big night out, you need to know when to cut your losses and run. Here are some clues for when you should take a little time out.
Do you know how you are getting home? Where your keys are? Your name? If you can't answer two or more of those simple questions and readily put your hand on the handbag, it's time to go. (But if you can't find your handbag, how do you think you are going to get there?)
You are dancing wildly, sensuously and passionately — even better than Kylie

and J. Lo put together. There's a touch of Britney in there too. You are sex to the max. (That's what you think.)

You want a fight. You've had too much of the Russian misery water and, hey presto, you want to sort someone out. Even worse, you reckon you could take them out. (Which is funny, since you can't even take the little paper umbrella out of your glass, and you've already nearly removed your eye with it when you tried to skol the Bloody Mary.)

Partying makes you look *fab*! Everyone else looks trashed after three hours on the dance floor, but you look better than ever! You wonder: how do I do it? (Everyone else wonders: *why* does she do it?)

You've found the deeper, spiritual side to the geek sitting next to you. What's more, the skinny little thing's looking really cute. What if he turns out to be the next Bill Gates? Or even Bill Gates himself? You begin to see yourself as secular Mother Theresa and give a comfort flirt to the freaky. (He's looking about as cute as you, probably.)

You suddenly take up smoking, thinking this is a really good way to cruise the room and meet men. (Reality check: because you bum the fags, you look mean as …)

Curse these Manolos! You take your shoes off because you think it's their fault that you're having problems walking straight. (Note to self: wear more friendly shoes for next expedition into the realm of the voddytonic. Wedges, perhaps.)

Any of these sound familiar? Then it's time to say goodnight, Gracie.

Dating: the bottom line

The most useful thing I learned in the mating and dating class: to stop mind reading. Interpreting what a man says can lead to terrible misunderstandings. The facilitator gave this example from cognitive therapist Aaron Beck, author of *Love is Never Enough*. An imaginary couple has gone from quiet reflection to threatened divorce in a matter of seconds and the car isn't even out of the driveway.

He is tired, and quiet on the way home from dinner.

She: *He's really quiet. He must be angry with me*. She becomes upset and withdrawn.

He: *She's so moody. What's wrong with her?* He retreats even further into silence.

She: *He's stopped loving me. I can't exist if he doesn't love me.* Cries.

He shouting: 'What's the matter now?' *Why does she always cry.*

She shouting: 'I'm going to file for a divorce.' *No-one will ever love me again.* Further sobs.

Nothing if not game, and still in the name of research, I decided to start at square one — and took a flirting workshop. Here is some of what the coach told a class of the walking wounded from the sexual revolution.

'Find something nice about another member of the class and compliment them on it,' instructed the teacher. Too late — I had already done that to almost everyone I had encountered that day before morning tea. 'Remember the other person's name,' the teacher taught, which was too late again. I'd already memorised everyone's name and then forgotten the ones in whom I had no interest.

By this stage, I was wondering what on earth I was doing in a classroom on a sunny Sunday. The women were attractive, confident and smart. On the whole, the men were insecure, not that attractive, and seemed to be resentful of the fact that women had not paid them enough attention in the past.

It was an extraordinary seminar, which included the use of the glance (give someone the once-over so they know they've had one, then look back again), a flick of the hair, which indicates interest from a woman, and the value of a reassuring light touch — as opposed to the pre-emptive lunge. It was enlivened in the afternoon by the appearance of a psychologist who specialised in helping people work through shyness. He made a lot of sense, but the smartest thing he said was some of the things my mother taught me when I was fourteen.

They were:

If you want to meet people at a party, pass the tray of food or drinks around. And keep passing until you have met everyone a couple of times. No need for an icebreaker then.

People love it when you make things easier for them in a social sense. If you go out of your way to make people feel more comfortable, you will do infinitely better than if you almost dare them to talk to you, and then to like you.

What would your mother have to say about rejection? Just that it's the price you pay for being alive.

If they knock you back, they're not smart enough to worry about. Move on to some one who is.

So, you've been practising your dating techniques, and nothing is happening? Should you ask a guy out? Why not? Coffee is good to start with. People might say it's manners to wait until you're asked, but truly, life is too short.

Unsexy beasts

The business of mating and dating can be so complicated some delicate souls just give up in terror and retreat to their jobs, a good book or restless travel to try to blot out the problem.

But mating and dating, no matter what the momentary discomforts, has got to be a better way (when it works out well) to ensure the survival of the species than the method evolved by one species of deep-sea anglerfish. The female of the species can be several thousand times larger than the males, according to *The Dance of Life*, by Mark Jerome Walters, and lives in the pitch black at a depth of around 600 metres. It can't be too easy meeting another anglerfish under those conditions. However, when a minute male angler gets within striking distance of a female, he sinks his fangs into her side and fuses to her body. Scientists discovered that the tiny parasitic appendages attached to the females are actually their mates. After the fusion, most of the male's body withers away until only the gonads are left. 'A steady supply of sperm, but a poor companion,' comments Walters.

It's even less fun for the male praying mantis, which after mating, has his head torn from his body and consumed by the female — useful protein to ensure the survival of the mother and therefore the offspring.

Still, if you are in the dating phase of life and it's starting to look like a cross between *Survivor* (outwit, outlast, outplay) and *Big Brother* ('It's time to go ...'), take heart.

Users will now refer to Charles Darwin, author *of The Origin of the Species by Means of Natural Selection* and *The Descent of Man*. As the distance between male and female of different species became greater, so the negotiations between them became more complex and more drawn out. Forced to couple, the alliance between female and male was shaky and underscored by a natural distrust. In 1871, Darwin suggested 'mating was more a bitter truce than a wilful embrace'. And that leads us neatly to the next chapter.

9
Love out-sourced

Looks matter

Books *are* judged by their covers. No, seriously, stop that shrieking. No matter how much you might think it's unfair, the User knows that how you look counts. That's why people with blue eyes generally do better than those of us who don't — it's called the 'halo effect'. Everybody who has ever looked into a pair of celestial blue eyes, or those the exact colour of the Indian Ocean off Perth, and suddenly found themselves gasping for breath, will know exactly what that means. Psychologists understand that a particular positive attribute or characteristic — such as blue eyes, blonde hair, height, or intelligence — can have such an effect on observers that they will also ascribe other, positive, values to the observed. The halo effect tends to rob an individual of the ability to apply objective judgement to another.

People who are considered 'attractive' do better on the whole than people who are not. A US study was done to see if life does, indeed, favour the fair. The results of that research, published in 1986 in *Mirror Mirror: The Importance of Looks in Everyday Life* by Elaine Hatfield and Susan Sprecher, were hardly startling. Hatfield and Sprecher found that while beauty is in the eye of the beholder, and standards vary between cultures and eras, it does make life easier for those blessed with it. (The halo effect can also work in reverse: blondes who have heard more than enough blonde jokes will attest to that.)

According to a survey by headhunters Morgan and Banks, some sixty-five per cent of people think physical appearance is more important for a woman's career success than a man's. Some 4000 people were surveyed on the question, and among the young, there was almost a seventy-five per cent agreement with the notion. Not surprisingly, as the respondents matured, they tended to disagree with the proposition. In the fifty-five plus age group, only one third of those surveyed said looks made more of a difference to women.

At the time, the then-New South Wales Minister for Community Affairs, Fay Lo Po' did some not unexpected huffing about the results when they were released, and was quoted as saying they demonstrated yet another hurdle for women. 'If NASA scientists had come from the ranks of matinee idols, we would never have been to the moon,' she said.

> *All of the animals except man know that the principal business of life is to enjoy it.*
> SAMUEL BUTLER, 1835–1902

That actually seems a bit 'lookist' itself. Does that mean a man cannot look like George Clooney and have a brain like the one found inside the skull of, say, Stephen Hawking, the brilliant author of *A Brief History of Time*, who is trapped inside a body crippled with a motor function disease? That Clooney-Hawking cross would be a marvellous creature to find, though the user knows she probably has more chance of being trampled by a unicorn in Pitt Street at rush hour on a Friday night. You can keep looking — there's that pesky triumph of hope over experience again — but don't hold your breath.

> *Appearances are not held to be a clue to the truth. But we seem to have no other.*
> IVY COMPTON-BURNETT, 1884–1969

But good looks do count more for women than for men. You just have to take a quiet shooftie at the tele to work out that men can look like unmade beds (be he newsreader, politician or businessman) and still be taken seriously, but women have to make some sort of Olympian effort to get anywhere at all. (That's quite a dispiriting thought, but some women deal with it all the time.)

If you ever see an objectively non-glamorous woman in a position of power and influence, you can be assured of a couple of things: she's marvellously bright and hard working. And if she has somehow transformed herself into a swan, she has a fantastic team of stylists behind her. Just take a look at Hillary Clinton for proof — she used to be as plain as a hospital sheet before Bill made it into the White House. With hair and make-up in place and a wardrobe full of power suits, she went for broke when her husband was President. When he left office, she has shucked off the First Lady role, won a US Senate seat and become a front-line power-broker in her own right.

Dating agencies

The relentless need to look good can be extremely tiring, as any User can attest. Combined with full work-days and hectic schedules, that can leave a lot of women with little time and less energy to find that Clooney/Hawking ideal.

So what's the answer to this problem? Out-sourcing! It makes sense, of course. You can, if you like, hire someone to clean the house, do the shopping, deliver dinner, paint your nails, de-flea the dog, and flog your butt around the local park for an hour every morning to get you fit and charge you hundreds of dollars a week for the privilege. So why not hire someone to take the chance out of romance for you?

Commercial dating agencies report a surge in the number of single, well-paid women availing themselves of these services. Previously, lonely hearts clubs used to be the province of the desperate and dateless; the people who had given up on trying to find romance in the usual way.

> *Bachelors know more about women than married men; if they didn't, they'd be married too.*
> H. L. MENCKEN, 1880–1956

Not to be unkind, but lonely hearts are generally alone for a reason. Such as, they want to be. Or they have been hard-wired *in utero* to be loners. Or they don't have the sort of small talk required to ease a member of the opposite sex into a friendship or, later, a relationship. Or they regularly picked partners so toxic that they retired from the field of love hurt and took up macramé, or organic bread-making, or even (heaven help them) bridge, as a displacement activity for sex.

But Nature abhors a vacuum in much the same way the community really does not adore a solo act. Even though single person-households are the fastest growing sector in Australian society and women today are twice as likely as their mothers to stay single throughout their lives, the pressure's still on.

Faster than you can say Kiss Me Quick & Associates, some of these loners are off to lonely hearts agencies. Many are undoubtedly successful, but others have been helped into romances for which many of them were absolutely unsuited. Which is when some of them discovered that the loneliest place in the world can be a double bed occupied by two.

> *The wind blows out of the gates of the day,*
> *The wind blows over the lonely of heart,*
> *And the lonely of heart is withered away.*
> W. B. YEATS, 1865–1939

If this goes on, pretty soon you'll be able to hire someone who will not only have a child for you (a surrogate parent), but also have sex for you, cuddle for you, exist your existence for you. If this is what they mean when they say women have come a long way, most smart Users would rather not be along for the ride. We'll be doing our own shopping, thanks, and taking our own chances. It might be a little bit hit and miss, but at least we'll be making our own mistakes.

And here's something to think about — what if the dream Clooney/Hawking mix turned out the other way around? George's brain and Stephen's looks? (That, of course, is an old joke, ascribed to either George Bernard Shaw and an actress, or to Albert Einstein and Marilyn Monroe. She: 'Imagine if we had a child. Your brains and my looks.' He: 'Imagine the reverse!') Perhaps it's better not to indulge in wishful thinking when it comes to eugenics.

Things not to expect from a dating agency

Successful outcomes. If you are not pretty or handsome, if you are overweight, underweight, have a squint, a goitre, a limp or anything else that could put you outside physical norms, you might not have much luck. Less than reputable firms will take your money, but if you complain about the length of time they take to make a match, or the number of inappropriate matches made for you, they will tell you regretfully that someone like you is difficult to match. Stories like these are the staples of television current affairs programs.

The man of your dreams. Honestly, do you think that he would be signing up with one of these? He's out sailing, or skiing, or building a mudbrick house in the country, not loitering in the foyer of Looking for Love Inc.

Brad Pitt does not go to a dating agency. People more in the mould of Hannibal Lecter, however, might be inclined to.

Things to expect from a dating agency

- That it could cost you a lot of money and might have absolutely no positive result.
- That true love will be, as always, elusive but not impossible.
- The real possibility that you could be rejected by some total loser. You would need a healthy ego to deal with that.

Infinity and beyond — dating in cyberspace

Tired of trying to meet the man of your dreams in pubs, bars and clubs? Fed up with finding instead a series of boys interested only in quick and ultimately unsatisfactory relationships? (It's fine, on occasion, but is that what you want for the long term?) Do you feel doomed to a life as a lonely single, with only the prospect of the odd, drunken encounter to look forward to?

Depressing, ain't it? But for many single women in their late twenties and early thirties, it's reality. And eventually, the thought of putting on their best frock and make-up and then putting themselves out there for the consideration of men who don't seem all that interested in anything except a quick shag can be enough to make them want to stay at home with a good book. But still, the longing persists. So what to do if you want a more worthwhile relationship with a human being but can't quite come at a dating agency?

> *The distance is nothing;*
> *it is only the first step which is difficult.*
> MARIE DE VICHY-CHAMROND, 1697–1780

How about a little arm's length marketing? You might never think about putting an ad in the personal columns, but increasingly smart Users are putting themselves out there and into the realm of cyber-dating. It's uncomplicated, and it is increasingly cool among people aged twenty-four plus.

Once again, in the interest of research, I joined the millions (some twenty million people in just in one month recently) around the world who have contemplated the notion of dating on the net and stepped into cyberspace. For women, it's a good place to be — here, at least, the odds are in our favour. On one site, in the eighteen to thirty age group, men outnumber women by about five to four. In the older age groups, the numbers are even more promising for women. If you are older and female, and you include your photo, then the odds of finding a companion are really running in your favour. The reason for the number of men? As usual, men are more accustomed to making the running in relationships, and are used to being the hunters.

A friend — let's call him Henry, to save his blushes — told me about a site that he was exploring. He's thirty-five and recently divorced; he works in an all-male and very macho field, doesn't like to go to bars, and so had little chance to meet women, so he signed up with one of the largest Australian dating sites. He met a few women on-line, had a few dates. 'The key is to have a look at the other person as soon as possible,' Henry said. 'There's no use wasting time if it's not going to work out in the end.' (Very goal-oriented, that man.) Within a few months, he was dating a thirty-two year old he had found on the site and was looking more cheerful than he had for months.

'It's easy,' he told me. 'You just sign up, send people electronic kisses, which tells someone you like them, they have a look at your profile and if they like the look of you, they email back.'

But what my friend did not bother to say, probably because he had no difficulty with it, was that before you log on, you really should have your email address and profile organised in your mind. I didn't and it took me about three hours to sign up.

Some people, however, don't try to be clever; they just include a shopping list description — *ChristianFatRunner* — to let people know exactly what is coming up. Men tend to imply that they are sensitive, such as *nice guy*, possibly ironic (*doesn'tdragknuckles*), or rampantly egotistical, such as *benzboy* and *legrandprix*. (Mmm … not good. But better, much better than *maverick69*.)

I picked 'beatricetoo' as my profile name after Dante's heroine and guide; the 'too' came from Dante's daughter, who was also known as Beatrice. 'What sort of person do you think will take a look at a profile called *beatricetoo*?' asked my friend Sam. 'All the Cedrics out there who might think that Beatrice was a little hottie are in old people's homes, don't have Internet access, and *their* little hotties are filled up with boiling water by nurses every night. Try *hunnybunny* or *jazzbaby* or anything, but get rid of *beatrice*.' Within hours, I logged back in and had changed my name to *smartandvsassy*. Then I waited.

> *Life is too precious to be spent in this weaving and unweaving of false impressions, and it is better to live quietly under some degree of misrepresentation than to attempt to remove it by the uncertain process of letter-writing.*
> GEORGE ELIOT, 1819–1880

And waited. And waited. Somehow, it turned out that I had managed the impossible — I had an Internet address on the site and yet remained invisible to all, including myself, because I had mistakenly locked my profile. The longer I remained mysterious, the more I liked it.

No-one could find me, but I could email others. So I did. It was like having grown-up penpals. I began to get used to having email from men who were not afraid to share their thoughts and feelings.

This is how it *should* work. You sign up, you write a profile of yourself. Send a photo if you like. You can choose to be on display, or not. You can restrict your photo to only those you have given a password to. You control the amount of detail you choose to give. So someone can choose you, or you can choose someone else, by sending them a message. And that might be the start of a wonderful friendship, or even a marvellous love affair. Stranger things have happened, and you needn't (at first) step outside your front door.

Some useful sites

If you put Internet dating into the question field of your search engine, you will discover there are thousand of sites around the world dedicated to matching up singles in cyberspace. You can also find 'specialist' sites that cater for everything from committed Christians to earnest lesbians or people with a penchant for interesting perversions. Here are some relatively white bread ones:

   www.rsvp.com.au
   www.lavalife.com.
   personals.ninemsn.com.au
   match.com
   personals.yahoo.com (US and Canada only)
   pearmatch.co.uk (Here, apparently, 'the world is your orchard'.)

Cyber-dating — start-up etiquette

Be quirky, not kinky. Give yourself a name that describes your personality or something of your interests and that will catch the attention of a potential date. *SummerBreeze* is evocative, and better than *WinterStorm* anyway. *FoxyLady* might be okay, if a bit twee, as long as your photograph supports the assertion. *TooSexy4MyPants* is the cyberspace equivalent of wearing a plunging neckline and will get you some attention you could live without. If you're literary and hoping for a literary partner, try your favourite author or heroine — it might strike a chord. Stay away from names with overtly sexual references — *MissKitty*, for instance (though the name worked in more innocent times for the woman who ran the saloon in *Gunsmoke*). And don't oversell yourself — *Superspy*, are you listening?

Never give your own email address on the dating site as your nickname. Using the site as a filter, at least in the first instance, is smarter.

Try to tell the truth, or as much of it as you can. (No reason why you can't accentuate the positive, eliminate the negative, though.) Fakes are easily spotted — like the Russian miss from Perth who said she was a lawyer and then said her educational level was high school. Cyber-dating is a perfect place to practise the Golden Rule: you wouldn't like to be lied to, so don't do it to anyone else. That said, there seem to be an awful lot of men on the dating sites who are 179 centimetres tall, and a huge number of women who are forty-nine years old.

Don't sex up your message to start with, unless you are a member of a more adventurous site. Discretion is best. This is not a message *crackafat* (who was probably in marketing or sales, to judge by the snap attached to his profile) had taken on board. (I cannot imagine how that worked out for him, and didn't have the stomach to email him to ask.)

Be amusing, if you can. But remember that sometimes humour doesn't translate quite as you might have intended. (Was the forty-one year old *Atomickitten* joking when she listed Syndey (sic) Sheldon, convicted felon Jeffrey Archer and Harold Robbins as her favourite reading?)

What if he's a fraud? You need to factor that into your thinking. For instance, does he only email you in the dead of night? Chances are, he's married.

Cyber-dating in practice

Okay, so you have found a likely candidate, corresponded a little, spoken over the (mobile) phone. Now it's time for the unveiling, and to meet in person. There are some sensible and simple rules that will keep you safe while you give your cyber suitor the once over.

Do you know who you are going to meet? What is his surname? You should have other pieces of information you can verify — his home address, for instance, and his home telephone number, possibly where he works. Use your own discretion about how much of this you reveal about yourself. If it starts to feel at all uncomfortable, just don't do it.

Tell someone, a member of your family or a friend, what you are going to do. You might also leave a printout of his emails with them, just in case. Make sure he knows that you have told someone about him and that that person is expecting a call as soon as you get home.

Meet in a public place and meet early. A coffee at lunchtime is best. If you are meeting at night, arrange to meet him no later than 7 or 7.30 pm.

Get yourself there — and get yourself home.

Keep your first meeting short. Make sure he knows it will be. Tell him you have to be back at work (daytime) or are meeting a friend for dinner.

Be light and flirty, not heavy and sexy. The right tone is really important.

If you feel uncomfortable, make your excuses and leave. Just chalk the meeting up to experience.

natural
selection

10
Different, not equal

Stand by for a self-evident and nonetheless shocking fact: men are not the same as women. And Users should all thank God for that. If they were, getting into the bathroom would be much harder, we'd all forget every birthday, anniversary and kid's sports day in the calendar (and then no-one would be speaking to anyone), no-one would ever pick up the dry cleaning and we'd all have to buy two full-length couches for in front of the television to accommodate the lounging around during the football match on Friday nights.

The differences between a User and a man are particularly evident in a number of areas — and the most obvious has to do with food intake. If men were like women, they'd understand about dieting. Men have rather a straightforward approach to weight loss (as they do to most things). It's simple: they diet to lose weight (if they realise they need to; but that's another story).

Women, on the other hand, have been known to diet for any number of reasons — among them, but not necessarily primarily, to lose weight. We might diet simply to maintain weight, or in fact, to balance weight we know is going to appear over the Christmas season, some two months away. (That's investment dieting.) And, of course, there is the solidarity diet — your girlfriend is on one, and you don't want to wolf down a piece of cake in front of her, so you go on a diet too. This sympathy diet might last just for that particular lunch, or if you have a lot of girlfriends on diets, you might find yourself accidentally dieting full-time along with all of them.

> *To be happy with a man, you must understand him a lot and love him a little. To be happy with a woman, you must love her a lot and not try to understand her at all.*
>
> HONORE DE BALZAC, 1799–1850

There is also the 'look at me' diet, a favourite of women who are already as thin as a cigarette paper, but who love to hear their luncheon companions saying: 'You can't be on a diet. You're too thin already!' (They can't get enough of that sort of reinforcement, but your response should always be to encourage them to pour just one more glass of wine down their birdlike beaks.)

Men will never go on a sympathy diet with you. If you have to lose the *avoirdupois*, baby, you'll find yourself all alone in the kitchen, except for a pair of kitchen scales and a very small piece of veal. (Beforehand you will have sorted out his menu of porterhouse steak with béarnaise sauce, mashed potatoes and salad, followed by bread-and-butter pudding and ice-cream.) Best then, if you are dieting, to make sure there is a lot of eating out going on — it's no fun preparing a meal for two when one is eating only half of what the other's enjoying and still doing all the work.

If you are on a diet, you will generally find men come in two varieties, one kind will say *don't worry, eat a proper meal, you look fine the way you are.* This, the very afternoon when you have gone to buy a new swimsuit and accidentally caught sight of yourself in the mirrors of the klieg-lit horrors otherwise known as dressing rooms. Those lights make slight cellulite look like the craters on the moon and are enough to reduce you to craving a comforting Mars bar. (By the way, according to some scientists cellulite doesn't really exist, but I'd like one of them to come over to my house and take a look at mine then tell me it isn't a real condition. Actually, I'd pay money for that sort of exorcism.)

The other variety is the man who, when asked, 'Do these pants make me look fat?' never manages to get the 'no' out fast enough or with the correct amount of conviction. He's the man who functions as a calorie controller, doling out the food and suggesting that the small portions are for your own good. 'Wouldn't want to pork up, would you, babe?' he asks, before helpfully slinging another slab of apple pie and cream on to his plate. Or he playfully pinches your stomach and makes sickening references to love handles. Do you do that to him? Well, maybe, but never at the beach, in the middle of a crowd, or in front of your boss. (Actually, you might want to do it to him at the Christmas party, but only in front of that woman he keeps talking about all the time.)

> *Well, of course, (men) are only human ... But it really does not seem much for them to be.*
> IVY COMPTON-BURNETT, 1884–1969

Size matters

Men seem to have very weird ideas about what women's bodies actually look like, and for that we can thank *Playboy* and *Penthouse* (remember, they are all airbrushed), American television and popular movies. Here's the drum, guys: most women do not look like Meg Ryan (cute and coltish and flat chested in her forties — doesn't this seem just the tiniest bit retarded to anyone?), Sophia Loren (it takes her about four hours to get coloured-in these days so she looks like the sex bomb she was in the 1950s), or Elle Macpherson (who has a body the like of which only about ten other women in the whole world have). The other three billion (minus ten) of us ordinary women — among whom numbered that size 16 sex goddess, Marilyn Monroe — will have to get by with bodies that are slightly less celestial.

But who can blame men when even shop mannequins are conspiring against us? If, like Dr Coppelius's doll, those mannequins came to life as real women, they'd barely be able to function. For a start, they would be too thin to menstruate. It's postulated that a woman shaped like a real-life Barbie Doll would have to walk on all fours just to balance those incredible breasts on her skinny little hips.

What most men don't know is that the average Western woman weighs seventy kilos and wears between a fourteen and sixteen clothes size, which means that it's hardly a surprise that a 1995 study found reading fashion magazines made seventy per cent of women overwhelmed by shame and guilt and depressed about their own bodies. (What is a surprise is that when fashion magazines want to show 'normal' sized women, many designers say they don't want their clothes shown on larger models — and there is even a consumer backlash that indicates most buyers actually don't want to see women like themselves in magazines, either.) It's getting worse, too: models twenty years ago weighed just eight per cent less than the average woman, while today's clotheshorses weigh twenty-three per cent less.

However, this lack of awareness among men about women's bodies does have an upside for the User. We can tell men that we are really a size ten or twelve, and they will believe us. Don't feel bad about doing this — most men insist to their women that they, too, are average-sized. (For your interest, according to Spanish research, an erect penis is around thirteen centimetres, fifty-eight millimetres. And those under seven centimetres, ten millimetres while flaccid should be worried.) This plan only comes unstuck when they go and buy you something in 'your' size and it doesn't fit. There is only so often you can blame a small make before you've named all the labels on the market.

> *Love is the history of a woman's life;*
> *it is an episode in a man's.*
> ANNE LOUISE GERMAINE NECKER, MADAME DE STAEL, 1766–1817

Stressed spelt backwards is desserts

Men will never understand the rules of dieting, and no matter how you try to explain them, they seem obstinately determined not to get what's going on here. The bottom line is: it's only a calorie when you say it is.

Eat alone whenever you can. There is a school of thought that argues if no-one sees you eat something, it is calorie-free. A Diet Coke or a Pepsi Max and a chocolate bar cancel each other out. If there are almost no calories in the drinks and loads of calories in the bar — that's creative calorie counting.

Eat with a guy. He eats *moussaka*, you eat roast chicken with the skin on. He has more calories than you. You can at least feel smug.

Foods eaten as emotional therapy, including hot chocolate, toasted cheese sandwiches, and the bottomless glass of vodka, have no calorific value. The exception is stress chocolate — eaten to relieve the fact you don't have a boyfriend. Those calories go straight to your hips, where they'll stay until you fall in love and can't eat — which is unlikely if you blow up to the size of a small family van while you haven't got a bloke. That's a really vicious circle. You'll have to wear long, loose shirts until you fall in love again. Worst-case scenario: you'll spend beach holidays in a caftan from *Here to Eternity*. Cultural note: do you think that Burt Lancaster would have been rolling around in the surf with Deborah Kerr if she'd been dressed in a *djellabah*?

Weight is relative. Fatten up your fella, and you will look thinner by comparison. Try this at home, and if it's effective, move the act to the work place. Start baking. Tell everyone it's a special recipe from the Heart Foundation — no sugar, low fat. And if they want to know why it tastes so good? Well, that's your little secret.

Fun foods have a zero calorie count because they are not strictly food intake. This includes popcorn (which is included on a Weight Watchers diet, but then that doesn't include the butter, or even the butter substitute), ice-cream and Minties. In fact, you can even *lose* weight while eating Minties — if enough of your fillings come out.

Foods licked from spoons and forks while cooking have no fat content. Or if you pick at something while watching someone else cook.

Anything eaten while you are standing up has fewer calories. Actually, this is true. It burns more calories to stand than to sit or lie down.

Further proof that men are different

Top ten things that a man will never understand

10 That a woman who already owns four pairs of black shoes, still finds another pair of black evening pumps essential.

9 That there are compelling differences between cream, ivory, eggshell and off-white which even the most visually illiterate should be able to see and appreciate.

8 That crying your eyes out is therapeutic, that it can be fun and even, on occasion, a guilty pleasure.

7   Fat clothes. And thin clothes. And clothes that don't fit at the moment but might any day soon, which is why they are still in the wardrobe and not headed for St Vincent de Paul.

6   That a salad, a diet drink and a double chocolate-dipped cone from Wendy's add up to a totally balanced lunch when carried in two hands.

5   That buying a designer anything for less than half price is a peak experience to be relived again and again so you can gain the maximum dollar value from it.

4   That every set of bathroom scales ever made is wrong, wrong, wrong and requires you to take off at least three kilos for the inaccuracy. And scales in hotels are notoriously more unreliable — take off five.

3   That a good man may be hard to find, but it's a sight harder to find a good hairdresser, which is why you never fight with your hairdresser and keep giving him presents. If more men understood this, there would be far fewer tragic haircuts on men.

2   Why a phone call between two women rarely lasts less than ten minutes even if those two women have seen each other an hour ago. Stuff happens all the time that needs to be classified.

1   Women. And that's why God invented other women for us to talk to.

> *I expect that Woman will be the last thing civilized by Man.*
> GEORGE MEREDITH, 1828–1909

Top ten things a woman will never understand

10 Why it is a miracle for a man to remember to observe important life events and buy an appropriate present. And why he doesn't understand that anything from Tiffany and Co. is acceptable — those trinkets in the blue boxes take all the guesswork out of giving.

9   Garbage night happens the same day every week. Why does he never remember from one Thursday to the next the timing of his date with the bins?

8   How any man can spend hours playing golf, more time replaying it over a drink, and then get up at 4 am to watch a televised

international competition. This is a game during which you can hardly ever see the ball and when you do, it is invariably in the wrong place. Professional golf is the most boring game in the world, played by some of the most tedious people ever and enlivened only by the presence of Tiger Woods.

7   Why it is only the total absence of all of the socks, shirts and boxers from the drawers and cupboards that triggers a man to do some washing or go shopping. And while we're on the subject, why do clothes that are holey and falling apart, and which belong in the rag basket, inevitably seem to invoke his everlasting passion and loyalty?

6   Why a man constantly 'needs his space' (usually the shed or the boat), but can never understand that a woman might, from time to time, occasionally require the same privilege.

5   Why his doesn't stay his. They're his suits so he should take them to the dry cleaner and he should take his own shirts to the laundry.

4   If women are supposed to be the vainer of the two sexes, why it takes him forty minutes in front of the bathroom mirror every morning before he can leave the house.

3   Given the above, why he doesn't notice the errant eyebrow/nose/ear hair. And what about that pelt across his shoulders?

2   He's big, strong, and smart. You tell him so on a regular basis. So why does his ego need so much care and attention from other women, particularly that Jezebel in accounting?

1   Why men think they're complicated, intense creatures with delicate existential sensibilities. To use a man properly, it's best to understand early that this is completely wrong.

And the four ages of women

From birth to age eighteen, a girl needs good parents.
From eighteen to thirty-five, she needs good looks.
From thirty-five to fifty-five, she needs a good personality.
From fifty-five on, she needs good cash.
SOPHIE TUCKER, 1884–1966

The Seven Ages of Man

At first, the infant,
Mewling and puking in the nurse's arms.
And then the whining schoolboy, with his satchel,
And shining morning face, creeping like snail
Unwillingly to school. And then the lover,
Sighing like furnace, with a woful ballad
Made to his mistress' eyebrow. Then a soldier,
Full of strange oaths, and bearded like the pard,
Jealous in honour, sudden and quick in quarrel,
Seeking the bubble reputation
Even in the cannon's mouth. And then the justice,
In fair round belly with good capon lin'd,
With eyes severe, and beard of formal cut,
Full of wise saws and modern instances;
And so he plays his part. The sixth stage shifts
Into the lean and slipper'd pantaloon,
With spectacles on nose and pouch on side,
His youthful hose well sav'd, a world too wide
For his shrunk shank; and his big manly voice,
Turning again toward childish treble, pipes
And whistles in his sound. Last scene of all,
That ends this strange, eventful history,
Is second childishness and mere oblivion,
Sans teeth, sans eyes, sans taste, sans everything.

AS YOU LIKE IT, WILLIAM SHAKESPEARE, 1564–1616

11
Mummy dearest

Eventually there comes a point in any relationship when the careful User must take a long, hard look at the parents of the object of her desire. And, in return, she'll have them cast one straight back over her. With any luck, everyone will be content, if not exactly happy. There is generally no way out of this inspection, unless he is an orphan (something women often say they add to the list of the qualities they are looking for in a man) or has parents living on the opposite side of the world.

> *People's mothers always bore me to death.*
> *All women become like their mothers. That is their tragedy.*
> *No man does. That's his.*
> OSCAR WILDE, 1854–1900

The question is — when should that meeting take place? The answer is — unless there are pressing geographical reasons — meet them as soon as you possibly can. If you are facing up to Lily and Herman Munster as the prospective parents-in-law, it's best to start getting used to the idea ASAP. And the User knows there is a lot to be learned about any man by seeing him in context within his family. That goes double for the way in which he treats his mother.

If she has done her job properly, this mother will have used her son from birth — in the nicest possible way! He will already be properly socialised (or as properly socialised as her patience and his Y chromosome will allow). Chances are though, that while she has done her best, he will still be a man. And that is both the good and the bad news.

And here is another piece of good and bad news — to most mothers, a son is a real prize. From the day of his birth, particularly in non-Anglo-Saxon families, he will have been idolised and adored by all his relations. (The only exception is his father when his son reaches adolescence, which is quite a different story.) Heaven help us, there's even a greeting in Italy that wishes the woman receiving it be the mother of sons.

What does a woman want in a man? Here's how it goes: good-hearted, handsome, clever, handy around the house, parentless or, if that's not possible, could he please be motherless?

Mamma's boys

In Italy, *il mammismo* (defined as an excessive attachment to the mother but, in practice, the cult of the mother) is rife — appropriately enough since this is the country in which the Madonna holds sway. (You know the joke — how do we know that Jesus was really Italian? He lived at home until He was thirty. His mother thought He was God, and — the clincher — He thought His mother was a virgin.) Interestingly, while the word *mammismo* deals with something essentially female-centric, it is in itself masculine — and that might have something to do with the fact that really only men are struck with this particular condition. Italian daughters are busy building the *mammismo* bank for their own sons.

(There is a fascinating side effect of *il mammismo*, which was reported in *The International Herald Tribune*'s Italian edition recently. With little encouragement to leave, young Italian men are staying with their parents longer and longer. So long, in fact, that they are in their thirties and older before they think about jumping out of their cosy nests. But the result is that mothers' anxieties about their sons, from their private lives to their business lives, communicates to their children, making a generation of coddled Italians reluctant to take chances because their *mammas* mightn't like it. This has produced, according to the *Herald-Trib*, a generation of Italian businessmen lacking in entrepreneurial derring-do.)

> *The best friend of a boy is his mother, of a man his horse; it is not clear when the transition takes place.*
> Joseph Mankiewicz, 1909–1992

The thing is, you can hear about *mammismo*, but until you see it in action, nothing prepares you for it. I was writing this chapter in Sardinia, where I had come to finish *Men: A User's Guide* and I was sent by my dear friend Bruno to stay with his mother. For a week, I hardly moved a muscle except to tell his *mamma* Italia what I would like to eat and then raise a fork to my mouth. Do I like *spaghetti alle vongole*? A little pastry for breakfast? Would I care for some fish for lunch? What sort of fish? *Mangi*! Eat up! *Dormi*! Sleep! It was like being in hospital, except that no one was sick. Would I prefer to go down to the bar for coffee, or would I rather she make it for me. (Yes, please, to the second. Signora Italia's coffee was brilliant.) Was there anything else I would like? (Yes, please. Can I take you home with me?)

Every day, my friend's mother cooked lunch for the members of her family who live in Cagliari, and there could be nine, ten or more people around the table every day. (It's more amazing when you think that Signora Italia was eighty-six years old, but acted as though she were a relative youngster of sixty-five.) At 2 pm, a tempest of activity burst through her front door — a son, a daughter, a daughter-in-law, a son-in-law, four grandchildren and assorted others. It was always a case of the more the merrier. Lunch was on the table — always *pasta* with sauce or *risotto* ('and would you like artichokes or something else with that?'), roasted meat or chicken or fish, always side dishes, always fruit, sometimes a dessert. 'Would you like some *gelato* with the strawberries? Or perhaps something else? What? You say. *Dimmi*! Tell me!'

Her sons- and daughters-in-law have reason to be grateful for this dedication to the art of mothering. It helps them immeasurably in the way they run their own family lives. To them, there's no point in being a mother unless you do it well.

> *Give up all hope of peace while your mother-in-law is alive.*
> JUVENAL, 40–125

A good mother-in-law can be worth her weight in gold. So why are there so many women who find they can't manage their partner's mothers and are secretly (or not so secretly) longing for the day those parents go to their eternal rest. Is it because mothers-in-law want the best for their sons, and are convinced that no other woman can provide it? Perhaps there is a trace of jealousy for being displaced from the prime position of a man's affection? Whatever the reason, the User will find a way around her mother-in-law so that everyone profits.

You don't have to be Freud to understand the way a man relates to women is a direct result of how he relates to his mother. Have you got a man with an *Oedipus* complex, a mother-in-law who idolises her boy? How can you make that work for you? And if your man has a problem with his mother, how might that be a problem for you? Obviously, there are as many different mothers as there are sons. And you will be able to tell a lot about the way a man will treat you as a wife. But what if you discover the man you love is still tightly wound in his mother's apron strings? He might be in love with you, but he cannot get by without his Mum.

> *The awe and dread with which the untutored savage contemplates his mother-in-law are amongst the most familiar facts of anthropology.*
> SIR JAMES G. FRAZER, 1854–1941

Remember the old saying — a son is a son till he marries a wife, but a daughter is a daughter for life. That saying has some appeal if you marry a man and you get the mother-in-law from Hell — you won't have to see that much of her. But generally, it's not such a good idea to try to separate a partner from his mother. Think about the babysitters you'll need if his parents are absent or estranged. So the User will try to incorporate his mother into family life — and a smart mother-in-law will try to do the same as regards her child's partner. Sometimes a well-policed, armed truce can function as well as a friendly alliance.

Dangerous liaisons

Can there be a more undesirable partner for a User than a Mummy's Boy? (Actually, there can: rapists, for example; men doing time in any correctional institution; or inmates of any other institution, including marriage to someone else.) For the sake of this argument, let's consider some of the biggest MBs of all time.

Oedipus. The ultimate mummy's boy, is celebrated in legend and on psychiatrists' couches. Briefly, his parents were warned before his birth that he would be the death of his father but instead of making sure their child didn't survive, they got a little sloppy about disposing of him. Years later, Oedipus unknowingly killed his father and then married his mother. It was enough to send the mother crackers when she found out, but Oedipus himself seems to have endured the horror without too much trouble.

Hamlet. The Prince of Denmark and hero of Shakespeare's eponymous play. He had every reason to be extremely cross with his mother, Gertrude, since she was complicit in the plot to dispatch Hamlet's father and marry his uncle, the assassin, but he did seem to become a little obsessed about her private life with her new husband. If he'd just focussed on Ophelia, not his mother, he might have lived happily ever after and one quarter of Shakespeare's tragedies would have turned into a pretty story about a handsome prince weaving garlands for his girlfriend and missing his father. A man who has issues with his mother's current sex life should really be disqualified from the User's thinking.

Napoleon Bonaparte. Talk about a stage mother! Laetitia Bonaparte had plans for all her children, and none of them had a single thing to do with staying on Corsica. How happy she must have been when, thanks to a stoush on the island, the family had to flee to France and Napoleon began his inexorable rise through the French army. But things didn't always go her way. She was the mother-in-law from Hell for the hapless Josephine Beauharnais, who was Créole (strike one), widow and mother (strike two), older than Napoleon (strike three) — and then she was out of the game as far as Laetitia was concerned. No chance for the heir and the spare there.

Eventually the drip, drip, drip of his mother's disaffection for his wife blended with his own dynastic need to secure the throne of France and so it was not any night, Josephine, and too bad if he had once loved her to distraction. *Maman* must have been delighted when Napoleon repudiated his first wife and imported Marie-Louise, his new imperially connected, nineteen-year-old bride from Austria. Apart from missing the glory, Josephine was well out of the scrum of Bonapartes. And at least the divorce meant she didn't have to share his exile: first on Elba (the Austrian consort went there with him before her Hapsburg relatives gave her an Italian duchy to make up for the pain of not being the empress of France any more), and then on to the windswept pile of St Helena, where he had neither wife nor mother to comfort him in his final exile.

Liberace. The apogee of Mummy's boys everywhere. Smiling, charming, oddly sexless, with hair that inflated the bouffant to new heights, Liberace was a talented pianist but also the template for MBs for generations to come. There have been a number of examples to be seen on Australian television, the darlings of women of a certain age. These men are about as sexy as pantomime dames — slightly prissy, plumpish, with hair that after the age of forty tends to an unnatural red, they are usually dressed in a vaguely too colourful manner. They can often be found at shopping centre promotions, singing for their suppers and delighting the ladies with their slightly *outré*, very camp, performances.

Prince Charles. Tragic that a man of fifty-plus years should be waiting for his mother to hand over her job so he can get on with the career he's been in training for all his life. Tragic, too, that he should have allowed his grandmother, in cahoots with one of her ladies-in-waiting, Lady Fermoy, to pick out his first bride for him — a girl who just happened to be the aforesaid Lady Fermoy's granddaughter. Talk about a conflict of interest. For a former Prince Charming, he certainly has been hag-ridden for most of his life. And still it continues with Camilla Parker Bowles, who is a bracing, no-nonsense matron with a certain air of the nanny about her.

12
Pick me! Pick me!

It is a sad fact of life that some people spend more time picking their animals than they do in choosing a potential new mate. They'll research the pet question to death — size of animal, ratio of animal to house space/yard space, exercise requirements of creature, personality quirks of both animal and potential owner, whether the animal will play nicely with children and share.

They tour breeders, take several trips to the local animal shelter, sizing up what's on offer, and come back time and again until their shopping list of qualities is near to filled. Not savage? Tick. Not stupid? Tick. Wormed? Tick. Spayed? Tick. Eyes not too close together? Tick. Some even manage to colour match the new pooch or moggy to the upholstery.

These same people go out partying and can be seen across the country any Friday or Saturday night succumbing to the charms of the first thing that rubs up against them or bounces into their laps. And that seems quite the wrong way to go about finding not only a mate, but a partner for any length of time. Choosing a new loved one just because they were there and persistent, or there and you noticed them, is seriously unsound, as anyone who has found themselves in an iffy situation after playtime can tell you.

Who would just go to a pound and take the first hound that bounced up to them with its tongue hanging out, or the first cat that wound its way through their legs and think that the arrangement was going to mean bliss forever? It's not such a serious matter — if things don't quite work out, you can return the unwanted creature anytime within its life and no one would think the worse of you for dumping the furry fury or the doggy psycho who just didn't fit in.

But in the dating jungle, some singles, well gone in drink, catch sight of someone and that's it. Game over, possibly for the rest of your natural life.

Making the correct choice always involves a little preliminary research.

When my friend Sam decided to get a dog, he did his homework. First, he bought a book by a friendly neighbourhood TV vet in which the relative virtues of different breeds were assessed. Despite this quite reasonable line of inquiry, he made a decision I thought at the time was a little odd. He picked a poodle.

His choice fell not, as it happened, on a standard poodle, whose size adds a bit of credibility to the package, and not a miniature, which would have been beyond ridiculous. What he wanted was one of those smallish, bright little toy things which always put me in mind of Brigitte Bardot (it's the haircut) and the South of France (that would be the diamante collars and the hairclips) or something you'd find on a bed with a zip up its stomach and a pair of shortie pyjamas inside.

Then he decided to do a field trip, which is how I found myself in the backyard of a house deep in the 'burbs, surrounded by half a dozen cockahoop chocolate poodle puppies. Poodles, when they are in a mass and left *au naturel*, might be as terrifying as any pack of ravening hounds, but the fact is that these looked like wind-up dinky toy dogs, something a Japanese manufacturer might have designed had she a penchant for canine topiary. It's so hard to take a dog seriously when it's wearing a hairdo that makes it look like a series of strung-together powder puffs.

Sam was looking more and more entranced by the idea of having a poodle of his very own. I, on the other hand, was going off them at a rate of knots. Just thinking about brushing one of those chocolate brown coats to get the lumps out was exhausting; a fact I was trying to point out to him. However it wasn't until he saw the snoods hanging up in the kitchen, over their personalised dinner bowls, that he started to see the reality of life with a poodle. Life really seemed far too short to put your dog into a hairnet before he chows down. These snoods, the breeder explained to Sam's questioning, were necessary to keep poodle ears out of poodle dinners. While a dog with Chum stuck to its chops is unappealing until it manages to wipe its face all over the best pale cream wall-to-wall, Chum on ears (spaniel owners should be nodding their heads by now) is even worse. But the thought of a dog with its ears whipped up in a net (or even held up with a couple of pegs) at supper was so bizarre, it became impossible to stifle the giggles.

We ran from the house, escaping both snoods and poodles, and he went back to the books. In the fullness of time, he researched various terrors … sorry, I'll try that again … terriers and came up with the West Highland White. This seemed just the sort of companion animal anyone would enjoy — perky, resilient, a dog with a sense of humour and boundless sympathy.

Having made his decision about the type of dog, he then set about researching the best place to actually acquire the dog. When he found her, a six-month-old bitch eliminated from the breeding pool because of a rather pronounced pair of bandy back legs (dog-breeders are so lookist!), he took her home. He remains satisfied with his choice and has never once wished that his West Highland White terrier was, say, a Labrador, or a German short-haired pointer, although occasionally he might wish she were darker and showed the dirt less.

Not being happy with their original choice is a problem a lot of women confront. They fall in love with a particular man, form a relationship with him, perhaps even marry him, and then some years later, it occurs to them that perhaps it might be better if their fella were a little less … what? … *male*? A little more something else? More in touch with his feminine side? Less in touch with his feminine side? Less involved with sport. More romantic. Less of this, more of that. On and on.

Here's the core piece of advice for making a happy relationship: when you pick a man, pick the right one, so you can happily gaze at him on the other side of the bed for years to come without resenting his maleness. It's better for you, and it's much better for him.

A vicar once observed that the moment a bride walked into his church, she seemed to get the wrong idea. 'She sees the aisle, the altar, and the bridegroom. Aisle, altar, him,' he said. 'She changes the spelling and the punctuation and comes up with "I'll alter him!"' (This does not mean you can't renovate your bloke — but the underlying structure is immutable, and you forget that at your peril.)

Make the right choice, though, and the 'I'll alter him' thought need never occur. Think of the time and trouble you will save if you just do some homework before you get out into the marriage market. You could be set for life.

> *Men who do not make advances to women are apt to become victims to women who make advances to them.*
> WALTER BAGEHOT, 1826–1877

The smart User will understand the point of the research versus haphazard approach to finding a man. The haphazard approach includes: 'He followed me home from the club and he's been here for four weeks now'; 'A friend didn't want him anymore and thought that I might like him'; 'He looked as though he didn't belong to anyone so I brought him home for a feed and a clean'; and 'My parents/the kids really like him'.

If you want quality in an animal, you would look at bloodlines, breeding and early training. If you want a nervy mass of energy, then just pick up any dog and take what you get. It's the same with finding a man. You will save yourself a lot of time and trouble if you choose a man who is worth your attention in the first place. And taking a look at some of the questions to ask when picking a dog is not a bad place to start.

The smart User's guide to picking the right dog

1. Is this the right sort of dog for you? Is it good with old people and children, does it need lots of exercise, a big garden? Is this a dog you are going to allow in the house, or is it a yard dog? Do you have the same energy levels as this dog — will he like to spend cold days in front of the fire while you just want to hike in the sleet?
2. Does it have a glossy coat, shiny eyes and a cold nose?
3. Avoid any dog that bounces out of a litter to greet you, then starts to slobber all over your shoes.
4. Equally, don't head towards the depressed and neurotic little cutie cringing at the back of the pack.
5. If it's snarling, ignore it and find one that's not.

6. If its eyes are too close together and you are not actually looking for a dog to mind a junkyard overnight, keep moving.
7. It looks like a bad dog, it sounds like a bad dog, and it acts like a bad dog. Crikey, the trifecta! The smart User knows this *is* a very bad dog indeed. This is a dog not-so-smart Users, unfortunately, know intimately.

> *There is no such thing as perfection. But in striving for perfection, we can achieve excellence.*
> VINCE LOMBARDI, 1913–1970

The smart User's guide to picking the right man

1. All of the points above add up to making a smart choice.
2. Plus, never take a stray home. You'll be ages trying to get rid of it. And you will not be able to take a bad choice, made in the dark under the influence of one too many Flirtinis, back to any shelter. Though, *in extremis*, you could try leaving him in the park and hoping he won't be able to find his way back.

If the man were a dog…

Labrador/Golden Retriever

Labrador rhymes with 'adore' for good reason. They adore their mates, and have the added advantage of being generally too lazy to pursue other women. This is a man who needs a lot of pats, so make sure he doesn't take off trying to find them. He tends to cupboard love and sticks to the person who feeds him. This can also lead to middle-age spread in his thirties. **Spotted:** he's easy to find in the crowd — he's fun and amiable and generally the centre of attention. He's sometimes a little muddy and dishevelled and generally has no sense of style at all and can get a bit dribbly. The Golden Retriever is quite close in style to the Lab, but he is generally more water-centric. The Golden

Retriever in human form lives in paradise. He floats through life, happy with an occasional outing and looking for a warm spot for a snooze. **Bonus:** will tend to put on weight, thereby making you look smaller by comparison. **Drawback:** the canine forms can suddenly turn like a mad yellow dog and take great chunks out of small family members, then adopt a 'my goodness, where did that come from?' look. To avoid this in your golden male, check the breeding.

Border Collie

The human Border Collie is a serious bundle of energy and needs lots of activities to keep him amused. If he's not occupied, you might get up one morning and discover that he's planned your holiday and it's something like trekking in the Himalayas. It's unlikely you'll be bored, but it is equally unlikely you will ever get any rest. He can go seriously mental if confined to the house for too long. **Spotted:** all over the place. You will need to be quick — he is. **Bonus:** he's an events organiser — the one who's into everything and can be found rounding up kids for a game of something that involves ten-a-side. **Drawback:** he sometimes looks a little woolly, but scrubs up well. Very hard on his clothes.

Dachshund

Your human dachsie suffers from small man's syndrome and can tend to be a little aggressive and snappy with it. On the good side, he will be very protective of you and yours. He finds it hard to get up on high beds with those little legs, so if you are seriously interested in one of these, think futon. **Spotted:** they like to stay close to home, and can be very possessive of their mates. **Bonus:** can be very bright, if occasionally overwrought. **Drawback:** you'll find you spend quite a lot of time reassuring him that he's medium height and much, much taller than Napoleon ever was. Or Jimmy Cagney. And that Elijah Wood is also small and perfectly formed and very good looking (for a Hobbit).

Rottweiler

The human adult male version of the Rottie comes in two versions — the gentle giant who doesn't know his own strength, and the bully. The second is a hardship posting. **Spotted:** watching big sporting fixtures. Cruising hardware shops. **Bonus:** nice square heads. **Drawback:** looking like Mussolini is not so useful these days.

Malamute
Along with the Siberian husky, the male human version of these animals tends to shed all over the house. They appear to be doing nothing at all, but they spend quite a lot of time in silent surveillance. You'll be surprised what they notice. Like that new dress you hid at the back of the wardrobe. **Spotted:** out of the back yard, taking part in big events and team sports. **Bonus:** can have beautiful eyes. Unless you get one of those with the mad orange irises. **Drawback:** the heat really lays them out. They have to spend the whole of the Christmas holidays flat in front of the television watching the cricket.

Jack Russell Terrier
Oh my lord, how did you get lumbered with one of these? Men made in the image of these small, excitable little guys are really difficult to keep track of. **Spotted:** it's a bit of a blur, really, because they are hard to keep an eye on. They can give you the slip really easily in a crowd. **Bonus:** lots of energy means lots of sex. And they are very easy to keep neat. **Drawback:** too much sex from an over-enthusiast Jack Russell can quickly become a little dull.

Poodle
Human males made in the poodle image are the worst sorts of charmers. They get everyone to do their dirty work for them, and appear after any fracas looking cool and collected. **Spotted:** they are very showy — try the races, television stations, the bar. **Bonus:** nice carriage and very smart. **Drawback:** well, you didn't really need to use a mirror while you put your make-up on, did you?

Cocker Spaniel
Your cocker spaniel-type man fairly redefines any currently held view of laziness. He'll always be underfoot and always be making some sort of mess and looking at you hoping you'll sort it out. **Spotted:** this is the style of person who wins those reality television survival games because they cruise under the radar and end up winners. Tune into the next edition of *Big Brother* for

examples. **Bonus:** very appreciative of anything you do for them. Incredibly sweet and loyal. **Drawback:** requires long snooze times.

Doberman Pinscher

If you want a relationship with someone who looks like a bouncer, then that's your lookout. Human Dobermans can just about block out the sun when they stand over you or, worse, lie on top of you. **Spotted:** front row of the All-Blacks. Real estate agents, and sales and marketing managers recruited from among the ranks of superannuated professional sportsmen. **Bonus:** if you go out and leave him at home, you can leave the doors and windows wide open. No one will ever get past this boy. **Drawback:** if he ever decides he wants a piece of you, he'll have a piece of you.

Boxer

Slightly aloof, the Boxer in human form is not Anthony Mundine, but a rather more civilised creature. He's pretty laid-back so don't rely on him to do much other than look handsome and have breathing problems. **Spotted:** inner-city gyms, but these are probably gay. Health food shops. Meditation classes as he tries to balance his personal Yin and Yang. Pilates classes as he tries to balance the back he threw out at yoga. **Bonus:** sweet, those brown eyes. Adorable, those pecs. **Drawback:** can be too self-involved and vitamin-supplement focussed.

Irish Wolfhound

Standby for a street angel and a home devil. **Spotted:** pubs, clubs, anywhere for the *craic* — the fun. **Bonus:** can be very pretty — think Peter O'Toole, the early years, or Pierce Brosnan — if they haven't had their teeth knocked out in pub brawls. **Drawback:** can look like an old sandshoe left out in the rain. That's Peter O'Toole recently and Van Morrison at any stage.

Greyhound

The human male who is a greyhound in disguise is a fiend for ball sports. If it moves, he'll watch it. Try to encourage him outside the house to play with his own ball. Small children are very useful for this sort of man. **Spotted:** on the pitch. On the golf course. On the field. In front of the television watching any ball sport. **Bonus:** can explain all the rules of any game to you. **Drawback:** to catch his attention, you'll need to wait for the ad break and wear a catcher's mitt.

Australian Blue Heeler

The male version of this dog is easily recognised. He's the one who's always saying 'C'mon, hurry up, let's go, we'll be late.' He's driven and he'll try to round you up all the time as well. **Spotted:** he's the organiser for the social club at work and the events secretary of the squash club. Anywhere there are people in need of organising. **Bonus:** very handy if you have a tendency to lateness. **Drawback:** annoying if you already know where you are going and what time you have to be there.

Old English Sheep Dog

The human male version of this deliberately obtuse animal can drive any sane woman to distraction. You will need to practise detachment if you want to hook up with one of these. **Spotted:** wine society tastings. The country. **Bonus:** nothing is ever wrong, so he doesn't complain. **Drawback:** nothing is ever right, either, so he never gives you a pat on the head. Or back.

The name game

You shouldn't pick a book by its cover, or a partner by his name, but there are names that put people off. A survey in 2000 discovered that psychiatrists were less inclined to be favourable to, or to believe, men called Wayne (and women called Tracey, as it turned out) than men called, for instance, Matthew, and women called Fiona. (This might have had something to do with the fact that more psychiatrists were, themselves, called Matthew or Fiona, but that is another question.)

13
Stereotypes and other clichés

Harlequin Enterprises, publisher of romance novels, recently polled more than 5000 women in fourteen countries on what they thought about their men. The results were something of a surprise: Australian men were rated second in the world's-sexiest-men stakes, after the Greek guys and ahead of those legendary lovers, the Italians.

Who would ever have thunk? Aussie blokes rated the second sexiest in the world! It's a miracle. Or a joke, depending on who you talk to. 'Do you think those readers have ever met any Aussie men in real life?' asked one astounded Australian woman who, while she loves her countrymen, finds it hard to see them as sexier than Italians — or Finns, or Latvians etc. She would have numbered any one of a dozen different nationalities ahead of Australians in the sexiest men alive stakes, but Harlequin hadn't asked her. Still, according to the American press, exports such as Eric Bana, Mel Gibson (yes, yes, born in America; who cares?), Heath Ledger and Simon Baker are giving Australian men a good name overseas.

The international view is understandable. The Australian bloke recognised by international readers (notwithstanding the annual Gay and Lesbian Mardi Gras that every February produces some of Australia's most buffed bodies, as well as some of its hairiest) is the stereotype they find in romance novels —

broad-shouldered, relatively taciturn and uncomplicated men with suntans, horses (or at least four-wheel-drive utes) and long, slow, sexy smiles. This is an image of masculinity Australia has been busy selling to the rest of the world for the best part of the last century.

> *If man is only a little lower than the angels, then the angels should reform.*
> MARY W. LITTLE, BORN 1880

It's a stereotype supported by some first-rate ambassadors over the years — think Errol Flynn, Rod Taylor, John McCallum. Still later, there were stars such as Bryan Brown (who looked in *The Thorn Birds* as though he could blow away that over-made up wimp, Richard Chamberlain, as though he were a puff of powder), Guy Pearce, Hugh Jackman and Russell Crowe. (Don't start that business about him being a New Zealander or we'll be at it all day — our Russ grew up here.) There is no doubt that these men are sexy (let's just pause for a minute to think about Russ's voice ... *mmmm* ...), but even their mothers, wives and girlfriends would find it difficult to promote Aussie blokes as the second sexiest group of men in the world. But then, people do want to imagine that what is a little beyond their grasp is better, so that is why — for those conditioned by Hollywood dream factories — the top three countries turn out to be Greece, Australia, and Italy.

Why? People (okay, women) in other places want to escape to those locations, and when they are there in their imaginations, they are looking for a little romance. It's SVS, aka Shirley Valentine Syndrome. Sick of cooking her insensitive clod of a husband his heart-attack inducing, greasy breakfasts, Shirley flees to Greece. There she finds a sexy local who takes notice of her and does not require a fry-up from her as an aftermath to their sexual encounters. It helps that the Greek in question is framed by the blue Mediterranean, while the pasty English husband is thrown into relief by a grimy light reflected off an industrialised landscape.

> *What passes for women's intuition is often nothing more than man's transparency.*
> G. J. NATHAN, 1882–1958

Greece is fabulous, and there are many women who would agree with the ranking of Greek men as the most attractive in the world. However, it's not so hard to make the case that the third-ranked group, the Italians, have been cheated out of a higher position.

I remember my Italian friend taking me by the arm in the vaulted hall of the *Villa Medicea* at Poggio a Caiano, not far from Florence. This country house, now part of the Italian national estate, was once the retreat of the Medici family. During the Renaissance, the Medicis, tired of the fetid swamp that their city turned into every summer, fled to this neck of the woods. Up on top of the hill, the weather was distinctly cooler, and the ruling family of the city could be safe from the malaria and other diseases that regularly gripped Florence.

This wonderful villa is a perfect location for a daydream. It's a model of Renaissance architecture with twin, grand staircases outside the house leading from the driveway to the first floor (the *piano nobile*) and the main reception rooms, where the nobility of the city gathered to while away those long, warm summer evenings. The surroundings were, to say the least, impressive — there was a della Robbia frieze and enough frescoed ceilings by Jacopo da Pontormo to satisfy even the most demanding art lover.

'Close your eyes,' said Silvano, tour guide. 'And imagine what it was like here in the early fifteen hundreds. You and I are receiving the guests for a great *festa*, a party,' he said in a conspiratorial tone. 'Can you see the shimmer of candlelight? The gleam of the silks and the brocades in the dresses of the ladies and the jackets of the men? Can you smell the perfumes and the incense of the night? Do you hear the musicians playing at the other end of the room?'

His hand closed under my forearm and even though it was a chilly afternoon in October, I began to feel quite warm. The exceptional luminosity of Tuscany in autumn (an Italian greengrocer said that to me once. Imagine getting that line of poetry with your tomatoes — *fantastico*!) diffused through the room and I was transported back to another time and place by the light and the power of his words and his touch. No wonder I was feeling the heat!

I could hardly wait to tell one of our mutual friends, who is actually married to an Italian. 'How romantic,' I sighed. 'How routine, you mean,' she said bracingly. 'A lot of them are like that.' She proceeded to illustrate her point. 'I had a girlfriend who was on a first date with an Italian. It was full moon and he took her to a bridge on the Arno, and then asked her to tell him the three things that she wanted most in the world but dared not tell anyone. She was absolutely smitten, and answered the question. No man had ever asked her a question like that in her life, and she decided it was true love.'

My friend knows a thing or two about romantic Italians, but she has lived there long enough to know that sometimes a romantic stereotype can also mask a certain lack of depth. 'She was still struck with him about a month later, when they were out on another date, and he took her to the same bridge, under another full moon, and asked her the same question,' she said. 'He'd forgotten he'd tried this routine on her before.' At that moment, the love-struck visitor realised that the bridge, the moon, the three questions, were simply part of her Italian boyfriend's repertoire, and he had overlooked the fact that he had already been there and done that with her.

It is no accident that Casanova, the world's most famous seducer, was an Italian. This great lover, whose name has become synonymous with libertine, boasted a string of conquests from virgin teens to nuns as he cut a swathe through eighteenth-century Europe. Venetian-born, the brother of two famous painters, Giovanni Jacopo Casanova made love his art.

He was an adventurer, a failed priest, secretary to a cardinal, violinist, alchemist, knight of a Papal order, spy, and received everywhere in polite society. His Christmas card list would have included addresses for the Vatican and the palaces of Frederick the Great and Madame Pompadour. (He should be admired not only for his amorous adventures, which were chronicled in his twelve-volume *Mémoires écrits par lui-même* but also for the fact that the great lover was a practitioner of more or less safe sex.

(And considering the sheer numbers of his sexual encounters, this was a smart move. The prophylactics of the time were fashioned from sheep gut and not exactly waterproof, so to speak, but they were certainly better than having no protection against a plethora of venereal diseases, among them syphilis and genital herpes.)

The Latin lover is a stereotype that is difficult to obliterate, thanks to the charm and the ease of Mediterranean men from Spain to Greece and back again, and, you'd have to suppose, because of the encouragement of their women. If that behaviour weren't usually well rewarded, it would have stopped aeons ago. (There is another factor at work, here as well. Because of traditional religious value and cultural restraints, young women were well protected before marriage. Roués had to try that much harder, so romantic love, the field of the later Crusader knights, became the art form that led to seduction.)

Ladies, pick your partners by nationality

The Aussie bloke

We know what these guys are like. The best are loyal, steadfast, hardworking and good humoured. The worst are lazy drunken layabouts with no manners, intent only on satisfying themselves. One such encountered by Anastasia was a busy barrister who appeared twice week to take her to dinner and to bed. 'He was smart, and occasionally funny. He was great with the wining and dining,' she said. But towards the end of their relationship, Anastasia was the one whining. 'He was the laziest lover I have ever had. He would come quickly, then offer just to hold me while I masturbated myself to climax.' His argument was that she was so much better at satisfying herself than he was — 'but he didn't really even try. Then he started to fall asleep before I came. It was easier having a relationship with the vibrator. At least I could throw that over the edge of the bed when I had finished with it and it didn't want to have breakfast in the morning or me to go to the football with it on Saturdays.' Anastasia found a solution: she started to go out with older men. 'They have more time to spend on a woman and are often not as fixated on their own orgasm,' she said.

Australian men also tend towards the conversationally blunt end of the scale. Sometimes they are just too honest. And when they are not, they can get themselves into a load of trouble. Ask one if your bum looks too fat in this and see him try to get himself out of trouble. It's an education.

If your partner is a typically Australian male and you want to have good sex for life, the ball (so to speak) is in your court. You will have to pay attention for the same amount of time, that is for life, to get the best out of this nationality. You will need to keep them up to the mark — even when you don't necessarily want to. If you don't, they'll turn into perfunctory lovers and you will start to resent them for it.

Pluses: they tend to be thick on the ground. And as loyal as blue heelers — particularly to their mates.

Minuses: they can be a bit thick, particularly where women are concerned. And sime of them are a bit scared of Aussie sheilas.

Prime example: Hugh Jackman. **Not so prime:** Sir Les Patterson, the carbuncular and stained former Federal Minister for the Arts. Leses outnumber Hughs by about a factor of 10,000:1.

Habitat: Hollywood, these days, for all-Aussie bloke actors. Otherwise, the species ranges across Australia and, while young, backpacks across Europe and surfs in Indonesia. More extreme versions can be found trekking in Nepal. As this specimen ages, he will be found increasingly on the golf course.

The English gentleman

Think of a couple of English stereotypes — the toff and the yob. Which one would you rather share body fluids with? Personally, Astrid didn't care. At 29, she was in England on a working holiday and eager to find a boyfriend. Perhaps a little too eager. 'Anthony was so sweet. When I met him at work in the City, I thought he was great — he had perfect manners, a wonderful speaking voice and he was extremely polite to me. If anything, he was a little too polite. We had been going out for six weeks, and he hadn't made a move.'

She was beginning to think her perfect new date was perhaps a 'confirmed bachelor'. Astrid was a girl who had grown up on the Gold Coast, and her experience of boys who didn't jump on girls at every opportunity made her think he might be gay, as most of the non-jumpers had been. But after nearly two months, Anthony finally succumbed.

'I just about dragged him into my flat one night in Shepherd's Bush and had his clothes off while he was still stammering he couldn't possibly. Well, I could and I did and so he did too. While it was sex that wouldn't have set the Thames on fire, it wasn't too bad for a first go.'

Astrid and Anthony continued to date. The problem was, nothing much more happened on the physical front. 'Anthony wasn't that interested, really. It was as though he didn't want to put me out too much. He was an awful lot of hard work for not much result. He was a great boyfriend and a lukewarm lover. He got keener and keener and wanted things to go further, but one night I was out with some mates and we ran into some guys and I went home with a

Scot. He was fantastic, and reminded me that all men were not as half-hearted as Anthony.' So it was curtains for Astrid and Anthony.

However, many red-blooded Australian women have discovered to their great delight another stereotypical English male: The reborn Goon, or one of the latest generation of the Goodies, or one of those other half-way good looking English humourists who manage to seduce a girl with their delicious senses of the ridiculous.

In my field research on cyber-dating for the Love Out-sourced chapter, I discovered, much to my surprise, a very funny and therefore very attractive, Englishman. This sense of humour was the thing that caught my initial interest. (Almost all. He also looked a total dish in his snap.) Some of the details have been changed, but you get the idea. This is part of what he wrote as an opening gambit:

Thank you for your enquiry. Please find the following details:
- Model was first constructed in the UK in 1962 but successfully underwent Australian conversion in 1989 and now has full paperwork.
- Well-maintained for years with usual dents and scratches. All major joints and parts regularly inspected and attended to.
- Duco shows some signs of wear due to sun and salt and roof has less coverage than new, but still respectable.
- While not strictly a sports model, it performs well in most environments but especially good on the beach and in remote locations. Used extensively for multi-tasking around the world.
- Contract requirements mean that this model is available for three months at a time, twice per year.
- Return on this investment is very sound.
- Easy to operate, fun to have, all that is needed is a regular supply of quality fuel and good rub down with an oiled cloth in the right places.
- Does not care for rough handling as some parts are delicate.
- Rewards tender loving care with same, providing the right driver with hours of fun and a lifetime of great memories.
- Stick shift operates and responds well to regular use …
 To make a booking please email …

You didn't seriously think I would give you the email address of this paragon, did you? I'm not that silly.

Of course, I emailed him in kind, under the heading of 'A stick-shift, you say.' I wrote: 'You have not mentioned boot space. Please note that there is not need for much room for baggage. My client assures me that she is baggage enough herself in any vehicle.'

Once the mindset of both the man on offer and the inclination of the User had been established, the friendship moved on appropriately.

Pluses: the English can be beautifully tailored in that understated Rover, bridge and green wellies way that makes the French long for the *'style anglais'*. Traditional prejudices about the personal hygiene of the English seem to have been resolved permanently and satisfactorily.

Minuses: funny can go only so far — The Goons were not noted traffic stoppers when it came to looks. The English are generally not known for being romantic (they say Latin lover, don't they, not Liverpool lover? Remember, a Liverpool kiss is a head butt!) although the exceptions more than make up for the rest. There can be a tendency to juvenile attitudes to sexuality (that's what nannies and boarding schools can do to a boy). Can also appear rather aloof and proper.

Prime example: Pierce Brosnan doing his James Bond. Since Brosnan is actually Irish, this is quite a nice twist. David Beckham.

Not so prime example: Hugh Grant. (Bad form to get caught with the really un-Divine Brown.)

Habitat: Hollywood, again, for the luvvies. You'll find the rich ones in the City (London) and in the countryside in August doing the huntin', shootin' and fishin'. On the pitch at Old Trafford, but be careful — it's highly unlikely you will find a prime example of British manhood among the fans in the stands. Backpacking in South-East Asia.

The Irish hero

For the User with a musical ear and a keen sense of the ridiculous, there can be little more fun to be had in the world than with an Irish boyfriend. Funny and playful when properly used, an Irishman can also be the sexiest thing on two legs — kind, attentive and adventurous. One of them kept me interested for far longer than strictly necessary by Scheherazade's stratagem — the *Thousand and One Nights* ploy.

You remember that scenario — in *Tales of the Arabian Nights*, Shahryar the despot discovers his wife has been unfaithful. Totally incensed, he orders her execution, along with everyone who conspired with her against him. After this, the king had major trust issues, but as he couldn't live without a wife, he married a new one every day and had her killed the following morning. (This would be something of a magnification of the French notion that orgasm is *la petite mort*, the little death). At that rate, he fast ran out of eligible women. Then one of the vizier's daughters — Scheherazade — decided to stop the slaughter.

She convinced the vizier to marry her off to Shahryar but she had a plan to save her own life and those of other women. The king married Scheherazade, but that night, her sister Dunyzad came to their room and asked for a story. The king listened as well and was so taken by his bride's tale that he insisted on hearing the ending. Clever Scheherazade kept him waiting for the final instalment for around three years. By finishing with a cliff hanger every night, Scheherazade managed to escape the grisly fate of her predecessors.

And three years is about how long my experience of *Finnegan's Wake* lasted as well. The main difference is that I didn't hang around to hear a particular Irishman read through to the end of it. I still can't read the book.

Pluses: can have a very sly way of looking at life and the world. Also, they have considerable natural charm tempered by real warmth.

Minuses: can have a very sly way of looking at yet another glass of Guinness, too. Can tend to the sentimental when in their cups and be over-fond of games such as rugby and golf. (This is a serious understatement.)

Prime example: Liam Neeson. Tall, fair, straight — and that voice!

Not so prime: Oscar Wilde. Also Irish-born, and not so straight.

Habitat: they tend to gather around watering holes. Try Irish themed bars on St Patrick's Day, or any night Ireland plays any other team at any game. Tend not to stray too far from their mammies at home.

The all-American boy

Clean-cut, sweet, well balanced — that's the published image of the American male. Even their serial killers, such as Ted Bundy, who murdered an estimated thirty-six women, and Jeffrey Dahmer, who killed fifteen men — looked remarkably clean-cut. The thing about most American men, though, is that they are not too adventurous. This is a group of people which, by and large, thinks America is the centre of the universe, that McDonald's is the thing to eat while on tour in Europe, and that Lycra leisurewear can disguise quite a wide range of figure faults.

But there are some goers among them as well, men like the writer Henry Miller, for instance, and Ernest Hemingway, before his failing sexual prowess haunted him enough to make him suicide.

Pluses: so polite! So articulate!

Minuses: too polite. Way too articulate.

Prime example: it used to be the heir to Camelot, John F. Kennedy Jnr. Now, we have to make do with Ben Affleck.

Not so prime example: Ben's best pal, Matt Damon — he's got a face like a potato and none of a potato's utilitarian charm. Remember, this is the man who dumped his girlfriend Minnie Driver on television.

Habitat: since they have no discernible vices such as drinking, you might have to gather up your strength and go to a health club in the commercial district of a large city to find one. Try New Orleans during the jazz festival for ones with rhythm, or for really woodsy ones, Alaska, during the running of the annual sled race, the Iditarod.

The French playboy

If you have ever had a French lover, you will understand the dual nature of heaven/hell. Anastasia found hers on the Rive Gauche. 'I was not looking. I was just there sightseeing after a hard afternoon trying to escape the attentions of a whole group of men of Middle Eastern appearance, who seemed to be offering me a position among their concubines.'

Walking between the Eiffel Tower and the Hotel des Invalides, a handsome, late twenty-ish man fell into step beside her. 'He asked me in French if I were enjoying myself, and I was so overcome to think someone might mistake me for a French woman, I stopped in my tracks and answered him. I wanted to practise my French, he wanted a cup of coffee, there was a bar right there.' And that, *mes amis*, was that.

'Madonna was playing on the jukebox, and I looked at him and I thought "you are such a nice man". He was slightly grave, a soldier on his way back to his barracks. He walked me around Paris for four hours, took me to dinner, walked me back up to my hotel just off the Champs Elysées. He left me at the door with a kiss, said he would call — and he did.'

For five days, Serge squired Anastasia out after work. He didn't try anything until the third day, when instead of leaving her at the door of the hotel, he took her upstairs to her room. 'For three nights, the chambermaid had been turning down both sides of the bed and doubling the number of towels in the hope that Serge would make me a happy woman. For three mornings she tutted at me for failing to take advantage of the hotel, the city, the gorgeous Serge.'

The night after he took her to bed for the first time, Anastasia met with the full force of approval from the maid. 'I felt like I had won a gold medal at the Olympics.'

Serge was an inventive and considerate lover, who was seemingly unstoppable. The thing about Serge was that he was a working holiday romance. 'He was adorable, but it would have been impossible in the long term. He would have looked silly outside France and I couldn't see myself moving there to marry him. So he took me to the airport after six days, and kissed me goodbye.' Serge cried as she left, but Anastasia was under no illusions — Serge, the *flaneur*, she sensed, would have been on the pavement the next Sunday afternoon, looking for the next foreign woman to seduce.

Pluses: can be incredibly appreciative of a woman. Generally smell sensational, particularly those wearing Guerlain. Also have a tendency to a certain natural style.

Minuses: can be incredibly appreciative of almost any woman. Also can tend to a certain indifference. (*Blasé* is a French word, after all.) Quite of lot of them seem to think they are channelling Jean-Paul Sartre.

Prime example: Gérard Depardieu. A beauty in his youth, he looks now like an overstuffed teddy. But he obviously knows his way around a dinner table, which is a very good thing in a man.

Not so prime example: Inspector Clouseau, as done by Peter Sellers.

Habitat: inside the Hexagon. They do not travel well outside France. The further they get from the Arc de Triomphe, the shadier they tend to be. Exception: the south of France in August. Very good in cutting single women out of packs, so be careful.

The Italian lover

These boys are the original Latin lovers — and they have worked hard to earn their reputations. They look wonderful, smell great, some of them can cook, they are appreciative, they can be fantastic fathers, and, best of all, they really pay attention. You will wait a long time to hear one of these boys asking 'Did you come?' They will know, because they care enough about it to make sure you did. (If you have had an Italian lover who didn't care about your end of the love making, ask yourself a question: Are you sure he's really Italian, and not a half Italian and half Swiss, from the north? That could explain some of it.)

An Italian lover will notice when you are not too cheerful, when you are wearing a new dress, a new hairstyle, a new pair of shoes. The only problem is that once you have one, you might never want to get out of bed again.

Pluses: there is an emphasis in Italy on appearances which they call '*la bella figura*'; this helps make them the best-dressed men in the world. They can also charm the birds out of the trees.

Minuses: you could have a Hell of a time getting to the bathroom mirror. Or finding a space for your clothes in the wardrobe. And that charm can tend to be a trifle indiscriminate.

Prime example: he was dead sexy, now he's simply dead, but Marcello Mastroianni defined sex appeal, Italian style, for generations.

Not such a prime example: Roberto Begnini. He's hysterically funny but way too manic!

Habitat: have you ever travelled on the inter-city, high-speed trains in Italy? Try it, and see what happens. The businessmen aboard can look splendid, like Caesar's legionnaires returning from Gaul. With any luck, one of them will teach you how to play *scopa* between Milan and Rome, and then take you home for a little more. Be careful — while *scopa* means broom and *scopare* means to sweep, it also has a rather more elemental meaning. Colloquially, it translates as 'to fuck'.

The Greek god

Greek boys were among the prettiest and most celebrated in the Ancient World, judging by the statues representing them — beautiful planes in their faces, classic profiles. It is still a thrill to see a prime example of one in modern times. They are not as mother-centric as their Italian counterparts, but having been adored by the mammas, the *theas* and *yayas* all their lives, they can tend to see themselves as gods in their own cosmoses.

As lovers, Greeks can offer certain cultural challenges, as Eliza discovered when she met and fell in love with one in Sydney. 'From the start, Con was restless,' said Eliza. 'He was always great with me, when he was with me. The problem was that he was always going out in the middle of the night to sit around and drink with his friends. They had body clocks which were totally different from mine. Con would want to make love as soon as I got home from work, when all I wanted was to settle down, have a glass of wine and unwind.'

By 10.30, Con's internal engine was revving to go again. But after a full day at work, then the commute home, the hour of hot and sweaty sex in the early evening, all she wanted to do was settle down with a good book and turn the lights off by midnight. 'We were time-challenged. And our energy levels were very different,' she said. 'On the weekends, things weren't much better. The only time we managed to get into sync was during the holiday we had together on Mykonos. It was brilliant, because I could sleep all day if I needed to and not worry about being out in a club at 3 am.' Then Eliza thought about what married life with her very own Greek god might be like. She's married to a calm, Anglo-Celtic accountant now, and still goes to Greece for her once a year fix of Mediterranean mayhem.

Pluses: when young, they can look as they have just fallen off the side of a Greek urn. Have an extraordinary capacity for having a good time.

Minuses: can sometimes fail to understand the concept that some of us, at least, need sleep. That means they will never let you go to bed before 4 am and that can make you look as though the Greek urn fell on you. The mothers can also be pretty persistent at trying to stuff food down your throat.

Prime example: ex-King Constantine. He's handsome, and a former Olympic sailor, and comes with fantastic contacts. Pity about the ex-business, though. And the fact he's actually not very Greek at all.

Not so prime example: Zorba was a classic, but in his later years, he proved there's no fool like an old one.

Habitat: you will have to be nocturnal to find these boys. They're out and about until late — if you have ever been in rush hour in Athens at 2 am, you will have seen them driving from one *taverna* to another. God knows how they ever get to work in the morning.

A good Jewish boy

One of the sexiest men I had ever met on a long-haul flight looked at me over an airport trolley and said: 'Are you Jewish? You should be Jewish'. I took it as a compliment, rather than a reference to the fact we had talked the whole trip. When he loaded my luggage on to his trolley and helped me to a taxi, I was gone! He also helped me out at the other end — nothing was going to be too much trouble for this guy, even though I was a *goy*. On the cab trip from New York's airport to the Plaza, he got more chat and I got a date for dinner the next night in the famous Oak Room.

Irving turned out to be incredible — sweet, kind, caring, a total *mensch*. But he had the mother from Hell, as it turned out. He had warned me about her, before he took me home to meet her at Friday night dinner in Brooklyn Heights. She was an orthodox Jew, he said, and quite strict about observance. If I had been wearing horns and a tail, she couldn't have been more horrified by my presence on her broadloom. She fed me, she talked to me, she was nice to me and then she was very happy to show me the door. Irving took me back to the hotel, his shoulders curved into a resigned little slump. I knew that there was never going to be any future with Irving for any woman who didn't pass muster with his Yiddish Momma. It was such a pity; Irving was exactly the sort of man you dream up when you write down the list of ideal qualities you would like in a boyfriend.

Pluses: can be incredibly loyal and fantastic providers. Their mothers — if you are Jewish or when they get over the fact that you are not.

Minuses: can be a trifle suffocating. Their mothers.

Prime examples: Jerry Seinfeld and Ben Stiller. They're cute, rich, amusing — so what's not to like?

Not so prime example: Woody Allen. Not cute, not amusing. So what's his point?

Habitat: anywhere in the world where there are good coffee shops, good cake shops, and good delis. These boys run on their stomachs.

putting
the
man
under
man-agement

14
The 'F' Word

If you think this is going to be about *that* 'f' word, you're wrong. It's more about some other 'f' words the User should know inside out — 'f' for flirt, 'f' for flattery, 'f' for anything from fear to fun to food to fakery — than anything else. You'll have to get a handbook from the local sex education clinic on the mechanics of sex if you've forgotten the basics of the seminal 'f' word. And if you have, don't panic: it just takes a little practice and some imagination. So get yourself the guide, some props and off you go. (And don't forget the fella — another 'f' word. It's generally more fun with two.)

If further details are required, read *Cleo* or *Cosmo*, though these days you'll probably find yourself confronted with a blow-by-blow description of how to pleasure yourself when you are alone (not that there is anything wrong with that), rather than share pleasure with a man in the hot and sweaty tumble of a double bed. Women's magazines, having gone through the 'how to please your man' phase, moved to the 'better sex for you *and* him', and then on to 'the best sex you've ever had'. The emphasis passed from the individual him, to the couple, and then to the individual her and masturbation without missing a beat. (Any further away from the mainstream of consensual sex and they'll be back in the lower depths and urging the delights of anal penetration on us.)

Sex is a lead indicator within a relationship — if it's not good, then the communication levels within that relationship will be under stress as well. (Though perversely, it seems it's possible to have great sex with someone you don't know, might actively dislike and would never be seen in public with — that was the basis of Erica Jong's vintage literary quest in *The Zipless Fuck*.)

Sex in theory is also simple. According to the accepted wisdom: men give love to get sex, women give sex to get love. If you believe that, it would follow that the User gives a lot of sex to get a lot of love in return. When that equation doesn't work out, smart Users quickly move to Plan B — withhold pleasure at appropriate times to indicate a certain displeasure.

To the smart User, sex is *the* area in which a man is definitely more useful than any girlfriend, mother, or packet of Tim Tams. The first two provide relationships that can help fill the communication void when you're between relationships — or even when you are in one. The third is a sex substitute: you remember the adage — if you can't have sex, have chocolate.

Nor is this chapter about another 'f' word, feminism, either, even though the smart User has absolutely nothing against the concept. What's not to like about equality of opportunity for women, socially, politically and economically? As an increasing number of Americans are fond of saying, 'It's all good', though that's generally about losing in a *Survivor*-type game show or at baseball, not feminism.

> *(Feminists) keep getting up on soapboxes and proclaiming that women are brighter than men. That's true, but it should be kept very quiet or it ruins the whole racket.*
> ANITA LOOS, 1891–1981

So, before you get to feminism, you have to go past the initial, and most important, 'f's: flirting and flattery. They are an essential part of the smart User's arsenal, and they are ready to use at all times. First…

Flirt!

Some women begin life as flirts. They get to the edge of their cots, peer over and think 'oh, look, someone new to enslave' and start practising. It doesn't matter upon whom or what their eye falls: male, female, the family dog. To some, flirting is as natural as breathing while others insist they can't flirt at all. Here's the news: there's no great trick to it. It's about knowing when to pay attention and be interested in the person you are flirting with. There is nothing more flattering to anyone than to have another human being interested in him or her.

(If you are absolutely not interested in other people, then flirting is simply not for you. You need to work on other ways to attract men, though it's hard to imagine why you would want to.)

Flirting ranges from subtle signs across crowded rooms, to the signals that separate a man from a group and draw him closer, to rather less subtle chat. It includes behaviour such as mirroring (your body begins to imitate the stance of the person you are flirting with), or hair flicking (hard for women with cropped hair), or light touches on the arm or back. When women use these signals, they are indicating they want to indulge in a little playfulness, which might or might not include something more. Many men seem to read these signals as an invitation to have sex with them in the nearest bathroom. Smart Users quickly work out who can play the game and who can't.

When chat gets too raunchy, flirting flies straight out the window and that spoils the fun. By its nature, flirting is light, frivolous and should make the people involved in it feel desirable, attractive and amusing. It should not make either party feel as though they are committed to carry through. An essential element in good flirting is…

Flattery!

Never underestimate the value of a judicious piece of flattery, because it really does get you everywhere. We're all susceptible to it (particularly the 'that outfit makes you look soooo thin' line) to one degree or another, but men seem desperately keen to believe a compliment, any compliment. (This is because of the fragile male ego.)

> *I can live for two months on a good compliment.*
> MARK TWAIN, 1835–1910

Never doubt that this line of attack works. Even the most egregious piece of sucking up can be well received. An example: recently, I was at a dinner to honour a distinguished Irishman who had not long before been knighted. In the vote of thanks, one of his compatriots referred to the newly dubbed knight as 'the greatest Irishman of his generation' which is, when you think about it, quite a declaration to make about a citizen of an island which has produced the Nobel Laureate for Literature, poet Seamus Heaney, and Nobel Prize Laureate for Peace, politician David Trimble, to name just two.

Anyone looking to the guest of honour's table hoping to see a demure look on his face ('Who, me?') would have been disappointed. Whatever reservations he might have had about being described thus were not for public display. But the event proved again, if proof were ever needed, that flattery is like oxygen to most of us. It is its own reward to the smart User. As another Irishman, Oscar Wilde, once said: 'A person who believes that flattery does not work, clearly has never been flattered'.

And there is a mantra that works to this purpose. It's the 'you're so handsome, you're so clever, you're so kind' trilogy. This forms the basis of a smart User's approach to a new man she's interested in. And it works on men she's had for a while, as well.

> *When to the sessions of sweet silent thought*
> *I summon up remembrance of things,*
> *I sigh the lack of many things I sought,*
> *And with old woes new wail my dear time's waste;*
> *Then I can drown an eye, unused to flow,*
> *For precious friends hid in death's dateless night,*
> *And weep afresh love's long since cancelled woe,*
> *And moan the expense of many a vanished sight;*
> *Then can I grieve at grievances foregone,*
> *And heavily from woe to woe tell o'er*
> *The sad account of fore-bemoaned moan,*
> *Which I new pay as if not paid before.*
> *But if the while I think on thee, dear friend,*
> *All losses are restored and sorrows end.*
>
> SONNET NO. 30, WILLIAM SHAKESPEARE, 1564—1616

(Lovely piece of flattery, this!)

It's the most amazing thing, but flattery never fails. Like TV vet Dr Harry training a puppy by positive reinforcement, smart Users can accustom men to this sort of conditioning.

> *Every woman is infallibly to be gained by every sort of flattery, and every man by one sort or another.*
> LORD CHESTERFIELD, 1694–1773

Pretty soon after you start using the Dr Harry method, ordinary men will start behaving like handsome, smart and kind individuals. It's a miracle. However, if for some reason, the process doesn't work, you've got a totally useless case on your hands. The smart User will just return him to the stockpile of men, happy in the knowledge that she has done her best, but sometimes, it's impossible to make a silk purse out of a dog's breakfast. Speaking of which…

Food

Food is good. The way to a man's heart has always been through his stomach, so perhaps you should start with breakfast. For some reason, men seem to believe that eating really is the right way to start the day, as many a single woman with not much more in the fridge than a bottle of vodka in the freezer section, two bottles of champagne and half a dozen bottles of nail polish (they keep longer) in the door has discovered to her cost. If you have kept a fellow overnight, he will think juice, cereal and fruit a proper recompense for his nocturnal activities. (Imagine the fuss if men got breakfasts which mirrored their performance!) So try to have fruit salad, muesli, eggs, bacon and thick toast on hand for a true champion of the innerspring.

> *I am not hungry; but thank goodness, I am greedy.*
> A NINETEENTH-CENTURY PUNCH MAGAZINE

Some of the most liberated women I know are among the best cooks. They regard it not as part of the general drudgery of life (which includes ironing, cleaning the kitchen floor and scrubbing the loo), but part of its rewarding creative process. Smart Users know that ability is extremely attractive, and competence in the kitchen is welcome, nurturing and a real asset when the world outside is quite the opposite. If you can't cook, take a class. How hard can it be? You follow a recipe, and things come out. If only everything else in life was as simple.

How to be a fake food goddess:

- Styling is everything. Get in a professional to make your kitchen look like the real deal.
- Buy a cookbook or two. Actually try to cook. Bury the most sensational failures.
- If this doesn't work, take a cooking class. Bear in mind that certain socio-economic groups will be found at different sorts of classes. Do you really want to learn about 101 ways with mince? Tofu for beginners? Or is mud crab with ginger or five easy recipes for *foie gras* more you?
- Get in the caterers for dinner parties or pick up some up-market takeaway on the way home from work. Throw away all the containers well before the guests arrive and decant the contents into your own pots. Always keep something which smells wonderful simmering on the stove to add to the effect.
- Learn to cook something really simple, like cheese biscuits. Guests will be amazed. Or find out where you can buy cheese biscuits that look home-baked.
- Keep the raw materials (vegetables, fruit, olive oil, fresh herbs, etc.) for simple meals at hand. It looks as though you would cook — brilliantly! — if only you had the time. Throw the mouldy bits out regularly.
- Grow your hair long, dye it dark chestnut, practice a sultry, English-accented purr and invite your guests into the kitchen. This all works for smart User and TV cook Nigella Lawson. Any man you are trying to use will be gone for all money once he sees you press the meat tenderly on the griddle.

Cooking is chemistry and physics, not rocket science, as a friend of mine knows very well. She met and fell in love with a man who was, apart from being extremely thin, absolutely ravenous all the time. It was a match made in heaven, because she was already famous as the woman who over-catered for everything. Then this boyfriend appeared on the scene, and suddenly there were no leftovers — ever. His previously insatiable appetite had found someone who was more than a match for him. She proved endlessly that abundance never goes out of…

Fashion

The smart User knows that men interested in fashion tend not to be too straight, which is why men who interest themselves in the detail of their wives' wardrobes are always such interesting creatures, in a Noel Coward sort of way. (I knew one who insisted his wife only ever wear baby blue, which was cutish when she was in her twenties and increasingly eccentric as she approached thirty-five. Thankfully, this was something she was aware of. She rebelled against the blue — which was his first indication that all was not well within their relationship from her side. The divorce papers confirmed that inkling some months later. She celebrated their divorce in the hottest pink you could imagine.)

If some men had their way, their women would be dressed like prostitutes on a Rostered Day Off or Mariah Carey at work (which, when you come to think about it, looks like much the same thing). They are the ones who respond to the elemental stimulus of tits and ass. Today, they should be satisfied with a walk down any main street in Australia on a mild day to see the under twenty-five female population exposing any and every body part to the elements and admiration or otherwise of total strangers.

However, most men seem fixated by breasts, which is why many Users, smart and otherwise, put theirs on display when they are out in a social situation. They're best revealed at night. During the day, exposed flesh is fine on the beach at Noosa and the further reaches of St Kilda, but not in general view. Remember, you will rarely, if ever, find a woman who dresses in the style of Erin Brokovich when she's at home with the kids on the weekend.

Smart Users pick their best attributes and work around them, and that makes *chadors* so useful for women with liquid eyes, bad skin and dumpy figures; and trousers fantastic for women with legs not quite up to the mark. Over the top of it all, you need only add a dash of fragrance and a little…

Fun

Which is, as any User knows, the key to keeping a relationship alive whether it's brand new, two years along, or ready for a silver anniversary. Life has a habit of getting very serious, very quickly, and sometimes you just have to do something really silly — and funny. Define your own fun, from eggbeaters to oddly shaped prophylactics. Keep the fun confined to you and him and never broadcast it, in Charles and Camilla fashion, via mobile phone. Find what makes you laugh: it will increase the longevity of any relationship.

A relationship without the right levels of fun can quickly degenerate into one with heightened levels of…

Fear

…from your nearest and dearest as they wonder what on earth you are going to get up to next. Fear has no place in a relationship, except as part of the way some successful relationships are strategised. Parents subconsciously manage children by tapping into the deep-seated fear in the child about losing the parental esteem. This is how it works: 'If I play hooky from school, go into town, spend the day in a games arcade smoking with other potential illiterates, that might be fun … but hang on a minute … if Mum and Dad find out about it, they'll think I'm a total drop-kick for lying to them, spending all my money on video games and hanging around with deadbeats. And if they think I'm an idiot, maybe they won't love me anymore.'

> *Freely pardoning the shortcomings of others although nowhere falling short yourself; in holding a companion no less dear because his standards are less exacting.*
> DESIDERIUS ERASMUS, 1469–1536

F for forgiveness?

Eureka! Here it is. The smart User knows that her man needs to fear the consequences of losing her good opinion and respect. This is how his thinking might go: 'If I go out for a drink with the boys after work, that's fine. But if I stay out all night, get drunk, spend all my spare cash, meet up with a couple of women who take me home and then I lurch into her place/our place the next morning reeking of alcohol and full of apologies ... well, perhaps she will think I am an idiot. Maybe if I do this enough times, she will not only stop loving me, but might actively come to despise me. Perhaps to maintain her good opinion of me and love, it would be a idea if I didn't behave like a English lager lout on a soccer tour to Amsterdam.'

To keep the fear level effective, the smart User does not tolerate bad behaviour. Full stop. Forgiveness is the province of God, not a woman trying to make a life for herself and/or her family. However, for the sake of sanity, the smart User occasionally appears to forgive, although she certainly will never really forget. That's called...

Faking it

And it's the thing smart Users do all the time, in various senses. If women ever stopped faking 'it', the world as we know it would come to a crashing end. Honestly, faking it is sometimes the best thing a woman can do for her relationship — or for a man she hopes to have a relationship with.

> *What force cannot effect, fraud shall devise.*
> RICHARD CRANSHAW, 1613–1649

What woman hasn't at some time in her life faked an orgasm, or wished that she knew what one was so that she could fake it? Or pretended that what she really wanted to do one cold and rainy afternoon was go to the football rather than stay home in front of the fire with a good book and a glass of wine? Or agreed happily to see an action thriller when she was longing to see a romantic comedy? Or appeared delighted when at three hours notice she has heard that one of his old mates from the country was coming to stay for a long weekend? It's all fakery, and if the purists say it's dishonest and undermines the basis of true communication within a relationship, Users say 'pish tosh'. Smart Users fake it all the time.

But there are some things a User should never have to do if she doesn't want to, and that includes faking knowledge of the rules of Rugby (apart from anything else, they change too often); the laws of cricket (test cricket goes on for the best part of a week! Relationships sometimes don't last as long). And if she doesn't care for fishing, she shouldn't have to see a fish with scales outside a fishmonger's window.

> *When one door of happiness closes, another opens; but often we look so long at the closed door that we do not see the one which has opened for us.*
> HELEN KELLER, 1880–1968

But all this happens after a relationship has been bedded in. In the beginning, you'll have to fake it. You need to acquire a smattering of knowledge about everything he's interested in to make him feel comfortable with you. You must, of course, never assume that he will even feign an interest in the things which interest you. You might take sailing lessons so you can spend Sundays together, but this is not a two-way street. You can never, for example, expect him to spend any time at your *Grandes Dames ou Femmes Fatales* course about women in French cinema so you can spend Thursday nights together. That is just not going to happen.

Here's the thing about faking it. You do it and then you keep quiet about the whole deal. When you fake, you can never share. The man never even notices what's going on. Now, that's the perfect outcome for the clever User.

Can you be feminist and User?

There is no question. Take Japanese women of the tenth century, for instance. While Japanese women generally are not regarded as feminist role models, in this period they were certainly years ahead of their European sisters. Among them was Sei Shonagon, a writer worth paying attention to, even today. She lived in the city of Kyoto, then called Heian Kyo, the City of Peace and Tranquillity, and wrote a very famous book called *The Pillow Book of Sei Shonagon*. In this, she recorded everyday life in the isolated city with a keen and sympathetic eye and a lyrical brush. It's a chronicle of life, snapshots, moments, relationships within a closed society, and above all — lists! Sei also demonstrated a remarkable modernity in her attitudes to men and their management within the strict rules of courtly behaviour of the time. Here are some of her observations, and some adaptations for the modern era.

Things that make the heart beat faster

Then:
>To see a gentleman stop his carriage before one's gate and instruct his attendants to announce his arrival.
>To wash one's hair, make one's toilet, and put on scented robes; even if not a soul sees one, these preparations still produce an inner pleasure.

Now:
>To see a gentleman stop his car outside your house and know that he is the designated driver for the evening.
>The ring of the telephone when you are awaiting a call from a new lover. Hiding from the telephone when trying to avoid an old lover.
>To wash your hair, put on your make-up, and put on multi-layers of fragrance. You will feel better about yourself.

Things that arouse a fond memory of the past

Then:
>It is a rainy day and one is feeling bored. To pass the time, one starts looking through some old papers. And then one comes across the letters of a man one used to love.

Now:
>It is still a rainy day. To pass the time, you decide to clear out the cupboards. You find an old shoebox full of letters from a man you used

to love. And then you wonder why your present loved one can't even manage an email.

Things that cannot be compared

Then:
> When one has stopped loving somebody, one feels that he has become someone else, even thought he is still the same person.

Now:
> The man you used to love, and the man he became when someone else started loving him.

Rare things

Then:
> People who live together and who still manage to behave with reserve towards each other. However much these people may try to hide their weaknesses, they usually fail.

Now:
> Since familiarity breeds contempt, it is increasingly rare to find people who live together and who still manage to behave with respect towards each other. This is even more rare when they are at a dinner party together and he begins to tell a story she has heard more than one dozen times before.

Embarrassing things

Then:
> A man recites his own poems, (not especially good ones) and tells about the praise they have received.
> Lying awake at night, one says something to one's companion, who simply goes on sleeping.

Now:
> A man who sings his own folk songs (not particularly good ones) and asks you to admire them.

Lying awake at night, you say something to your bedmate, who simply goes on sleeping. Not even a sharp elbow to the midriff will disturb his slumber.

Surprising and distressing things

Then:
All night long, one has been waiting for a man who one thought was sure to arrive. At dawn, just when one has forgotten about him for a moment and dozed off, a crow caws loudly. One wakes with a start and sees that it is daytime — most astonishing.

Now:
Most of the night long, you have been waiting for a man you thought was coming. At dawn, just when one has forgotten about him for a moment and dozed off, he does. You wake with a start, see that it is daytime — and he asks you if you came too. No longer most astonishing: he never gets it.

Moving things

Then:
Two young people are in love with each other; but someone is in their way and they are prevented from doing what they want.

Now:
A proposal, not a proposition. A man in love with his woman.

15
Unified Theory

If you enter 'Unified Theory' (something most sane people would rarely do) into the query field of your favourite Web search engine, you will not find a simple explanation of the expression. It is clearly not in the hearts and minds (let alone the business plan) of physicists to let the rest of us in on the secrets of the universe without some pain. Some untrained ratbag might just run off with the plans and have too much unauthorised fun poking around in its theoretical nether regions.

In response to your query, *inter alia*, you could find the treatises of various Canadian geeks aged nineteen and a half who are trying to make a name for themselves via a third-year quantum physics class at McGill University, or even discover the website for the rock band called Unified Theory. Discarding the CD liner notes, you can trail through the swamps of these less than limpid thoughts about what Unified Theory is all about. Basically, it contends that underlying the rules and theories of physics, there should be a point at which they all, from *alpha* to *omega*, converge, and everything becomes crystal clear. The Big Bang? Unified Theory will explain the why and the wherefore — easy peasy — as well as tell you why snowflakes are shaped the way they are.

So it takes in everything from Einstein's Theory of Relativity to Newton's Laws of Gravity and spins it all into the fabric of space, time, mass and … I'll spare you the rest. Unified Theory has created quite a few black holes in my brain, which had just about closed up after reading Stephen Hawking's

A Brief History of Time. (It doesn't help if you enter 'Simplified Unified Theory' into the query field either — I tried it.)

In researching this book, I spent some considerable time here and on the other side of the globe trying to work out if there was a unified theory when it came to being a smart User. I asked English, Irish, French, Italians, Greeks, and Americans; I even asked a couple of Moroccans on the Paris Metro at one stage. Anyone I thought who might have an insight into what the basic principle of using might be was asked the question.

> *When first we met we did not guess*
> *That Love would prove so hard a master.*
> ROBERT BRIDGES, 1844–1930

So there I was one warm June night, perched on an antique chair in a palazzo in Florence (the view out of the French doors and across the garden was the floodlit campanile of the Church of the Santo Spirito — which is some punctuation point in the night sky as well as a phallic addition to a view), a glass of the Frescobaldi Pomino Bianco in a hand which had just been kissed half a dozen times by some men any smart User would love to get her paws on. I was talking to an English art student, aged twenty-six, there to study painting. Without a steady boyfriend at that time, she answered the question bluntly: 'Treat 'em mean to keep 'em keen,' she said. It's a theory we've all heard about, but is it the unified one?

The diplomat's wife who was the third part of our triangular conversation nearly fell off the antique sofa — she had the look of a woman who carefully negotiated her relationship with her husband and treated him with respect and generosity. 'Well, if you're too accessible, they lose interest in you,' said the pale-skinned beauty. 'And if they are too nice to you, you lose interest as well.'

> *People who are not in love fail to understand how an intelligent man can suffer because of a very ordinary woman. This is like being surprised that anyone should be stricken with cholera because of a creature so insignificant as the comma bacillus.*
> MARCEL PROUST, 1871–1922

Apparently, Unified Theory these days is simple, even if it sounds like the perfect excuse for sadists to behave badly and then say it's all just part of the plan to attract and keep a man. Actually, it works beautifully if you are involved with a masochist, but there aren't really too many of those you'd want to date.

It's been around for years, this theory, but it has some surprisingly modern adepts. Take Catherine Zeta Jones for instance. The Welsh actor took leave of her senses and set her cap at Michael Douglas, a self-confessed former sex addict who at one stage checked himself into a rehab facility to treat his passion for passion. Rather than become a notch on his by-now shredded belt, Catherine took any mother's advice (which is always 'Don't sleep with him, he won't respect you') and made Douglas wait. And wait. And wait. According to the American scandal sheets, she made him wait nine months before she finally 'allowed' him to seduce her at his villa on Majorca.

> *A woman begins by resisting a man's advances and ends by blocking his retreat.*
> OSCAR WILDE, 1854–1900

This nine months business worked also for *Friends'* Jennifer Aniston, who decided she fancied Brad Pitt and got their agents to set up a date. Jen, also taking the advice of the mother figure within, made Pitt wait for sex as well. According to the same American gossip sheets, it wasn't until a holiday in Mexico on Valentine's Day that Jen and Brad finally consummated their relationship. (Jen also kept a couple of other shots in her arsenal, as well. She researched her man — so easy when he's a high profile personality — right down to his family background and his relationship with Gwyneth Paltrow. Then, she gave him small, thoughtful presents that demonstrated how tuned into him she was. It worked.)

While acknowledging it's incredible that such a level of detail about the private lives of public people should become known (or written about), what is also clear is that the 'treat 'em mean-ish' strategy seems to have worked in both these cases. Also incredible that that mother's advice could also be so effective in the twenty-first century.

❝ *By keeping men off, you keep them on.* ❞
JOHN GAY, 1685–1732

It seems as old-fashioned now to make a man wait for sex as those archaic (or are they time-honoured?) pieces of magazine marital counsel from the 1950s about how to keep your man interested. You must have heard some of them: a friend remembers reading one which urged women to greet their husbands at the front door wearing a dress (which they had whipped up themselves) made of cellophane. There are a couple of things wrong with that idea from the start. First of all, who can sew these days apart from your nanna? Think of the explanations you'd have to go through as you handed her the fuchsia cellophane sheets and the Butterick pattern 7540 for a shirtwaist dress.

You might also think about having an oxygen cylinder handy — some men after a hard day at work might not be quite up to the adrenalin surge caused by someone jumping out from behind a door at them in a cellophane dress.

❝ *Megaera: Oh! I won't bear it another moment. You used to sit and talk to those dumb beasts for hours, when you hadn't a word for me.*
Androcles: They never answered back, darling. ❞
GEORGE BERNARD SHAW, 1856–1900.

And yet, women's magazines in the 1950s were always giving women advice on how to treat men properly, how to make them feel like kings.

Housekeeping Monthly of May 1958, is alleged to have given the following tips to its readers — presumably the Users of the day. I think it's a bit of an Internet trick, but it makes some interesting points. (The italics are my later additions.) Personally, I think the Unified Theory far easier to remember, and thus administer. But still:

- **Have dinner ready.** Plan ahead the night before to have a delicious meal ready on time for his return. This is a way of letting him know you have been thinking about him and you are concerned about his needs. Most men are hungry when they come home *(actually, so are most* *people, including women)* and the prospect of a good meal (and especially his favourite drink) is part of the warm welcome.

- **Prepare yourself.** Take fifteen minutes to rest so you will be refreshed when he arrives. Touch up your make-up (*this indicates you had time to put some on during the morning*), put a ribbon in your hair (*no mention of cellophane frocks here*) so you will be fresh looking. Remember, he's been at work with a lot of weary people. *(So whatever you do, don't look as though you had anything to do yourself during the day.)*
- **Clear away the clutter.** Make one last trip through the main part of the house.(*And make sure those messy kids are well out of sight.*)
- **Gather up school books,** bags, papers, run a dust cloth over the tables. *(Make sure all traces of the children are gathered up as well.)*
- **Prepare and light a fire** during the cooler months for him to unwind by. *(Very cavewoman. But if you don't have a fireplace, perhaps you could wheel the Weber into the sitting room).* Your husband will feel he has reached a haven of rest and order, and it will give you a lift, too. After all, catering to his comfort will provide you with enormous personal satisfaction. *(Be careful not to light a [figurative] fire under him, either, no matter how much you might think he deserves it. This will not add to the feeling of a haven of rest and order.)*
- **Prepare the offspring.** *(This sounds like the first step of a recipe: Prepare the children by dusting them in flour, then browning then in a fry-pan over a low flame.)* Take a few minutes to wash their hands and faces, comb their hair and change their clothes. *(Stepford wives deserve Stepford children, too.)* They are little treasures and he would like to see them playing the part. *(What drug was this writer on?)* Minimise all distractions. At the time of his arrival, eliminate all noise of the washer, dryer and vacuum. *(It must have been like living in a hotel with free sex for these guys.)* Try to encourage the children to be quiet. *(None of this nonsense about trying to encourage the children to express themselves.)*
- **Be happy to see him.** Greet him with a warm smile and show sincerity in your desire to please him. *(Actor Melanie Griffith still practises this on her husband, the Spanish matinee idol Antonio Banderas. She told a writer that she always smiled whenever she saw her husband. If your*

husband looked and sounded like that, you'd probably be smiling too — very sincerely.)

- **Listen to him.** You may have a dozen important things to tell him, but the moment of his arrival is not the time. Let him talk first — remember his topics of conversation are more important than yours. *(And that's because he's the man and you're not.)*
- **Make the evening his.** Never complain if he comes home late or goes out for dinner or other places of entertainment without you. *(This is the sentence which makes me think a man wrote this. Can you imagine a woman saying, 'Yes dear, of course you can go out to dinner without me. Have a nice night and don't hurry home.')* Instead, try to understand his world of strain and pressure and his very real need to be at home and to relax. Your goal is to try to make your home a place of peace, order and tranquillity where your husband can renew himself in mind and spirit.
- **Don't greet him with complaints and problems.** Don't complain is he's late for dinner or stays out all night. *(Yeah, right. Like that was ever going to happen, even in the 1950s.)*
- **Make him comfortable.** Have him lie back in a comfortable chair, or have him lie down in the bedroom. Have a cool or a warm drink ready for him.*(Do not pour it over his head.)* Arrange his pillow *(try not to arrange it over his mouth and nose)*, offer to take off his shoes for him, and speak in a low, soothing and pleasant voice. *(Try to sound like the human equivalent of ambient music.)*
- **Don't ask him questions about his work** *(this goes double if he's in the Mafia)* or question his judgment or integrity. *(He might become annoyed or irritated if you start to ask how a policeman on a sergeant's salary can afford a new Mercedes Benz)*. Remember, he's the master of the house, and as such will always exercise his will with fairness and truthfulness. You have no right to question him.
- **A good wife always knows her place.** *(And that place is cooking, cleaning, tidying and pouring drinks, when she is not acting as a human doormat.)*

Between the 1950s and the first decade of the twenty-first century, a few bridges have fallen into the water between the detailed instructions of *The Good Wife's Guide* and the Treat 'Em Mean Theory. The Unified Theory has the advantage of brevity and requires no subservient behaviour on the User's part.

16
Let's talk about sex, baby

Quick! Hold page one! Working women are too tired for sex and can barely remember what it was like. And women raising children are getting crankier and crankier with their husbands. (What a shock!) When they are looking at cutting themselves some slack, for something to jettison from their busy lives, increasingly they choose intimate relations with their husbands. This is the basis of a piece of research which came of out Adelaide University recently (which actually did make page one of the papers, but more of that a little later), although a quick chat to almost any woman would give you much the same result, assuming you know her well enough to raise the subject. Feeling like sex tonight? No thanks, we're married with children.

It's one of the great paradoxes of the modern age: sex is everywhere in public, and in increasingly fewer places in private. Go to the cinema, look at a billboard — sex is inescapable. Thank God we can go to our own homes and get away from all that hot and sweaty sex! Okay, maybe you can't if you turn the TV on, or open the pages of a magazine, but at least at home, you can turn the lights out and pull the sheets over your head. And if your partner asks you if you are 'feeling like a little cuddle?', you can say 'I'll pass, thanks. Julia Roberts just had one for me.' Don't feel too bad — this sex boredom is nothing new.

> *The reproduction of mankind is a great marvel and mystery. Had God consulted me in the matter, I should have advised Him to continue the generation of the species by fashioning them of clay.*
> MARTIN LUTHER, 1483–1546

Simulated sex saturates the twenty-first century landscape in a way it never seems to have done before in the Western world. Which is not, of course, to say that our forebears never thought about it — if they hadn't, we obviously wouldn't be here. But somehow, all we see now is sex, and it looks as if everybody else is having our share. Even the famously unable-to-get-a-bloke Ally McBeal occasionally scored, but those moments were, thankfully, mostly off-screen.

If you talked to women, you would be surprised at what they say. Here it is, in short: Single women not in a relationship have the possibility of exciting and satisfying sex. What they don't know is the where, the when and — possibly — the who. This triple uncertainty can sometimes drive them into the arms of extremely unsuitable men in bars in the very early morning, a course which necessitates some pretty fancy footwork a short time later as they drag on their shucked-off garments and head for the door. (Obviously, this exercise is difficult if you have entirely forgotten yourself and invited him home to listen to your Enya CDs. You have to be pretty dexterous to be able to shed a one-nighter with any degree of grace.)

Single women can also, on occasion, be jealous of their paired-off sisters, because they are convinced that the marrieds have the security of knowing where their next cuddle is coming from. And that sounds pretty good to the singles. Married women, or women in stable relationships, however, come from a different position altogether — they might know from whom the sex is coming (and they might even know when — every Friday night without fail, and every Sunday afternoon, depending on whether the Grand Prix is on or not) and the where (always in the marital bed) but for the most part, the sex to them might not be too exciting. They, therefore, envy their single sisters the unexpected, exciting sex they imagine they constantly have.

Take my friend Jacinta, for instance. (Obviously, Jacinta is not her real name — unfortunately it's hardly anyone's name. If I used her real name she would be minus one husband.) Anyway, Jacinta, working mother, married these ten years, was having a bit of a moan to me about her husband. 'It's like being married to your brother,' she said. 'We get along really well, but when it comes to sex, honestly, it's a bit of a chore.' But Jacinta has not lost her appetite for a sex life. 'I'd love to have a lover! Even three!' she joked. (I *think* she was joking.) But where would she fit in three lovers into her busy home/work/mothering/wife schedule? 'I'd manage. And think of the fabulous underwear I'd have!'

But here is the news flash — hardly any one is having hot sex these days. Most of us, like Jacinta, just dream about it. Single women without partners don't, because for the most part it's tricky and can be dangerous (thanks to the threat of STDs, that little payback at the end of the twentieth century for all that free love in the 1960s); and married women don't have that much either, because they're too tired, too preoccupied, or too something-or-other (which might just be bored or cranky with their husbands, but they would be unlikely to tell you that) to make the effort.

> *It has to be admitted that we English have sex on the brain, which is a very unsatisfactory place to have it.*
> MALCOLM MUGGERIDGE, 1903–1990

It's something to think about, this level of unsexiness in a world for which sex has become a marketing tool. Buy a car, a holiday, a pair of men's shoes, anything, and it's almost certain to have sex attached. The pressure on real women to be seductresses like the almost-naked women their partners are constantly exposed to is enormous. Which is why real women are finding less and less time in their lives for it, and that brings us neatly to Dr Barbara Pocock and her research.

Sex and its partner, frustration, were the unexpected guests at the feast when Dr Pocock conducted a survey for the Centre of Labour Research at Adelaide University. Dr Pocock wanted to find out about women and work, and so she interviewed 150 women for her report, *Having a Life: Work, family fairness and community in 2000*. While she didn't specifically set out to find out about the sex lives of her subjects, the topic kept coming up.

The pressures of modern life seem to be squeezing the very breath out of intimacy. People were either too tired, or too stressed, or totally uninterested, said Dr Pocock's report. 'Women find they can't be a terrific worker, a wonderful mother, and have a great sex life under the current arrangements.'

What Dr Pocock found was that women had discovered the trick in the idea of 'having it all.' That was the catchcry of the 1980s, when women were starting to really make their marks in big business, in government, in areas where there had been relatively few of them before. But having succeeded in their jobs, and gained the status, the social relationships — and let's not forget — the money that work delivers, they discovered that having it all meant something ever more pernicious — doing it all as well.

There was obviously some considerable upside for men in having their wives at work — the money as well as more interesting wives. But when it came to taking up the slack left when a housewife became a working mum, many were notably reluctant to come to the aid of the party.

And Barbara Pocock discovered the consequences of that in her study. The underlying message is that government, institutions, workplaces and men are yet to understand the changes which have taken place in women's lives. Unless something is done, the birthrate will decline even further than it has. The benefits of motherhood, mixed in with the sheer volume of other work that women have to do, sometimes seem outweighed by its negatives.

This survey of Dr Pocock's raised some eyebrows, and even a few hackles. It's not natural for women not to want to be mothers, said some callers to talkback radio stations. 'Whingeing bloody women' seemed to be the consensus. (It's a constant to blame women for the situations they find themselves in because of social pressures. In the middle of thinking about this particular subject, I went for a walk around the block. There, in the bookshop window, was a volume entitled *Mothers who work: Are they to blame*? Blame for what? And is there ever any idea that a working father might be culpable for whatever it is that women are?)

According to Dr Pocock's report, the thing which got working women most exercised was the question of housework. Even when men were SNAGS (sensitive new-age guys) they weren't too whoops at it. They did a bit, just enough to keep their women off their backs most of the time, but the underlying point of it was if their partners complained too much, they could point out with some justice they do much more that Tom, Dick or Harry.

The pressure of work outside the home, as well as work inside, has put the most incredible pressure on women to perform — mother, paid worker, housewife, wife. And since it is simply not possible for women to say to their bosses, 'Sorry, it's not you, it's me, I just don't feel like work today, I've been too busy at home,' or to put the children on hold while she takes a little time out, something has to give — and that's the intimacy between husband and wife.

The women in Dr Pocock's research group indicated a growing level of dissatisfaction with partners who were either unable to see the amount of work which had to be done around the home and didn't pitch in, or who saw what was happening and simply decided to do as little as they could get away with. Also according to her report, women were distressed by their long hours in paid work and housework, added to which was the responsibility of raising the children. All of this was building into anger and resentment — the natural enemies of sex. You try having meaningful sex with someone while you are really cranky with him for not cleaning out the garage, or for not putting through a load of washing without separating the coloureds. (Boo, hiss for all those currently pink or grey shirts.)

No wonder fictional women are having the sex that real, busy women are not. When one of those *Sex and the City* chicks gets a little action, the audience has a vicarious thrill without the crankiness or distaste which can sometimes inexplicably accompany sex with the man you love.

Yes, yes, you say. For the last thirty years, this has been the double-edged sword of the women's movement. Greater financial independence, combined with greater responsibility, has produced greater pressures on women, relationships, families and work. Dr Pocock writes that to revive the spark, a lot has to change, starting with men. The Nile will flow backwards before that happens, but good luck to her! She will need all she can get — thousands of years have seen very little change in men.

> *To say that you can love one person all your life is just like saying that one candle will continue burning as long as you live.*
>
> COUNT LEO TOLSTOY, 1828–1910

The difference now is that we still embrace the notion of romantic love, or a love that stays constant until death. It was all very well for this idea to take root and flourish in the medieval courts of love — young knights then needed to attach themselves emotionally, not physically, to the ladies. (Husbands who locked their wives into chastity belts while they were away might have rendered a physical attachment impossible, anyway. A woman in such a contraption might not have had to do much housework, but she would have been very moody when the lord and master came home swinging the key.)

> *There are few virtuous women who are not bored with their trade.*
> FRANÇOIS, DUC DE LA ROCHEFOUCAULD, 1804–1864

It wasn't such a bad thing, then, this notion of romantic love. People didn't live very long, so the notion of loving someone until death did you part wasn't onerous. Disease or a stray spear could easily shorten a lifespan, which was only about forty on average. Now we put such pressure on romance we expect the most fragile form of love to endure through thick and thin and up to seventy years or more. Good luck to us, as well as Dr Pocock.

Some tips for the exhausted

Choose a partner well

Take a long-term view. The User picks a mate she thinks will be a stayer, not a sprinter. Try this: Gaze at a prospective loved one and squint. Imagine him in a checked flannel dressing gown with a cord tie. Are you seeing cute, which is attractive, or comfortable, which is certainly not? You could be seeing like this quite a lot over the years, so make sure you like the view. And you should have made sure that he's smart. There is nothing sexier in the long run than a clever, funny mind. Abs of steel are fab for about ten years, but eventually they turn to abs of flab and after that you might need another diversion. If you allow for this at the outset, you will have made your life so much easier.

If your sex life has all the tension of a wet flannel, withdraw your labour

Go on strike. Remember Lysistrata, who organised the women of Athens against war by telling their menfolk that there would be no sex until they stopped scrapping with the neighbours? You could tell your partner that there will be no more sex until he pulls his socks up. (You decide what that might mean. And remember, you can do this several times until you negotiate your way to a more equitable division of labour.) This strategy has a double benefit — it means there is a reason for the lack of sex, not simply tiredness and uninterest. It also means that when you decide to call off the strike, there could be a resumption of relations with a certain extra *frisson* of passion involved.

Ignore the problem, not the man

Since you can change no one's behaviour but your own, the smart User knows that instead of getting overwrought by his lack of attention to the housework, she should try to ignore it, not him. (Not the housework, his attitude towards it.) This might require you to get into the zen of cleaning — no mean feat — because, to be honest, it's not that amusing. But since no one but you is going to do it, and you can't stop doing it because if you did the whole house will fall in around you and everybody else, you might as well adjust your thinking. (Actually, will the whole house fall in around you? Try not doing it for a week and see what happens. Will anyone notice? Will you be able to stand the horror of it?)

Escape the pressures that add up to a sex life of zero

Take the seductress in you away for a weekend for some fun and relaxation. As the Elizabethan adventurer Sir Walter Raleigh wrote: 'Romance is a love affair in other than domestic surroundings'. Light the candles, draw a bubble bath, open the champagne and pamper yourself and your partner. It's such a cliché — but it works.

Reclaim your private life

Users know that, in the end, a successful sex life depends on them and on them alone. Turn on your own sexuality by turning off those skinny strumpets on *Sex and the City*, and don't let proxies have the sex you deserve. And make a note to yourself: Get new underwear. Even if no one else sees it, at least you will know that you're the very devil on the inside!

> *We would rather love alone,*
> *Kiss untaught and chance the stumbling.*
> ROBERT HERRICK, 1591–1674

Good sex, bad sex

Good sex takes its time. Equally, sometimes it can be pretty urgent. To use an analogy your favourite Usee might understand, what you do depends on whether you are playing a five-day Test or a one-day game. The first is more about strategy, the second, run rate. Both have their place.
Good sex is constant. Whatever its pace, good sex is frequent sex. You can't have sex only every couple of weeks and expect it to be fantastic every time. Imagine an opera singer not rehearsing for a month and then expecting to sing *Tosca*, cold. It's not going to happen, and something might get strained!
Bad sex insists. Good sex cajoles and seduces.
Routine sex declines through tedium to bad sex. Good sex is always reinventing itself.
Good sex doesn't need bells and whistles. Though sometimes a toy, some candles and some massage oils are a really good idea.

It is not possible to have bad sex during a dirty weekend away in a five-star hotel or a luxury resort next to a sandy beach. Or given Edward Bulwer-Lytton's formula: 'Midnight, and love, and youth, and Italy!' (Well, it might be. But at least you will have starched sheets, the view and room service to comfort you.)

Good sex shouldn't take that much effort. Men are almost always up for it. As Dr Johnson said: 'There are few things that we so unwillingly give up, even in advanced age, as the supposition that we still have the power of ingratiating ourselves with the fair sex.'

A is for aphrodisiacs

How about trying some chemistry and giving a love potion a try, and if the idea is a little outrageous, just ask yourself what that bottle of Thierry Mugler's *Angel* is, apart from exactly that.

The ancients managed to mix some truly disgusting things together in an effort to improve their love lives — powdered rhino horn is still, despite the best efforts of anti-poachers in east Africa to stamp out the trade, a highly prized performance enhancer in the Far East. Bits and pieces of animals — ivory, reindeer antlers, bats' wings, sea dragons' tails, eye of newt (ignore the last one, I was just getting carried away) — were also pressed into service. It's all a bit messy, really.

Perhaps it's easier to stick to chocolate as the ultimate aphrodisiac these days. It doesn't carry any form of World Wildlife Fund protection order, it's cheap and you can get it at the service station at 2 am. Chocolate is the great turn on — just ask any woman with a passion for it — and has been recognised for its qualities for almost 2000 years. The Mayans, who migrated into the north of South America around 600 AD, were the first chocoholics. They thought chocolate was the food of the gods and established cocoa plantations in the Yucatan.

According to Aztec legend, cacao seeds (*xocolatl*) came from paradise and so consequently wisdom and power came from eating the fruit of the cacao tree. It was also reputed to be something of an aid to love-making: Montezuma reportedly drank a frothy chocolate drink before going to visit one of his wives.

Modern chemistry seems to bear out the ancient wisdom: chocolate contains caffeine, which acts as a stimulant; theobromine that stimulates the heart muscle and the nervous system; and phenylethylamine which is reputed to be a mood enhancer and an anti-depressant. Taking the three of these together in chocolate can give extra energy, make your heart beat faster, and make you feel jumpy and slightly giddy. And that all sounds like the very definition of love!

There are, of course, other forms of vegetable matter (fruit, herbs and spices) which are supposed to raise the levels of sexual interest among the users. Here are some, none of which taste as good as chocolate:

Kava: that's the revolting stuff the Queen is ritually handed every time she sits down for a ceremony with a South Pacific chief. No sign of her falling for any of them in an inappropriate way, however.

Durian: your nose finds this fruit before your eye can locate it in markets across South-East Asia. It smells diabolical, but it is said to have the power to increase the libido among those brave enough to swallow it. Good luck!

Marijuana: this is said to raise the desire by lowering the inhibitions; it seems to help people who want to sleep together end up sleeping together.

Fenugreek: prescribed by modern naturopaths to cure snot — according to naturopath Mim Beim it's a mucolytic and that is why it is put in hay-fever remedies. It has the rather unattractive property of making you smell like a curry when you take it. Thanks to its ability to increase breast milk production — in this function it's called a galactogogue — it was once thought by Muslim women to enhance the shape of the breast. (Rather like a natural version of the Wonderbra.) Girls in Central Europe also found it useful to wear bunches of the herb when they were with their lovers, though its effect might have had more to do with the fact that it has a deodorant aspect (that would be the masking odour of the curry, perhaps) rather than any potential aphrodisiac quality it might have.

Saffron and chilli: the Puritans frowned on the use of spices, because of their ability to inflame the senses, which when you consider the damage that a really hot chilli can do to the delicate mucous lining of the mouth — and other parts of the anatomy — this is not such a silly idea. The rare and pricey saffron has been pressed into service since the ancient Phoenicians added it to cakes eaten in honour of their fertility goddess. But that might be taking your plan to manage a man rather a little too far at this stage.

Mint: not normally seen in lists of allure-enhancers, but it surely deserves a place. How many of us resort to a mint mouth freshener, brush our teeth or suck on a Tic Tac as we are about to approach an attractive man with intent?

Oysters: these molluscs are said to have properties that enable a man to maintain his interest in a woman — and that might have something to do with the minerals such as zinc which they contain. However, one thing is certain: a man who knows you are feeding him oysters to enhance his performance will sometimes become a self-fulfilling prophecy.

Among the rest: Naturopath Mim Beim nominates the following — Korean ginseng, *damiana*, *yohimbe*, and *withania* (*ashwanghandra* is the Ayurvedic word), which is meant to give one the sexual tenacity of a stallion. Basically, she says, you have to look at increasing testosterone (which ginseng can help with), basic energy levels and also circulation to the penis (vitamin E, *ginkgo biloba* and ginger helps with this). But you might find a new underwired bra on you and a good night's sleep for him could have the same effect.

basic history for users

17
Some great Users in history

Cleopatra, Queen of Egypt, 69–30 BC

Hollywood cast a super-kohled Elizabeth Taylor as the sultry siren of the Nile, but recent research depicts Cleopatra as short, dumpy and with very bad teeth, which makes the power she exercised over the most powerful men of her time — Julius Caesar and then Mark Antony — all the more remarkable.

One of the Ptolemies (a Greek family no outsider was considered good enough to marry into, making incest — brothers required to marry sisters, uncles their nieces — a necessity to maintain the dynasty), Cleopatra VII was first married at seventeen to her ten-year-old brother, Ptolemy XIII. When she went to war with him, he ended up dead. No matter, there was another just like him at home, her next husband, the eleven-year-old Ptolemy XIV. After he was deposed with the help of Caesar, the father of her son Caesarion, Cleopatra was confirmed as the ruler of Egypt.

Caesar had secured Egypt, but politics in Rome had become volatile. In competition with Crassus and Pompey (the other two-thirds of the Triumvirate) for position and power, he had recognised that a liaison with the Oriental queen was one way to shore up his personal stocks and take control of Rome and her Empire.

Cleopatra was obviously equally pleased to take Caesar as her lover — at the very least she was relieved from the duty of having to marry her brothers to hold on to the throne. But Caesar was murdered in 44 BC in Rome, which rather changed her game plan. After the battle of Philippi, she was summoned before the victor, Mark Antony. As conscious of the potential of the Egyptian power base as Caesar, Mark Antony fell for her completely, throwing away Rome's regard and, in the end, half the known world for her favour. Eventually, he was forced to face his brother-in-law Octavian in a naval battle at Actium. When he lost, he fled back to his mistress.

Cleopatra is said to have been so seductive that when Mark Antony was (wrongly) told she was dead, he decided he couldn't go on without her and fell on his own sword. As he died, he learned she still lived and he demanded to be carried to her. Restored to the woman he loved, Antony expired in her arms. Cleopatra was apparently unable to work her magic on Octavian, and unwilling to be a captive feature of the triumphal march into Rome of the man who would be better known to history as the emperor Caesar Augustus. She either took poison, or, more picturesquely, clasped an asp to her bosom and died from its bite. She was just thirty-nine.

This was a woman who knew how to manage men. Desperate to attract Casear's attention, but exiled from the pharaonic palace in Alexandria, Cleopatra had herself rolled up in a carpet, stowed in boat, rowed across the port and delivered to his feet. Her bravado worked. Caesar was intrigued by the young queen and made her his consort in Egypt, concubine in Rome.

When she wanted to impress Mark Antony, Cleopatra challenged him to outdo her in throwing a banquet. He gave a costly affair, full of lark's tongues and hen's teeth, and then she followed with her own party, a rather more restrained event. When Mark Antony tried to claim the victory, Cleopatra produced a priceless pearl, dissolved it in a goblet of vinegar wine and swallowed the lot. Game over.

Cleopatra's lesson: Cleopatra, no matter how many rolls of fat she had around her neck or how hooked the nose that our only contemporary source indicates she had, was a bright, energetic and very determined woman. (She was also an accomplished murderess; her sister Arsinoe was dispatched after the Ptolemy brothers, on Cleopatra's instructions. In Egypt at the time, it was a case of the survival of the fastest to call on the assassins.)

She strategised the openings of her love affairs with Caesar and Antony in the same way the Roman generals planned their battles. She knew she had only one opportunity with both the powerful men who became her lovers to impress and she made the most of her opening gambits, using flattering grand gestures on both occasions.

Having yourself delivered in a rolled-up carpet to the object of your affections might not be a good idea in these days of uncertain courier deliveries and mail-room delays. Just look at what can happen to a bunch of roses on Valentine's Day trapped in the mail-room overnight and then think about spending hours there, wrapped in a Persian. You'd emerge with carpet (as opposed to bed) hair, definitely not recommended for making a good first impression. The pearl sacrifice needs to be rethought, too. Don't risk casting a real pearl before someone who is more swine than swain.

Cleopatra's enduring lesson to women in the twenty-first century is that brains beat beauty when it comes to being popular. (Having great assets would also help, but they are not always within in the grasp of most smart Users, unfortunately.)

Theodora, Byzantine Empress, c. 500–547 AD

According to Procopius in *The Secret History*, Theodora was the daughter of a bear trainer who worked at the hippodrome in Constantinople. She had already been a dancer, actress (code word at the time for prostitute) and courtesan by the time she travelled, aged sixteen, through North Africa. On her journey, she converted to Monophysitism, the doctrine that declared Christ as wholly divine and not partly human and partly divine as the Orthodox religion taught.

When she returned to Constantinople at the age of twenty, she gave up her racy ways, got a job as a wool-spinner and turned into a born-again spinster. It was then she met Justinian, a local government official. Theodora was, according to Procopius, 'short and pallid ... her glance was invariably fierce and intensely hard', but an image of her in the mosaics in the church of San Vitale in Ravenna shows a sloe-eyed *houri* in a serious headdress. She is also said to have been intelligent and extremely amusing.

The reserved and austere Justinian immediately succumbed to her allure and made her his mistress and, after he overturned a law forbidding Roman government officials to marry actresses, wed her in 525. Two years later, he became emperor and she his co-ruler.

She was more than his equal. Theodora is credited with having saved Justinian's empire during the Nika Revolt. She convinced him that to die as ruler was infinitely better than to live as nobody. Justinian, courage restored, unleashed his loyal troops against the rebels, killing 30,000.

Theodora's lesson: Theodora had the worst possible beginning: born to the dregs of society, raised to sell sex for money. (In a particularly crowd-pleasing routine, Theodora is said to have allowed trained ducks to pick grain off her prone, naked body). But it doesn't matter where you start; it matters where you end up. Nor does it matter what people say about you — when she became empress, her enemies rewarded her with the title 'The Greatest Whore in Christendom'.

But her record as an able administrator and an early women's liberationist speaks for itself. She pushed for a law that forbade forced prostitution, set up homes for former prostitutes, passed laws which protected women in divorce cases and allowed them to inherit and hold property and, more controversially, made death the penalty for rape.

Theodora wasn't beautiful either, but clearly she was sexually adventurous. She focused on the men in her life. (Perhaps a little too extremely in one case. Procopius writes that after Theodora's long-lost and illegitimate son presented himself at the palace to start bonding with his mother, he was never seen again.) And she knew that sometimes a man just needs a little encouragement to help him win life's battles.

Some interesting sexual tricks might help, too — but the duck thing is not recommended for Users in medium to high-density housing.

Eleanor of Aquitaine, Queen of France, then Queen of England, 1122–1204

Eleanor was the heiress of her era, a duchess who inherited lands from the Pyrenees to the Loire. Reputedly beautiful (we'll never know this for certain, since the only remaining image of her is carved into her tomb at Fontrevault), intelligent and hardheaded, she was one of the medieval world's dominant personalities.

First, she married Louis VII of France, by whom she had daughters, Marie and Alix, and whom she managed to shed when her eye fell on Henry, Count of Anjou and Duke of Normandy. They married in Poitiers cathedral in 1152 when she was already thirty and he was in his sexual prime — nineteen. Together, they had eight children: William of Poitiers; Henry, known as the Young King; Matilda; Richard the Lionheart; Geoffrey, Duke of Brittany; Eleanor (later the Queen of Castile); Joanna (later the Queen of Sicily); and John, finally king of England.

Her elevated position in French and English society did not assure Eleanor a life of peace and comfort. Henry grew tired of her and her machinations after she had reached menopause (she was constantly trying to promote her sons and grandsons to his thrones) and had no qualms about locking her up, a fairly stock-standard response to a rival in these turbulent times. Henry had many ambitious heirs who would have liked to set their mother free and at the same time make free with her lands — and his.

Even today, Eleanor seems a beacon of modernity in the late Middle Ages. She made many of her own decisions, was well able to run her own duchy and her husband's or sons' kingdoms during their many absences. (This strength of character wasn't always appreciated in a period when women were mostly chattels, often sequestered and sometimes kept locked away from the world to keep them, their virginity or their fortunes, safe.)

On Henry's death, she became regent for her son, Richard, but there was just so much she could do for the soldier king known as *Le Coeur de Léon*. She found him a bride — Berengaria of Navarre — but couldn't change her son's basic nature and kindle his interest in a woman. No surprise that there were no heirs, and that meant Eleanor's youngest (and least favourite) child became King John of England.

Eleanor is something of a favourite of feminists today. She had no real say in her first marriage, but she certainly picked her second well. At the start it was a twelfth-century rarity — a perfect match between the rich and powerful. Henry was virile, ambitious and obviously hell-bent on success and she was much the same. Theirs was an over-heated love match between equals — at least in the beginning — and an uncontested success. Eleanor had not only married two kings, she was the mother of three more and the mother-in-law of another two.

Eleanor's lesson: Eleanor was a formidable physical specimen. In a time when childbearing was a dangerous activity and the average lifespan for a woman around forty, her production of ten children and life span of seventy-eight years were remarkable. Part of her extraordinary success revolved around the fact she outlived her husband, most of her children and some of grandchildren. Be healthy, get fit and stay that way, mentally and physically.

And as Eleanor discovered, it's not a good idea in the long run to fall for a bully, no matter how handsome, rich or successful he is. Now a man might not be able to imprison you, but there are other ways he could clip a woman's wings — and who these days has five sons and a few sons-in-law who can be relied upon to rescue a queen in a quandary?

Catherine de' Medici, Queen of the French, 1519–1589

The wife of one king of France, Catherine was the mother of three more — Francis II, Charles IX and Henry III: not bad going, even for a woman born into Florence's powerful de' Medici family of bankers, patrons of the arts and Popes.

At thirteen, she married Henry, the younger son of Francis I, but despite the fact that she brought cuisine and a slew of chefs to the French court with her and introduced the locals to the ways of the fork (for which the French should have been permanently grateful), she was slighted continually by her new countrymen. (Perhaps that is because also in her retinue were some very dangerous people — her assassins. The clever Florentines had rolled two of their prime skills, glove-making and poisoning, into one. Gloves soaked in poison made a convenient and undetectable means to off the opposition.)

But even after her husband's succession to the French throne, Catherine still had to put up with second best — his beautiful and glamorous mistress Diane de Poitiers was always first in his heart.

Henry was mortally wounded in a jousting accident in 1559 and taken to the Place des Vosges in Paris to die. After his death, Catherine was not entirely generous to his mistress.

Catherine's lesson: Catherine did not call for her chief glove maker immediately she was widowed, but she still exacted payment for years of humiliation. She forced Diane de Poitiers to swap the beautiful chateau of Chenonceau, which had been the love nest Henry shared with his mistress, for the marginally less lovely chateau of Chaumont. Diane spent much of her remaining life playing shepherdess and moving the *mouflons* (wild sheep) around Chaumont's fields, making pretty patterns against the green.

Catherine had her chance to settle the score and knew her best weapons were her brain and a little kindness. She knew forgiveness is good for the soul, but you don't have to forget. It can drive people crazy if you forgive them — or even just appear to.

Elizabeth I, Gloriana, The Virgin Queen, 1533–1603

Elizabeth's long life and reign over England is an absolute triumph considering her start. The daughter of Anne Boleyn, Elizabeth must have inherited some of her mother's charm as well as some of the smarts of her father Henry VIII, to have survived and prospered as she did after that same mother was judged a traitor and beheaded, and Elizabeth herself declared a bastard. By keeping her head (literally as well as figuratively) and then keeping it down, she outlived her half-sister Mary (who wasn't called Bloody Mary for nothing) and her half-brother Edward, to eventually ascend the throne.

The beginning of her reign was no picnic either, with religious conflicts, foreign pressures and a near bankrupt treasury. As well, there was the question of succession to sort out as Mary, Queen of Scots was creeping around the north of England, whipping up Catholic sympathy and support.

Elizabeth was frequently urged to marry and breed. Various kings and younger sons of kings were offered up for her consideration. From the age of fifteen to fifty-five, she declined them all, preferring to maintain the image of the Virgin Queen.

That is not to say she did not have her share of intimate friends. First, Robert Dudley, the Earl of Leicester, whom she might have married, had not Sir William Cecil talked her out of it. Dudley was an attractive if dissolute man, whose wife,

Amy Robsart, rather conveniently fell down the stairs at home and died. Some said suicide, while others suspected Dudley of her murder. His relationship with the Queen had its ups and downs, but his incompetence as a military commander eventually sidelined him as an influence on her. After his death in 1588, his stepson, Robert Devereux, the Earl of Essex, became the Queen's favourite. She, however, never lost sight of her real passions — power and the throne. When Essex joined a rebellion in 1601 and tried to raise the city of London against her, Elizabeth seemed to have had few qualms in signing his death warrant — despite their closeness.

Elizabeth's lessons: Elizabeth learned from her own life, and those of others. The young Elizabeth watched four stepmothers deal with her father, Henry, with varying degrees of success (a couple of divorces, another beheading, widwowhood for the last) in terms of managing their man. Then there were the half-siblings, seditious cousins, ambitious uncles, imprisonment as well as assorted plots and attempts to remove her from the succession, to deal with. Elizabeth was extremely bright and recognised that she would keep her throne by the goodwill of the people. To that end, she introduced administrative reforms and religious tolerance.

She knew she could be queen by terror and subjugation, but that is only a short-term arrangement. To rule in someone's heart can only be done by agreement with the subject. Even though her mother died when she was an infant, Elizabeth learned that frequently repeated lesson: 'You catch more flies with honey than vinegar'.

And what about Dudley's dramatic end? There's also a lesson there for today, too. It's simple: when a relationship is over, it's over. Fortunately, these days, the ex-boyfriends don't have to be dead, only be as dead.

Catherine the Great, Empress of Russia, 1729–1796

Born to a German princeling, Catherine was sixteen when she married Peter, heir to the Russian throne, in 1745. It was a union that was no great shakes from the beginning and Catherine soon began to take her pleasures in extra-marital relationships. Peter wasn't too happy about that behaviour, so after he acceded to the throne in 1762, she was effectively banished into a separate household. In the same year he was deposed and shortly after, the mad and maddening Peter was murdered, possibly at Catherine's instigation and certainly to her relief. Installed as empress, she was then free to carry on relationships with other favourites — notably Potemkin — and rule as she pleased.

Catherine lived for nearly seventy years and was said to have been a woman of 'great ability, though she had in full the vices of her time and station'. Among those 'vices' was a weakness for tall, handsome men. She reportedly allowed only Russians and the Irish in her personal guard, where she drew frequently on their 'personal' services. (After intensive field research, she decided Celts and Slavs were better endowed than other races.)

On a more serious note, Catherine imported thinkers who brought the Age of Enlightenment into Russia — great for the scholars and the French Revolution of 1789, but it didn't do her own peasants much good. They had to wait until 1917 for theirs.

Catherine's lessons: Here was a woman who never let a man stand in the way of ambition. Catherine the Great is not remembered today because she was another Saint Cath, or Kate the Good, but because in her appetites, desires and actions, she lived exactly as she pleased. She knew that to be really sexy, a man must also be bright, like her French scholars. And sometimes she made do with beefcake handpicked from the personal guard. Life is about balance.

> *Women are never disarmed by compliments. Men always are.*
> OSCAR WILDE, 1854–1900

The Hon. Jane Digby, adventuress, 1807–1881

A true beauty, Jane was married at seventeen to Lord Ellenborough, a man twice her age. Bald and a widower, he was never going to be a good choice for the headstrong romantic who confided in her diary at nineteen: 'Thus, though righteous heaven above forbids this rebel heart to love, to love is still its fate!'.

Her husband neglectful, Jane embarked on a series of affairs. When she met an Austrian prince, Felix Schwarzenberg, she fell right into his arms. It was not the best choice she could have made. The prince was the original 'cad', said to have earned the nickname because he was as fast as the leading racehorse of the time, Cadland.

The scandal deepened when Jane, pregnant with Felix's child, fled to meet him in Paris. The prince was not interested in marriage (couldn't be, he was already taken), and not even the birth of a second child, a year after the first, could hold them together. Lord Ellenborough petitioned the House of Lords for a divorce, which was eventually granted. Jane continued to live in Paris, took lovers (among whom was the writer Honoré de Balzac, who wrote her, as Lady Amanda Dudley, into *Le Lys dans la Vallée*).

In 1831, she left Paris and the prince and headed towards more husbands — the Baron Karl Venningen and then Count Theotoky — and other lovers such as an Albanian brigand, King Ludwig of Bavaria, and King Otto of Greece. (When Jane embarked on her affair with the King of Greece, his queen, Amalie, noted that not only had Jane captured Athens, but she has taken the King as well.) Failed marriages, doomed affairs, children scattered about Europe — nothing seems to have dented Jane's resilience.

But in Syria she finally found the man of her dreams, Sheikh Abdul Medjuel el Mezrab, a Bedouin young enough to be her son. The sheik was not tall, dark and handsome, but small (he was only around 160 centimetres), dark and beaky — what a nose! Still, she loved him and stayed a sexpot to the end. She was wondering when she was in her mid-seventies why her husband had not slept with her for more than a month.

Jane's lesson: When things didn't work out, as they tended not to, Jane kept her spirits up by moving on, and usually up, the social scale. She eventually became the matriarch of her husband's Bedouin tribe, an adviser to the explorer and writer Sir Richard Burton, and respected resident of a wonderful house in Damascus. She shows us the value of perseverance and proved you have to kiss a lot of princes until you find the right frog for you. Do your best to enjoy the trip, even if, like Jane, you don't have a clue where you are going.

Wallis Simpson, The Duchess of Windsor, 1896–1986

Bessie Wallis Warfield was born in Pennsylvania and died ninety years later in Paris, in a beautiful house in the Bois de Boulogne that is said to be where Dodi Fayed took Diana, Princess of Wales, on the last night of their lives. Bessie might have been born in relative obscurity, but by the time she died, she was known as Wallis or the Duchess of Windsor, and she was one of the most infamous women of her time.

During her career, she married three times: first to American naval Lieutenant Earl Spencer Jnr, then in 1928 to Ernest Simpson, an American-born businessman who lived in London. There, she fell in with a set of bright young things. Among them was the Prince of Wales, whom she met at a house party in 1930 given by his mistress, Thelma Furness. The prince had enjoyed a series of lovers, but his history didn't trouble the American divorcée.

When Thelma had to go to America to visit her sister, she took her friend Wallis to lunch as the Savoy and asked her to take care of 'her little man.' Wallis didn't have to be asked twice — and that was the end of Thelma in the prince's heart and bed.

He had glamour, wealth and position but he was also a shy and diffident man. His confidence was evidently bolstered by the worldly and sophisticated Mrs Simpson. Her enemies claimed that she had been everything from a spy to a prostitute in Shanghai (this is supposed to explain her sexual skills) and a Nazi collaborator. The Prince of Wales ignored the chat, and remained oblivious to the consequences of his determination to marry the woman he loved.

The Prince was convinced he could keep both throne and lady and began to insist (at her behest) on formalising their union. His parents were horrified, his younger brother Bertie, the Duke of York and his wife, Elizabeth (the late Queen Mother) scandalised. But Wallis and Edward pressed on. Eventually, she divorced Mr Simpson. The prince abdicated in 1936 and was given the title Duke of Windsor. They married in France in 1937.

The main players in one of the love stories of the century, the duke and duchess lived together for thirty-six years — always as exiles. First, he was governor of the Bahamas during World War II, which kept him out of the way of Hitler's designs to install him and his consort on the throne of a defeated England. Eventually, they ended up as paid-for celebrity guests at parties from Miami from New York.

Wallis's lesson: Wallis was an accomplished woman who demonstrated that you should never leave a lover in the care of another woman. A hostile takeover inevitably follows.

She understood perfectly the basis of her husband's nature. His mother, Queen Mary, was a remote and chilly figure, and he liked 'being mothered'. (He also liked needlework, which was surely a clue that he might be some testosterone short of a full dose of male hormones). By fulfilling his needs, she retained his devotion.

Coco Chanel, couturière, 1883–1971

When Gabrielle Chanel was twelve, her mother died and her father decamped. As a ward of the State, she was consigned to French orphanages, where she remained until she was nineteen. She later remembered the first home in Brive as a place where she learned what loneliness was really like, but also where she developed the power of her imagination and will.

Chanel went to work for a milliner when she was twenty, and thus began a stellar, sixty-eight year career. In 1909, she opened her own couture house with the backing of a rich lover. By 1916, she was ready to revolutionise women's clothes. She took jersey, which had previously been used only in male undergarments, and used the fluid fabric to make women's fashion. She also translated what was formerly men's tailoring into simple and elegant lines, liberating women into pants. Coco Chanel also invented the LBD — Little Black Dress — for which many Users have reason to be grateful when they consult their wardrobes just before a big date. If all that were not enough, she virtually invented designer fragrances such as Chanel No5, No22, Gardenia, Cuir de Russie and Bois des Iles. 'Wear perfume wherever you want to be kissed,' she advised.

During World War II, Mademoiselle Chanel made a bit of a miscalculation when she took a German officer into her bed. This was largely a matter of attire (those uniforms!) and proximity since the German high command had taken over the Ritz on the Place Vendome, while Chanel lived in a suite in the back section of the hotel, overlooking her *atelier*. It took her some years after the war (during which time she lived in Switzerland) to get over the stigma of fraternisation. It wasn't until 1954, when she was seventy-one, that she came back into fashion.

Coco's lesson: Very modern and very French, she had a series of lovers, some of whom she lived with openly. But Chanel desperately wanted to marry, saying: 'There is nothing worse than solitude, growing old without a shoulder to lean on. Marry, marry! Even if he is fat and boring.' Among her targets was her lover, the Duke of Westminster. He refused on the grounds that she was too old to bear the heir and the spare he needed to carry on the title.

The Russian composer Igor Stravinsky offered to leave his wife and marry her, but Mademoiselle refused. She knew in her heart that no matter how much you want to marry, just any (and anyone's) husband is not good enough. It has to be the right one. And, like Chanel, the User should always play fair. Chanel always wore her signature red lipstick to signal danger and give the faint-hearted a little time to get out of the way.

> *She, while her lover pants upon her breast,*
> *Can mark the figures on an Indian chest.*
> ALEXANDER POPE, 1688–1744

Pamela Digby Churchill Hayward Harriman, American Ambassador to Paris, 1920–1997

At nineteen this debutante daughter of an English aristocrat attracted the attention of her first husband, Randolph Churchill. A somewhat dumpy redhead, she was a favourite of his father, British Prime Minister, Winston Churchill. Pamela moved in with her parents-in-law after her son Winston was born. She soon became the PM's confidante; it was said she knew more about the progress of the war than almost any other civilian in London. Pamela, a famed wartime hostess, took a string of American lovers, including the millionaire Jock Whitney, the broadcaster Ed Murrow, and Bill Paley, who was eventually to own the television giant, CBS.

She divorced Randolph and, at the age of twenty-six, went Continental. She developed a reputation in France as an international *femme fatale*, enjoying affairs with, among others, the playboy prince Aly Khan, the heir to the Fiat fortune, Gianni Agnelli, and the French financier, Baron Elie de Rothschild. To make Elie jealous enough to marry her, she took other lovers, including Spyros Niarchos, the Greek shipping magnate, and the French author Maurice Druon. Pamela was known as '*La Grande Horizontale*', a woman who exchanged sexual favours and political contacts for considerable material benefits.

Her campaign for Elie de Rothschild failed (his wife wouldn't let him) so, at thirty-nine, Pamela married the agent and producer Leland Hayward. His death, in 1971 at the age of sixty-eight, left her poor at fifty-one and looking for another husband. She found one in an ex-wartime lover, Averill Harriman, and married the mega-rich seventy-nine-year-old former diplomat within the month.

Averill was a grandee in the Democratic Party, and Pamela became a Washington hostess with real power. When he died in 1986, he left Pamela more than US$115 million and an unassailable position in society. Thanks to her assiduous fund-raising and cultivation for the Democrats, President Bill Clinton gave her the plum job of American Ambassador to France in 1993. She died four years later after she suffered a stroke in the swimming pool at the Ritz hotel in Paris.

In the end, she was magnificent. She had reinvented herself over and over, thanks to enormous energy and a brilliant cosmetic surgeon. By the time of her death, the formerly dowdy redhead was blonde, highly groomed, svelte, beautifully dressed, and rich enough to make sure her colourful history was rarely spoken of.

Pamela's lesson: Pamela was a woman of many parts: wife, mother, mistress, gold-digger, fund-raiser, diplomat, friend of the rich and famous, and close to the centre of political, economic, and industrial power for more than sixty years. There must have been something in the genes: she was great niece of the scandalous Jane Digby, although unlike Jane, Pamela was no beauty to start

Some great Users in history

with. But ugly ducklings can turn into *femmes fatales* if they work at it. And as Theodora discovered, it doesn't matter where you start, but where you end up that counts.

Pamela Harriman was an Englishwoman who had been the intimate confidante (and more) to some of the most powerful men of the twentieth century. Along the way, she earned the title of the last of the great courtesans. But Pamela had something else — something as old as time. She knew how to please men and devoted herself to making the men in her life feel like gods. She had to concentrate, but it paid off for her.

18
And some great losers...

Some women, like the Users in the previous chapter, really put the 'man' into manipulation. Then there are others who, by dint of events and their own natures, provide some cautionary tales to modern would-be Users.

Lucrezia Borgia, daughter, sister, wife x 3, 1480–1519

Lucrezia was behind the eight ball right from the start. She was the puppet of her powerful family who used her in their efforts to expand their influence. She was the daughter of Pope Alexander VI and the sister of the infamous Cesare, a boy given a cardinal's hat by his father at the age of seventeen. She was just thirteen when she married one of the Sforza family, the Lord of Pesaro, in 1493. Four years later, her father annulled that marriage and gave her instead to a relative of the King of Naples. In 1500, her father and brother had her new husband assassinated. Finally, she became the wife of Alfonso, a son of the Duke of d'Este, later Duke of Ferrara.

By this stage, her reputation had been damaged for all time. She is known through history as a poisoner and is accused of incest and adultery, even though she is recorded in contemporary accounts as a kind mistress to her subjects and patron of the arts and learning.

Lucrezia's lesson: There are not that many arranged marriages in Western society these days, and ever fewer murders of inconvenient husbands. Users make their own, informed choices. Father doesn't always know best, particularly when it comes to picking husbands, not even when *papa* is *il Papa*.

Caroline of Brunswick, uncrowned Queen of England, 1768–1821

In 1795, Caroline had the world at her feet. Through a series of dynastic marriages, her family had links to the British ruling family, the Hanoverians. So when it came time to find a princess for the Prince of Wales, Caroline was a logical choice. There was only one problem — the bridegroom. The future George IV was a hedonist who had secretly married Mrs Maria Fitzherbert, a Roman Catholic, in 1785. Since this was done without the King's Consent, as required by the Royal Marriage Act of 1772, the marriage was invalid and the prince was required to renounce Maria — which he did, very reluctantly, and only for a time.

It wasn't a good start for the sanctioned Royal marriage and matters failed to improve. It became plain that the Prince Regent loathed Caroline. One reason, reportedly, was that, even for the time, the new Princess of Wales had particularly relaxed standards of personal hygiene. Still, in 1796 she gave the heir to the throne an heir, Princess Charlotte. After that, the prince put aside his wife, sending Caroline to live by herself.

Spurned, she escaped to Europe, and was seen often in company with an Italian nobleman. This count, Bergami (damned by a writer of the period as a man 'without dignity or scruples') was known as her personal adviser, but his attentions were perhaps more personal than advisory. Caroline was soon spotted, on a tabletop, dancing topless for the count.

The press of Regency London had a field day. Princess Caroline had fled England to gain some respite from the personal vilification from her husband and his spies, who were busy collecting information he could use to put her aside permanently. This investigation — which in 1806 declared her imprudent, not criminal — became a persecution that followed her to the end of her days.

Caroline wandered across Europe until she found the Villa del Garrovo (now the Villa d'Este, one of the world's leading resort hotels), a sixteenth-century cardinal's palace built on the edge of Italy's Lake Como. Caroline was seduced by its beauty, and bought the *casino* (some little house!) in 1815.

Among its tranquil gardens, she found the peace and acceptance that had previously eluded her, and bloomed. According to Joseph Nightingale in *Memoirs of the Public and Private Life of Queen Caroline,* the locals loved her.

He noted that Caroline, who couldn't do a thing right at home, had 'a cultivated mind, a ready and sure judgement, a brilliant imagination and unvaried gaiety in all her movements…'

After the death of George III, Caroline returned to England in 1820 and was offered an annuity of some £50,000 to renounce her claim to the title of queen and live permanently abroad. She refused, and turned up at Westminster Abbey during her husband's coronation ceremony in 1821. George, who had done his level best to discredit and divorce Caroline for twenty years, had the doors barred against his despised wife.

Caroline's lesson: When her husband dumped her, Caroline conducted herself pretty much as she wished — which is exactly what Catherine the Great did. Unlike Caroline, though, Catherine was an enthroned autocrat and widowed. As a princess, Caroline seems to have missed out on learning the Golden Rule: do unto others as you would have others do unto you. She shouldn't have been surprised, then, that her husband refused her the crown. He was paying her back in kind and doing exactly as she had done — suiting himself. It was a right Royal tit for tat.

> *Man's love is of man's life a thing apart,*
> *'Tis woman's whole existence.*
> LORD BYRON, 1788–1824

Dorothy Parker, writer, 1893–1967

One of the leading wits and raconteurs of her day, Parker penned memorable lines such as: 'Men seldom make passes/At girls who wear glasses', 'You can lead a whore to culture but you can't make her think', and 'Brevity is the soul of lingerie'.

But a lifetime of being smart, funny and sexy was undercut by a quote attributed to Parker in her obituary in *The New York Times* on 8 June 1967. Parker of the rapier-like wit was something of a fool for love. She wrote: 'Women's life must be wrapped up in a man, and the cleverest woman on earth is a fool with a man.'

It didn't start that way. Born in New Jersey in 1893, her career took off when she got a job at American *Vogue* in 1916. The following year she landed the job of theatre critic with *Vanity Fair* and married Edward Pond Parker II. After four years, *Vanity Fair* gave her the flick. The reason was her terribly acerbic, if terribly funny, reviews. '(She) ran the gamut of emotion from A to B,' she wrote of a Katharine Hepburn performance in 1934.

Out of a full-time job, she had to begin her life as a freelance writer, and so became *The New Yorker*'s book critic, the Constant Reader. It wasn't until after she wrote her successful first books, *Enough Rope* (1926) and *Sunset Gun* (1928) that she divorced Parker; but she kept his name. Life in the smart set of New York spread out in front of her and she helped found New York's legendary literary salon, the round table at the Algonquin Hotel, with Robert Benchley, Robert E. Sherwood and James Thurber.

Parker married her second husband, Alan Campbell, in 1933, and moved with him to Hollywood, where they collaborated on screenplays such as *A Star is Born*. After his death, she moved back home to New York. It's as well for her legacy as a wit that she is better remembered for lines such as 'It's a small apartment. I've barely enough room to lay my hat and a few friends,' than that business about how a woman must be wrapped in a man.

Dorothy's lesson: It doesn't matter how clever a woman is, a man can still make a fool of her. The smart User, like Dorothy, knows that there is generally an imbalance between lovers, always one who loves more than the other. Unlike Dorothy, the smart User tries to make sure that she is the one who is adored. It's more comfortable that way.

Edith Piaf, singer, 1915–1963

Piaf's sad end was predicted by her grim beginning. In between, her life was a sequence of high art and low farce, punctuated with some sublime musical moments, violence, sudden death and addiction. She was born in the street, two policemen acting as midwives to her mother, a part-time singer and prostitute. Little Edith was soon palmed off, sent to live with her grandmother, a madam who ran a brothel in Normandy. Unsurprisingly, she took off when she was old enough, hitting the road with her father, a performer. He recognised the talent in the child and put her to work singing for coins in the street.

Piaf was pregnant at sixteen to a soldier who deserted her before the delivery of her dead infant. But by the time she was in her early twenties, things were looking up. In 1935, Piaf was discovered by a nightclub owner who dubbed her the Little Sparrow (*La Môme Piaf*) and dressed her in the simple black dresses that became her signature.

When, a year later, the nightclub owner was murdered, she moved on to a married man. By 1939, she had left him to marry Paul Meurisse, another singer. Jean Cocteau used their violent and twisted relationship for his stage piece *Le Bel Indifférent*. In 1940, Piaf performed the monologue on the French stage.

World War II interrupted her career temporarily. Piaf later claimed to have been a member of the *Résistance*, but her critics have said she spent part of the war, at least, doing what she always did — playing up to men. This time, they were dressed in the uniforms of Gestapo officers. Both feckless mother and singing father turned up again. While the relationship with her father was described as balanced and happy, she was often required to drag her slatternly mother out of bars.

Over the years, Piaf transformed her pain and despair into art and gave voice to millions of voiceless others. Her career prospered, and songs such as *La Vie en Rose* and *Je Ne Regrette Rien* now make her the second most requested artist in the world, after Frank Sinatra, among nostalgia buffs.

In 1951, Piaf was in a terrible car accident, which left her with a serious problem — an addiction to both morphine and alcohol. Desperate and drunk, she cruised bars and dives in Paris, picking up men for sex. The following year, she married the singer Jacques Pilles and they remained together until her death in 1963. The final bitter reality was that Pilles was also an alcoholic.

Edith's lesson: She invested over and over in misery, choosing men who were violent or alcoholic or both. The smart User will never get into a relationship with a man who is either violent or addicted. Piaf retained and reinforced her role of victim through some really dreadful choices. In doing so, she was never able to rise above her own past.

Rita Hayworth, love goddess, 1918–1987

Rita Hayworth was a vamp: a curvy, sexy woman draped in clinging silks, who looked like she could be bought and only the price had to be settled. But inside, she was desperate for a settled home-life. Trying to achieve that goal, she married five times to men who never looked like good husband material, among them, the tortured genius Orson Welles, playboy prince Aly Khan and band leader Artie Shaw.

She was practically born into show business and taught to dance at six by her entertainer father. At twelve she joined his troop; by fifteen she had been discovered by a talent scout and signed to Fox Studios, where she made her first film. Then in 1941, Rita made *You'll Never Get Rich*, a film in which she danced with Fred Astaire, and her career took off. She also came to the attention of the filmmaker Orson Welles, and married him in 1942 — a relationship that was described as Beauty and the Brain. This seems to have been the happiest time in her life. 'During his courtship of her, she was positively illuminated. When she was expecting her baby, she was like a goddess walking far off the earth, touched with glory,' one observer wrote.

Rebecca Welles was born in 1944, but by the time Rita made *Gilda* in 1946, the marriage was over. 'I admire (Orson) greatly, but we don't get on,' was all Rita said. And then she met Aly Khan, playboy prince and son of Aga Khan III. After a tremendous, trans-Atlantic scandal, which effectively destroyed her image among the American film-going public, they married in 1949. Rita gave birth to a daughter, Princess Jasmin Aly Khan. That marriage didn't last, either.

Rita Hayworth began to suffer from early on-set dementia in the 1960s, and was eventually diagnosed with Alzheimer's disease in 1980.

Rita's lesson: 'Men go to bed with Gilda, and they wake up with me,' said Rita, making an astute distinction between perception (the glamorous character she created in the film *Gilda*) and reality (herself). She never found the man who saw past the image and found the real Margarita Cansino underneath. A smart User makes smart choices — among them picking a man who loves her, not the idea of her.

> *Being a woman is a terribly difficult trade, since it consists principally of dealing with men.*
> SIR JAMES G. FRAZER, 1854–1941

Marilyn Monroe, sex symbol, 1927–1962

Raised in a series of foster homes, Marilyn Monroe's self-esteem generally hovered around zero, which made her easy prey to Hollywood opportunists later in her life. But despite that early damage, Norma Jean, Jim Dougherty's pretty little wife, was determined to become Marilyn the star.

First, she was a model (her nude calendar of 1949 remains a classic) and then an actor. Her debut film was in the Marx Brothers' *Love Happy*, but it was when she made *All About Eve* in 1950, opposite Bette Davis, that her career ignited. She perfected her dumb blonde routine as Lorelei Lee in *Gentlemen Prefer Blondes* in 1952, starring opposite Jane Russell and made *How to Marry a Millionaire* shortly after.

She met and fell in love with baseball player Joe Di Maggio, who, in the full glare of exploding flash bulbs, courted her for two years. Married in 1954, their union lasted only nine months. In 1956, she married the playwright Arthur Miller. That didn't last either.

While her career contained gems such as *Some Like it Hot* with Tony Curtis and Jack Lemmon, and *Bus Stop*, it was her private life that was becoming more and more dramatic. Among her alleged lovers were Frank Sinatra, US President John F. Kennedy and his brother, the Attorney-General Robert Kennedy.

It came with the territory of being the nation's number one sex symbol, a tag Monroe never disowned. 'If I'm going to be a symbol of something, I'd rather have it sex than some of the other things we've got symbols for,' said Marilyn.

She lived up to her role during a party for President Kennedy at Madison Square Gardens. Marilyn was stitched into a skintight dress and whispered the song *Happy Birthday, Mr President* for him. Sexy and slightly bruised looking, this was a new take on the blonde bombshell. Dress and tone left little to the imagination.

Marilyn's lesson: If she had hung a sign around her neck reading 'I am sleeping with the most powerful man in the world,' she couldn't have made her affair more obvious. The clever User knows sometimes it's smarter to stay home and wait for a man to call, rather than go out and make a public spectacle of herself. But Marilyn, living up to her reputation of sex goddess, may have made a fatal choice. There are still people who argue Marilyn was murdered to keep her affair with the president a secret. Some secret. She would have been better occupied working on her self-esteem and dealing with the depression which dogged her through life.

Sylvia Plath, writer and poet, 1932–1963

When the American writer Sylvia Plath first met the English poet Ted Hughes, she bit him on the cheek. It should have been an omen for what followed between them. The relationship between the two high-profile writers began with blood and would end in tears.

There was something off-kilter in Sylvia from the start, a situation not helped by the death of her father when she was eight. A professor who taught biology at Boston University, he had convinced himself he had cancer. Instead of seeing a doctor, he rested in the family's Massachusetts home until it was too late to treat the correct diagnosis — diabetes. His death affected her for the rest of her life. Sylvia later said of her father, 'He was an autocrat. I adored and despised him, and I probably wished many times that he were dead. When he obliged me and died, I imagined that I had killed him.'

A perfectionist and a precocious talent, Sylvia had her first poem published when she was nine. She was intelligent, popular, active in the school newspaper, a drama student, won a scholarship to Smith College, and spent a summer as a guest editor at *Mademoiselle* magazine — the work experience that provided the basis of her best-known novel, *The Bell Jar*.

But in 1953, Sylvia became depressed and swallowed a near-fatal dose of pills. She was subsequently treated with electro-shock therapy and psychotherapy.

Despite all these traumas, she finished her degree and won a Fulbright Scholarship to Cambridge University in 1956.

There she met (and bit) the devastatingly handsome Hughes, a future Poet Laureate. They married and she devoted herself to her husband, her work and starting a family. In 1960, her novel *The Colossus* was published, and she gave birth to their first child, Frieda.

The stormy marriage came apart when Sylvia discovered Ted had been having an affair, and it finally ended after the birth of their second child. Sylvia was penniless, living with the children in a small London flat. There, in 1963, she poured all her energy into her best-known novel, *The Bell Jar*. When she had finished it, she finished herself by putting her head in the oven and turning on the gas.

Sylvia's lesson: Dark, brooding, handsome and poetic might make for a fascinating boyfriend, but do not necessarily add up to good husband material. The User knows this lesson well: don't confuse a relationship for therapy, a lover for a psychotherapist. Equally, don't be tempted to become your lover's mental healthcare professional.

Diana, Princess of Wales, 1961–1997

Some women are not only hazardous to themselves, but they are also tragic role models to others. Prime among them is Diana, Princess of Wales, whose real life tragedies were not unlike those that students of French literature have discovered between the pages of *Madame Bovary*.

Emma, you will recall, was the heroine of Gustave Flaubert's novel about a young woman who grew up in provincial France in the middle of the nineteenth century. Despite her relatively minor station in life and dodgy family connections, she attracts the attention of a doctor, one Charles Bovary.

Life as the wife of a country doctor is not nearly exciting enough to satisfy Emma's romantic longings, and she embarks on an affair with one lover. When he fails her, she finds another. She falls hopelessly into debt, thanks to some clandestine dealings with the local chemist. When she recognises the jig is up (the bailiffs carrying away the furniture was the clue), lost and lovely Emma poisons herself and dies horribly.

Diana's story has slight reflections of Emma's. She, too, married a solid, earnest man with a more elevated position in life than her own. After various problems in their relationship (she grows increasingly unstable and self-destructive), she finds that her husband has retreated to the arms of a former mistress. In retaliation, she takes a lover — an army officer. (This same Major James Hewitt later shows himself to be a total bounder when he co-authors a *roman á clef* about the affair and then threatens to sell her letters to the tabloids.)

Disappointed by husband and lover, she is accused of being a spendthrift by her husband's staff (all those in-palace hairdos, manicures, frocks and handbags!). Things look as though they might be working out when she starts seeing a man most kindly described as a playboy, Dodi Fayed.

While Diana didn't commit suicide, she did commit something close to social suicide when she went on television and admitted to interviewer Martin Bashir that she had been an unfaithful wife.

Diana's lesson: Sex outside a relationship can mean many things inside it — boredom, revenge, opportunity, drunkenness, a mistake. But owning up can be selfish and damaging to everyone involved. If she had been a different User, Diana might have denied everything, stayed married and had the lot — the acceptance if not the admiration of the royal family, the love of the people, and eventually the crown matrimonial of the queen consort. She could have followed the pattern of history — royals turning blind eyes to the serial, extra-marital pursuits of their partners. If you are, like Diana, unfaithful and in need of absolution, find a priest, not a journalist or a television interviewer.

comes
the
man,
comes
the
makeover

Reply: (Sunday; November 27, 2011; 3:50 P.M.)
"Comment/Reaction/Thought for the Day"
N°5 1-2-7-8: "Response: Your Take "Food for Thought"
"Original; Sun. 27 Nov 2011 12:39:25 -0800 (PST)

5. Please forget about the New York trip --- buying a suit for him Wakabwa mani yerona zwakakwana.
6. I am not toying to intimidate you, but to be HONEST with you, if you make that NY trip buying a suit that will be the END of ANY MONETARY ADVANCES from ME for EVER !!!
7. THINK TWICE before you get into this DEBT !!!
8. You have just got into Chibwerere cho furniture... under standable.

1. Nyaya yaw atowa yandinwara you DO NOT have that kind of money yekutodza munhu
2. Joyce does NOT help you in financial matters --- mumbo mumbo
3. Why would you have "burning" desire to buy for brother NO NO him enough "feeding" for him, them is enough. NO NO !!!
4. Feeding enough is enough
5. PLEASE forget about the New York trip --- buying a suit fo
6. I am not trying to INTIMIDATE you but to be HONEST. END OF ANY MONETARY ADVANCES from ME for EVER.
7. THINK TWICE before you get into this DEBT.

19
Manners maketh the man

A friend of mine went home to her parents to announce that she had accepted her boyfriend's proposal of marriage. He was an admirable man in many ways, well educated, kind, solid and they were particularly well matched. But they were both very young, which was an obstacle for her family, who would have been more comfortable if the intended couple had been about five years older. 'Still,' said the mother with some relief, 'it could be worse. At least he's a nice, clean Anglican and he's got good table manners.'

If only more men knew how often their romantic fates revolved around the question of manners — in both the long and the short term. Good manners are dead sexy, and more likely to get a woman into bed in double-quick time (it's part of the secret of James Bond's success) than almost any other quality. (This is not including torrid sexual encounters conducted under the influence of too much alcohol — then good manners would dictate just wobbling the other person into a taxi, saying a fond goodnight and then getting yourself safely into bed ASAP as well.)

Good manners are made up of petty sacrifices.
RALPH WALDO EMERSON, 1803–1882

And in the long term, good manners can help maintain a relationship. For instance, it is not good manners to point out to loved ones that they are a barbarian at the table (no matter how long you have known them and how many times you have had to put up with them using the knife as a spoon), and it is not good manners to flinch from their touch. Equally, it is appalling manners to hit someone, and it can be a crime. All of the above can make a person rethink their commitment to their partner (or, in the last case, should).

But beyond charmers who are instinctively labelled poofy by the less cultivated, very few men understand the power of behaving well. Just ask any woman, they'll tell you what oafs men can be. (I know, I know, I hear you — oafish behaviour is not limited to men. But the faults and foibles of women are not our concern here.)

The list of men's crimes against etiquette is endless, and it starts from the *minutiae* of daily life. I had hoped to get through this whole shebang without mentioning one dreaded issue, but it is impossible to avoid. Men: don't leave the toilet seat up! This behaviour shows not only a lack of consideration it is also a safety hazard, as anyone who, half-asleep in the middle of the night, has fallen into a toilet bowl will tell you.

This lack of manners is most obvious at the table. Many men seem to have learned their table manners watching *The Simpsons* and *Roseanne* repeats where open-mouthed debate is *de rigueur*. Parents who spent the required amount of time drumming appropriate behaviour into their children's heads clearly were just not around. These are people who think there is something sissy about behaving properly with a knife and a fork, keeping their elbows off the table, not speaking with a full mouth.

> *The society of women is the foundation of good manners.*
> JOHANN WOLFGANG VON GOETHE, 1749–1832

Funny business, manners. They're like an irregular verb conjugation: I have good manners, members of my family have passable manners (my mother has done the best she could, given the pressure of everything that was going on), and almost everybody else has the manners of swine in rut.

Manners are also notoriously treacherous, shifting from culture to culture, and age to age. Take the progress of that essential utensil, the dining fork. Developed in eleventh century Tuscany, the use of the fork was initially condemned by the Church which contended that only fingers, created by God, were worthy to touch God's bounty. For centuries, they remained a costly, scandalous novelty sometimes waved about in English courts and occasionally used for duelling. As late as the seventeenth century, forks were regarded as an effeminate affectation among men.

But while some of the accepted norms change, the concept that manners themselves provide the context in which a society can organise its relationships does not. They are simply a code of behaviour, which either admits individuals to or excludes them from social rituals.

Perversely, while good manners are rarely noticed (and since it is impossible to insist upon them, because to do so would be impolite, they must necessarily be their own reward), bad manners attract the glare of public attention and opprobrium faster than you can put a knife in your mouth and pick your teeth.

Melbourne writer Stephen Downes was blunt:

> For a quarter of a century, people in many Western countries have grown to maturity without manners ... When I was young, manners were taught at home around the dinner table. (Dinners were festivities families held each night during which they ate together and talked about the day's events — don't laugh, a lot of people have forgotten them.)

He wrote in his book, *Charming Up Profits*.

> Manners were also taught at school ... [but] in the sixties and seventies, teachers became more professional. They wanted precise job descriptions ... But somehow, one of the previous functions of school — that of role model for life — was crossed off the list. Most people in the street were well mannered then, too, and their behaviour rubbed off. You only had to look to learn. And if you didn't bother learning you were told in no uncertain terms that what you did was unacceptable.

By his 'guestimation', people forty-five to fifty or older have every chance of having acceptable manners. Younger that forty-five? Welcome to the Twilight

Zone for manners, where it's likely the residents have no idea of what to say, how to be, and simply can't be taken anywhere. Which probably includes almost all the men whom you would want to date.

> *Good breeding consists in concealing how much we think of ourselves and how little we think of other people.*
> MARK TWAIN, 1835–1910

Exactly why should we care about relatively arcane practices involving fish knives, when to drink port and where to wear suede shoes? Because good manners mean better social relationships — in business and in private.

Manners good and bad have been with us since we started to hunt as pack animals, and then sit down to a convivial meal after, Stephen Downes told me in an interview at the time of the launch of his book. Those first codified forms of behaviour were essential for the survival of the pack as a whole.

'Because food was essential, ways were determined not only to share it carefully and fairly, but to ensure that everyone could eat without interference and that the plump chop on your plate was not stolen by some muscly Neanderthal from whom you could never retrieve it,' said Downes. If those hadn't been enforced, the strong and the aggressive would have taken all the food for themselves, leaving the weaker (women, children, the aged and the sick) to starve. Here, in his view, were the first rules of etiquette, the first accepted codes of social behaviour.

Sensible manners, collectively agreed upon, about what and who not to eat, preserved primitive mankind, and allowed the evolution of humanity.

But if the man in your life has the manners of one of Attila the Hun's crack rape and pillage units, what can you do? It all depends on how old you are and how old he is.

If you are the mother of a boy child, you have years stretching in front of you as you attempt to socialise this male and make him fit for company. It's something which, if you haven't largely accomplished by thirteen or fourteen, you will have to make do with what you did achieve.

If you are fourteen and you've got a sixteen-year-old boyfriend with bad manners, it's likely that you will put up with it because either you don't know that boys can behave any better, or you are so delighted to have a boyfriend that you don't want to say anything to put him off.

At twenty, you should be more discerning if your boyfriend or partner has manners that aren't quite up to scratch. You could try leading by example, but he might not be paying that much attention. Personally, I think the Dr Harry Cooper method with dogs has always a lot to recommend it — a happy mix of praise and positive reinforcement. That's when the subject is rewarded for good behaviour, and gets the big ignore for bad. It's a miracle what the avuncular TV vet can do with a fractious pooch, a little psychology and a handful of doggy treats.

This is the way you'll have to retrain any man over the age of twenty-five, as well. You'll just have to be careful he doesn't catch you at it and turn on you like a mad dog. It takes patience and perseverance, but in the end it's worth it. And his good — or improved — manners will save your nerves.

Essential modern manners

1. It is a sign of respect to dress appropriately for various occasions. If your husband/lover/partner comes dressed to go fishing when you are expected, say, at his parents for dinner, don't go there with him. (It's easier for women in live-in relationships to manage this. Women being collected for a date are sometimes subjected to truly outrageous shocks and disappointments.)
2. It is always good manners to stand back and allow another person to go through a door ahead of you. This has nothing to do with the fact that women earn as much as men these days, can get into a boxing ring if they want to, or can now serve in frontline combat. It has to do with allowing someone else precedence. The same goes for giving up your place to the aged, the infirm, the pregnant. It's about taking care of others before self-interest. If he always barges ahead of you, or any other person, ostentatiously allow every one else to precede you. (Feel free to disregard this instruction in the case of a fire.)

3   Wasting someone's time is bad manners. If he is late for an appointment with you, or worse, stands you up, get the message. In the future, tell him that you will wait for him only for a specified amount of time — fifteen minutes in the street, thirty minutes at home — without being advised of his revised time of arrival. If he persists in this behaviour, either forget about him or never include him in your plans.

4   This is my favourite courtesy: men stand when a woman leaves or joins a table or enters a room. It speaks volumes about how they were raised, and how they conduct themselves. If your man does not do this, admire the behaviour in others. You do it yourself, for elderly people. If he asks what on earth you are doing, tell him it is a sign of respect and see if he gets the message. This might seem antiquated to some, but it is a charming reminder of the days of chivalry.

5   Acknowledge someone's efforts on your behalf. Say thank you and mean it. Remember, thank-you letters are always acceptable and appropriate after an event, big or small. There is one exquisitely mannered man in Australia who writes his before he goes out, then posts them on the way home. That's tremendously polished. You can't nag people into this sort of sophistication — but make sure he sees you writing your bread and butter letters.

6   Your partner spits in the street. What should you do? First of all, what were you doing getting involved with such an oick in the first place? If it's a new relationship, get out while you can. If the relationship is ongoing, you'll just have to dump him. There is nothing so hideous as a man who hawks and spits.(This is something I have never seen a woman do. What's the story with men that they can't control the expectorating muscles?) When you see someone else do this when you are together, launch into the World Health Organisation's stats about the rise and rise of TB. Or just clasp a hanky over your face.

7   Be careful you don't go too far, though, with this manners business and turn your bloke into a puppet — all show and no substance. You could end up with what Beatrice describes in *Much Ado About Nothing*: 'Manhood is melted into courtesies, valour into compliments, and men are turned only into tongues'. There is a happy medium between a

well-mannered man and a well-mannered milksop. He will be grateful, as he finds he is getting ahead at work and in his social environment.

Help, help

One churl's lack of manners is another man's window of opportunity. Doyens of the done thing have been selling guides to good manners for generations. You could even find etiquette lessons in the 'silver fork' novels of the eighteenth century, described by the American-born crime writer and ex-English literature professor Donna Leon as being 'books with simple plots written to explain to people who made a lot of money how to behave in polite society. They were written when all the money poured into England from the colonies, and the fat wives of Yorkshire weavers had to be taught which fork to use,' she writes in *A Venetian Reckoning*. (Imagine now if people used television as a model for behaviour — *Big Brother*, perhaps?)

Better to refer to Emily Post, who wrote the bible of manners *Etiquette: The Blue Book of Social Usage* in 1922, or of her literary granddaughter, Judith Martin writing as Ms Manners. Mary Killen, who writes weekly (with her tongue firmly tucked in her cheek) in *The Spectator* for those who are terrified of doing something incorrectly and being thought the worse for doing so, can also be useful.

The making of manners

If the Doomsday talk about manners sounds familiar, it is. Take out the technology and you will find complaints about how the decline of standards have been a frequent refrain through history.

As early as Egypt in 2500 BC, strict rules of behaviour governed the kingdom and the relationships between pharaoh, functionaries and slaves were codified. It's hardly likely those rules were formulated because the Ancient Egyptians thought contemporary manners were peerless. The opposite is far more likely.

Where there is a period of social dislocation, an increasing emphasis on the forms of good conduct is likely. Confucius wrote during such a period in the fifth century BC in China, describing the principles of good behaviour and emphasising the stability of the family unit as the cornerstone of society.

His was the maxim that continues to provide the basis of good manners and The Golden Rule across all societies to this day: 'What you do not like when done to yourself, do not do to others'.

Civilised conduct reached its zenith when the Crusades rekindled an interest in formal codes of behaviour from the eleventh century. Courtly love bloomed; prescribed, restrained behaviour ruled.

The first etiquette books appeared during the thirteenth century, when the merchant class was expanding, the middle class developing and more people in the upper class had access to court and needed to know exactly what to do so as not to betray their roots.

The intellectual flowering of the Renaissance, combined with the invention of the printing press, meant tracts on manners and behaviour were widely available for the first time. These were the first etiquette books. (The word *etiquette* comes from the Old French, meaning a ticket.)

Men caused the first rules of etiquette to come into being. In effect, the first etiquettes were orders indicating where a soldier had been billeted. The rules attached to billeting, regarding the proper behaviour toward a host, his wife and daughters, his property and his livestock, were developed, perhaps because of previous improper usage of the above. Etiquette came to have a far broader meaning, describing how society should behave in myriad situations.

Manners in context

Manners, like most things, belong to a time and place. They are also relative. Here are some instances of old-fashioned behaviour.

Ancient Egyptian behaviour

From the Prisse Papyrus, Instructions of Ptahhotep, grand vizier to the Pharaoh Isesi, written around 2500 BC.

- In the company of a superior, laugh when he laughs. (Good advice for yes-women of any era.)
- With a boss, let thy mind be deep and thy speech scanty. (Clearly they knew how to get ahead, even 4000 years ago.)

- With a wife, be silent, for it is a gift greater than flowers. (Smart, those ancient Egyptians.)
- When in Rome, a commoner eats with five fingers. A person of elevated station uses only three, never sullying the little finger or its neighbour. (This is possibly the beginning of the cartoonish tendency to stick out the little finger when drinking tea.)

Thirteenth-century manners

- A number of people gnaw a bone and then put it back in the dish — this is a serious offence. (Then, as now. A *Seinfeld* episode centred on a girlfriend who put something she had chewed back on Jerry's plate, and he put it in his mouth. The 'erks!' went on for twenty-two minutes.)
- Refrain from falling on the dish like a swine while eating, snorting and smacking the lips. (Which indicates there were quite a few who did just this.)
- Do not spit on the table in the manner of hunters. (The food is dead. It is not going anywhere.)
- When you blow your nose or cough, turn around so that nothing falls on the table. (No hankies, then?)

Fourteenth-century good behaviour

- A man who clears his throat when he eats, and one who blows his nose in the tablecloth are both ill-bred. (And possibly contagious. Bubonic plague? TB?)
- You should not poke your teeth with your knife, as some do; it is a bad habit. (Not good for the enamel, either.)
- Some eat unwashed. May their fingers be palsied. (This seems a little harsh, but the fourteenth century was not renowned for its fairness.)

Fifteenth-century etiquette

- Do not put back on your plate what has been in your mouth. (Things that go in the mouth are always better not seen again. There is, of course, a notable exception to that rule.)
- Do not chew anything you have to spit out again. (See above.)
- It is bad manners to dip food into the salt. (And even worse to double dip!)

Sixteenth-century manners

In writing *On Civility in Children*, the philosopher Erasmus of Rotterdam created one of the most comprehensive guides to instilling good behaviour into the young. Among his recommendations:

- If you cannot swallow a piece of food, turn around discreetly and throw it elsewhere. (A bin perhaps. Or down a handy hound's throat.)
- Turn away when spitting lest your saliva fall on someone. If something purulent falls on the ground, it should be trodden upon, lest it nauseate someone. (Oh look, manners when it comes to spitting. Who would ever have imagined?)
- You should not offer your handkerchief to anyone unless it has been freshly washed. Nor is it seemly, after wiping your nose, to spread out your handkerchief and peer into it as if pearls and rubies might have fallen out of your head. (Children only are allowed to fascinated by their own effluvia.)

Eighteenth-century good form

According to *The Gallant Ethic*, in which it is shown how a young man should commend himself in polite society.

- Use the napkin for wiping the mouth, lips and fingers when they are greasy. For wiping the knife before cutting bread. For cleaning the spoon and fork after using them. (Very dainty indeed.)
- When the fingers are very greasy, wipe them first on a piece of bread, in order not to spoil the serviette too much. (Very sensitive to the problems of the laundry maid.)
- If you pass a person who is relieving himself, you should act as if you had not seen him. (And, perhaps, as if he had not seen you.)

20
Once were cockscombs

Fashion is not just a metaphor, it's political, and has been since before Republican Romans insisted on a white toga for a man, a purple-edged one for a senator. And since the beginning of time, men have been among the fashion forward of any society. As you gaze upon the object of your affection — standing there in a Hawaiian shirt and a pair of baggy trousers over the top of leopard-print jocks — you might, however, find this hard to credit.

Most men today are fashion-challenged. They still think that if another bloke looks good he's probably gay, Italian, a drug dealer, or any combination of the three. But the User knows that there are some men who manage to take the sartorial biscuit and have a certain manly presence, and don't look as though they're trading in illicit substances or want to date a friend of Dorothy's.

> *What would ye, ladies? It was ever thus. Men are unwise and curiously planned.*
> J. E. FLECKER, 1884–1915

That's the lesson the current Afghan Prime Minister Hamid Karzai demonstrates. An unlikely fashion icon, to say the least, the former warlord caught the professional interest of the design overlord at Gucci, the American Tom Ford. Ford declared that Karzai was 'the *chic*-est man on the planet' and suddenly the world started paying attention to not just the cut of his jib but also the cut of his jacket.

There was more to Karzai's outfits than first appeared. He favoured a series of capes (*chapans*), one of which seemed to be a variant of the Black Watch tartan, and another in green with embroidered detailing around the neck, which featured long arm flaps. Underneath was a Western-style jacket over loose, traditional Afghan clothes. The ensembles were invariably topped off with a shearling Persian lamb cap. (Very Paris, Winter 2001/2002, as it turned out.)

Deconstructing this rig reveals Karzai's plans for the future of Afghanistan rather than any desire to boost himself into the world's best-dressed men lists. The tall and elegant son of a noble Pashtun family came from Kandahar, in the country's south. His capes are common dress in Mazar-e-Sharif, on the northern border close to the borders of Uzbekistan and Tajikistan, and the cap is from Kabul, closer to Pakistan. He might be chic, but he's also a walking wardrobe expressing a hope for Afghan unity. People not reading Karzai's clobber for his political agenda might think the man is simply an Afghani fop and needs to be taken into custody by the figurative fashion police for showing off.

Once, clothes were indeed so political that there were literal fashion police to enforce sumptuary laws — those that governed consumption. From China and Japan to England, France, Germany and Italy, there were rules about who could wear what and when. In Italy, the birthplace of the concept of *fare la bella figura* (making a good impression) those laws were very inventive. In Venice, for instance, after the Great Plague in 1347–48, dark blue or green clothes were banned in an attempt to force *La Serenissima*'s citizens back to general happiness.

In Florence, the city fathers blamed the flood of 1333 on the usual suspects — avarice, gluttony, usury, and drunkenness among the general populace as well as over-luxurious women's clothing. (Despite further sumptuary laws being enacted, the floods continued — go figure.) In Genoa in 1415, the Great Code forbade the use or pearls or precious stones. (Citizens could pay a tax [*gabelle*] and avoid the strictures, but the fashion police were kept busy checking and enforcing the rules.) In Nurnberg — halfway between Munich and Frankfurt — during the fifteenth century, no man over the age of fifty was allowed to wear red buckram, no man under thirty-two allowed to trim his cloak with beaver fur and, for decency, jackets had to reach six centimetres (two inches) below the crotch.

> *Naked came I out of my mother's womb, and naked shall I return thither.*
> BOOK OF JOB

But if you were wellborn, there was certainly no holding back in terms of personal decoration from the time of Henry VIII (born in 1547). By the time of Louis XIV (born 1643), the taste among the upper classes for conspicuous consumption was remarkable. But then various historical factors combined in history to make people in general, and men in particular, more sober in their dress. The Age of Enlightenment saw the trend growing, predating a similar sentiment expressed by Giorgio Armani at his men's wear show in Milan at the beginning of 2002: 'I'll tell you something. Luxury disgusts me'. (Now he says!)

According to fashion historian Colin McDowell in his book *Dressed to Kill: Sex Power & Clothes*, social life of the eighteenth century had become boringly repetitive in the upper echelons, and more and more just an excuse to dress up. The aristocracy retreated to their country estates — the main point of distinction they had from the increasingly wealthy bourgeoisie — where a different wardrobe, and a rather more practical one, was required.

Outlandish costumes in fine laces and embroideries, once commonplace, were more and more satirised by writers and playwrights, and eventually 'worn only by the most dedicated followers of fashion — the fops and the effeminates', writes McDowell. The Revolution of 1789 also contributed to the demise of the well-turned out chap in France — after the guillotine started falling, dressing up in public could be a serious health hazard.

> *Those who make their dress a principal part of themselves, will, in general, become of no more value than their dress.*
> ANON.

There have been various attempts to revive the dandy over the past 200 years. Wilde's aesthetes, at the turn of the nineteenth century, for instance and, in not so dim memory, the Carnaby Street Mod look (very Cliff Richard) of the 1960s and glam rock in the 1980s with the rock group Queen. But not until the last few years have so many men been paying so much attention to their appearance — and it's a trend that started with the young.

If you have any doubt, just have a look at swimming star Ian Thorpe. Still in his early twenties, he's a constant ambassador for Armani here in Australia, and not even the most daring member of the *de facto* fashion police would dare call him a fop or effeminate. This is something Australian men could aim for, and if your Australian man is not making the effort, you'll just have to help him achieve his true wardrobe potential. What follows is the smart User's guide to polishing up a man for fun and fantasy! But first, you need to polish up those search and rescue skills…

How to judge the book by his cover

Smart users know that the same rules apply for men as women: he gets just one chance to make a first impression.

Start with the suit. You should be impressed with his suit if you meet him in working hours. Careful — not all eligible men are suits. Creative types and men in IT, plumbers, firemen, sailors, will all have a different working outfit and you will need to accommodate that. It's much harder, too, for a man to make much of an impression in his after-hours clothes, since there is so much scope for personal expression, not all of it good. (Some of even the most reasonable men have 'leisure clothes' which defy description.)

But the suit can be a great identifier, since it's the uniform for many men. He should be wearing a good one, in grey, navy or black, plain or pinstriped. The only people who can wear light coloured suits with anything approaching *panache* are Italians or the French. Almost everyone else looks like they are trying too hard. The same goes for those coloured, checked sports jacket you see all over Europe and look fantastic there. Such a shame that they don't travel.

Smart users recognise value for money. The impression you get is what he has paid for. A man will never look sharp if he is wearing cheap clothes. Investment dressing really pays off. When you are looking at a man, with a view to becoming his User, you should be able to pick a bad bet from a good one. (I know it sounds shallow but a little personal marketing is a very good idea — particularly if the marketeer is aiming at the top end of the market.) When you crush part of a cheap suit in your hand (if you've just met, this could be tricky. He might think you're grabbing his bum, rather than road-testing fabric), the wrinkles will remain. The garment won't hang properly and, lacking a lining, it will soon pull out of shape.

Now to shirts. Shirts on attractive men generally come in two colours — white or blue (pale or mid- is fine, not navy, thanks.) Men who are very sure of themselves can pull off other pastels — in fact, one of the handsomest men in the world presented himself at lunch recently in a pale lavender shirt and a pale grey suit. He broke two of the cardinal rules of dress (the suit rule and the colour of the shirt rule) and looked dropped dead gorgeous for his sins.

Men who own tracts of land in the country can wear fine gingham shirts (blue is best, since red checks seem to heighten the look of sunburn or a slight alcoholic flush). Men who look as though they belong on tractors can have a go as well, and even expand the repertoire into fine stripes. Otherwise, checks need to be treated with some reservation, unless you really want to look like a Canadian lumberjack (and that would be some fantasy to be out in the woods with!)

Shirts for dangerous men with messy table manners come in black or dark grey, but these have a distinctly old-fashioned and underworld air about them. This is notwithstanding the fact that designer Tom Ford single-handedly resurrected the tone on tone look for Gucci some seasons ago, and some fashion victims are still investing in the plan. Striped or plain shirts with white collars and cuffs mean one thing — run for your life. This guy is probably in television or advertising, and there you don't even want to start. Sometimes, though rarely, a barrister or a doctor can get away with this look, but it really is for men with a great deal of front.

Check the collar closely. No matter what the colour, it should be neat, not frayed. You might have a passion for a man in an English spread or cutaway collar (okay, so that's me), but button-down is fine too. The collars you do not want to see on any man are the ones which are so long and sharp that they look as they could pierce a nipple if the wearer moved his head the wrong way too quickly. His cuffs should be neat, not frayed either. Doubled is nice, with cuff links. How you approach a man in a short-sleeved shirt depends on you. Generally, they are accessorised with pocket-protectors, which should give you a bit of a clue about the personality of the wearer. Escape while you can.

Allow a man a T-shirt under a suit jacket when he's Tom Cruise or he is telling you he has chartered a yacht for a two-month cruise in the Med and he's practising with part of his holiday wardrobe.

Check the shoes. Always look down. You can tell a lot about a person from their shoes. Is he wearing wing tips? Does he even know what wing tips are? Is he wearing loafers with tassels? (One of my more particular friends made it clear to quite an eligible man that she was not entertaining his attentions any longer because of his taste in shoes. 'I've not spent my life waiting for Mr Right to throw myself away on a man who wears a navy blazer and a pair of tasselled loafers,' she confessed later.) What you want to see are shoes which are no strangers to polish and a bit of elbow grease, and which are not down at heel. A man who takes care of himself from the feet up is a very good find indeed, even if there are tassels on his uppers.

Also, be careful of the colour and the leather choice of these shoes. Brown suede is acceptable when he's hunting grouse on his own estate in Buckinghamshire and his name is that of a whole English county and is prefixed by Duke of, as it is for Users. But suede is out for men in town altogether unless they are tweedy academics. Anything but black is out for hard-soled shoes. It can so easily go wrong — a dark night or morning, they reach into the wardrobe for the black shoes, put them on and then it's not till lunchtime when they look down and see they have accidentally teamed their dark brown shoes with their dark grey suit. That is the sort of thing that can put the aesthetically aware off for the rest of the day.

❝ *Great men are seldom over-scrupulous in the arrangement of their attire.* ❞

CHARLES DICKENS, 1812–1870

It's pretty obvious that men can go mad — and often do — with playtime shoes. It's hard to imagine why they think the latest in yoof-culture trainers are actually for them, since they are neither yoof-ful, literate in the culture, or in training. Those trainers look great on adolescent boys who play the game and whose feet are growing at such a rate that the trainers have very little time to subside into a grubby heap. On the other hand, adult men can wear theirs for years and years, and shouldn't. The same goes, by the way, for top-siders and canvas sandshoes. To look good, they have to be neat, clean and not like things you'd find in a skip.

No bowties. The only man who looks halfway sympathetic in a coloured bow tie is Ronald McDonald. After him, anyone who tries to wear a bow tie during the day looks like a complete idiot. When confronted by a man wearing one of these disasters, try to stifle the desire to dissolve into a fit of the giggles and make sure you look him straight in the eye. One of the most unconvincing men I ever knew was devoted to his bow ties, and his ensembles were not assisted by the fact that his hair was cut into a longish brush cut — a toilet brush. All other ties should be restrained, silk, and at the dry cleaners occasionally.

Never let him borrow anything from your wardrobe. First of all, you wouldn't want it to look better on him than it does on you. Secondly, you might take a long hard look at any man who wants to dress up in women's clothes, even if he claims it's just for a fancy-dress party. Make him get dressed up as a gladiator instead — much more fun for you than if he's trying out his Barbra Streisand routine!

DIY bloke renovation

The phone rang and on the end of the line was Brigid, the matchmaker. 'Do you like football?' she asked brightly. Like so many things in life, I thought, it depends, really. Could anyone like club level football, where nothing ever happens? No. But non-stop excitement played by experts is another thing altogether. Brigid, who could never be described as a natural fit with the football crowd, was offering the second version. 'It's the grand final at the Football Stadium on Saturday!'

I was about to say thanks but no thanks when she added the sweetener: she announced she had discovered my perfect match. And she would introduce us at the game. He's bright, she said. And he's charming. Most importantly, he's single, been divorced for some two years — which as any woman knows, is the minimum time for a balanced human being to get over the rubble of a ruined marriage. 'You'll love him,' she said. As she spoke, I was already beginning to plan what to wear.

Now, not everyone has an Irish matchmaker, and as a group they have a certain reputation. Not as fierce as the *Hello, Dolly* Levi types, the Hibernians are a little more on the whimsical side. They tend to romanticise features and qualities that others might see as undesirable. Which might mean that while the man she was suggesting was indeed both very bright and very charming, there might be something of an oddity along the lines of, for argument's sake, a hump. 'There's a hump?' I asked. What hump? She'd never noticed a hump. A hump worked for Quasimodo as he swung off the bell ropes in Notre Dame, but he didn't win Esmeralda. She assured me he didn't have a hump, or at least one that could be discerned. She hadn't checked all the elevations, but she was pretty sure this guy was hump-free.

There might have been any number of other things he might have been: absent-minded, plain as a pikelet, bald, a mass murderer. How could you know? How could my matchmaker know? As far as she was concerned, a perfect match began and ended with single — anything else was a bonus. He could have been covered with body hair as thick as a beaver pelt, been the size of a sumo wrestler, or just signed up for a men's support group. Anything was possible, since she was responding, you understand, to the very essence of the man. Which is great, since everyone needs a little latitude. But sometimes it's just as well to start close to normal. We all get odder, sooner or later. I just wasn't too sure her idea of normal and mine were even close.

Not to be discouraged, she set up a date which wasn't supposed to look like or feel like one. Her target had a box at the stadium, so she got me on to the guest list — and I don't even like to think about why or how she sold me. I tried but had to stop, in case I started to fulfil an imaginary shopping list based on someone else's description of me. Too hard.

So on the appointed day, I put on the navy linen, the little plaid navy and tan flats, stuffed the mobile phone (to call a cab for a quick getaway in case the whole thing went horribly wrong) and the lipstick (an Yves St Laurent gloss) into the Louis Vuitton (did you guess this match was Rugby Union?) handbag and climbed into the taxi two and a half hours late. Which was my first hint that I really didn't want to do this, or meet this man. The box was at a nosebleed-inducing altitude at the football stadium. As I hit the final steps toward heaven I heard my name, with an Irish brogue wrapped around it, floating down from on high. Then, I fell into the arms of my host.

He was, as the matchmaker had said, charming. Reassuringly, there was no obvious sign of a crooked back and I knew immediately that I found this man attractive: I couldn't speak, and it wasn't just the asthmatic after-effect of the trek up the stairs. The matchmaker had actually missed out mentioning his immediate defining physical characteristic. This man's eyes were the colour of the sky we were almost able to touch. Think cornflower. Think the blue on the Virgin's robe. Think blue eyes at once so piercing and so deep that not staring becomes impossible, and the shock of looking into them almost physically uncomfortable.

It turns out that Michael was an able host, had no discernible signs of madness, and didn't mind being asked silly questions about the flow of the game every once in a while. He had been living alone for some years, had no children, and was a researcher with a particular interest in Third World medicine.

The very best thing about this paragon of virtue and humility? In the middle of all his glory, he looked like an unbuttoned leather sofa. His honey blonde hair was over-long, his cotton shirt pulled up and out of the back of his Levis, which concertina-ed around his ankles. His leather shoes were scuffed. In short, he was disorganised, not so much a perfect ten as a perfect mess, which was truly perfect indeed!

Here was a man who would never be clogging up the front of the bathroom mirror, a man who would never be spending his money — or anyone else's — in expensive little boutiques where cashmere argyle socks cost $155 a pop or a pair of hand-tooled brogues cost the same as a small secondhand car. The names Ermenegildo Zegna, Ferragamo and Gucci meant nothing to him. This man would never read *GQ* or *Esquire* or any other men's fashion magazine masquerading as brain food. He had a *Spectator* mind in a Timberland frame. Best of all, he was a man in need of physical redrafting, and I was in the mood for just such a renovation. I could feel myself beginning the preliminary drawings.

Now I know there might be some people who consider this train of thought, this line of action, tremendously presumptuous. And, of course, it is. It requires arrogance disguised as altruism. The renovator must consider the subject under-utilised, under-resourced and underdone for there to be any fun at all in the game. If the subject doesn't like it, they can always say no. And I would hope they would see this hobby of mine as keeping me out of trouble and saving them hours of time, if not their money.

These male makeovers can go horribly wrong, of course. You can edit a guy from the ground up, neatening, straightening, getting the colours and the shapes right and then some opportunistic woman comes along and snaps up the reno for free! This is one of the hazards of the game: your only consolation is that the silk purse you've made from a sow's ear can last only for as long as the fabric of his new wardrobe. When he goes back to replace your styling, he's going to exercise his own taste and that was the very thing that got him into trouble in the first place. So unless his new decorator is clever, he's going to relapse, and she's going to see him without any disguise. Never gloat if this happens.

Because of the dangers of investing heavily in a male makeover, many women would never even contemplate trying one. Anna is twenty-seven and fairly flexible when it comes to men. She admits to only one immovable dislike. 'I can't take back hair. Before I can make a sensible decision about a man — whether I am going to keep him or put him back, I have to wax him.' (This takes some finesse, since she has to wax before their relationship enters a more intimate stage. In the summer, she takes them to the beach for an early date. In the winter, she gets them to try on a t-shirt for her.) 'I actually used to pretend it was part of foreplay, but no one ever really fell for that. Then it turned out that the guys who were keen on me and planned to stick around always agreed. But the blokes looking for a one or two or three-night stand just wouldn't stand still for it,' she said.

'It was like a litmus test about their intentions. It's painful, but if they put up with that, then they must like me.' The waxing plan waned in the end, though. One suitor, a brilliant lunatic, was really in love with Anna. But he would never let her wax his back. His argument was she should accept him as he was. She couldn't. He found someone else and Anna ... well, Anna's still waxing relative strangers in the hope of finding her smooth-skinned prince.

Michael, on the other hand, didn't look as though he needed my ministrations at all. In fact, he needed only minor adjustments — nothing structural — to realise his full potential. However, this would require some delicate negotiation. First of all, I had to start going out with Michael, before I could start arranging the makeover. Past experience teaches us that there are certain basic conventions that need to be observed.

I had done a renovation on fiancé number two that was gold medal material. When I found him in a pub (which should have been a sign, but unfortunately took five years to register), he was wearing R.M. Williams moleskins and the dodgiest shirt you could imagine. I have a very clear recollection of it: brown, with an all-over pattern of small dancing ladies. His aftershave, if it wasn't Old Spice, it was down in that league. The horror, the horror.

Despite the obvious drawbacks, a ruined glamour had settled around him. Within days, he had moved in. His entire baggage consisted of a dozen or so books and a couple of plastic garbage bags full of ghastly clothes. Within weeks, I'd sorted his wardrobe into the St Vincent de Paul's pile (which was almost everything) and the rest (which was not much more than three pairs of trousers). It was a not inexpensive business to replace the rubbish with cavalry twill trousers, new wool sports jackets, cashmere sweaters, shirts with French cuffs.

As I sometimes travelled for my job, I shopped for the loved one waiting at home. Guilt prompted some of the purchases: regretting his absence and thinking how much he would have enjoyed Paris meant silk from Charvet; the feeling that it was such a pity he couldn't see Dublin at dawn presaged the compensatory purchase of tweed jacket.

On it went. The process was like a transgender Pygmalion and Galatea, with him (in the updated, musical version) cast as Eliza Doolittle and me as the increasingly cranky Professor Henry Higgins. His old ties were polyester, the new ones all Italian silk. His aftershave now was decidedly up-scale, Chanel's *Pour Monsieur*. I was like a child playing dress-ups with my favourite doll. Unfortunately, that doll, having discovered a whole new world, fell in love with his own, regilded, reflection. His favourite words turned out to be not my name but 'bespoke tailoring'.

He looked spiffy. But going out with him was a trial, since he had a wandering eye and, dressed to kill in his new clothes, he attracted the attention of women too lazy to find and renovate their own chap. As I watched him cutting a path through crowds of female admirers, I made a firm resolve that I would never invest in anything permanent (which is the reason why I was never stuck with the bill for his root canal work). Eventually he moved on, taking with him a wardrobe that would have done a dandy proud. I was sorry to see the back of his tight jeans as they walked down the stairs but my bank manager was doing cartwheels of joy. Now that I had given up a hobby more expensive and just as dangerous as ocean racing, perhaps I could buy a house.

Since then, I have confined myself to superficial makeovers for chaps. With the return of fiancé number one for the second time, I was rather more circumspect. But much of that had to do with the ten years or so which had passed between our first engagement, when he was an intern, and the second, when he was a divorced father of three. When he was in his twenties, he was easier to dress, but there was no money to do it with. Towards his forties, he'd lost his sporting shape. Life was spent on the benches and he had started to gather a little condition. In both cases, I confined myself to ties, sweaters, and shirts (apart from a desperate attempt to get him out of shorts and trackie daks around the house) and caps to hide the growing bald spot. Still, he did have all his own teeth.

Along the way, I'd discovered some home truths about renovating a man, discoveries which are essential if you are serious about being a successful User.

Rule 1 — Subtlety is the key

You must never let him know he is under renovation. Even an innocuous question from you such as, 'Do you like this shirt/tie/suit/Hawaiian shirt?' must be put delicately. In the beginning, you never know where that item of clothing came from, or what sentimental values are attached.

Your response to his questions should be non-committal: 'I've always loved you in aqua'; or 'Bright patterns are so cheering' need to be practised to rinse out the irony. Never say, 'That's a really hectic blue', 'That shirt's a bit lairy' or 'You look like one of Al Capone's gang in those stripes'.

Or you might prefer to tackle the problem itself — in sporting terms, play the ball, rather than the man. If you were playing the man, you might say: 'God, why did you buy that awful shirt? You know you look shocking in donkey brown!' Congratulations: in two short sentences, you've alerted him to the fact you hate the shirt (he'll know who to ask when the thing goes missing), attacked his taste, and told him he looks terrible.

Instead, hit the ball: 'I think that shirt might not suit your complexion quite so well in the winter/summer. Maybe with the change of season you'll look really marvellous in blue.' This says to him that you have his interests at heart, the fault with the shirt lies not in his taste but in the changing of the season, and reassures him about his looks in another colour. No one in the world could resist all those ideas at once.

Or, less securely, you might take a leaf out of his book, the one that says when you are confronted with a vision of ugliness, your appropriate response is, 'Do you like that?' He might not immediately understand the subtext, though you know the question has the same meaning as, 'Are you going to wear that?'

Renovation requires stealth. Always tell him he looks great ('You're so handsome' is your regular refrain) and that he is as close to perfect as any human being has a right to be. As he is lulled into a sense of security, you can move on to the next step.

Rule 2 — Target the enemy

Identify those pieces in his wardrobe that you cannot live with. And then work out the strategy to get rid of them. While some brave souls immediately ransack the wardrobes of their new loved ones, this has always seemed a little risky on the first date.

The quickest way round this, of course, is to throw everything out and pretend he's been robbed. But this is hard to carry off with any degree of conviction — and the police might get involved. The same goes for a small, localised fire in his wardrobe. Hard to explain, harder still to contain. You might take the softly, softly approach, 'losing' something at the dry cleaner one week, accidentally shrinking something in the wash the next. This program works, but it takes nerves of steel over some period of time.

One clever User, who never smokes, keeps a packet of cigarettes handy in case she ever needs to blow tiny burning embers over an offending jumper or shirt. 'Oh, look, moths', she'll mourn, before hurling the holey garment out. The same woman has discovered that men will never again wear a tie that a woman has appropriated and worn as a belt. She'll wear the tie she doesn't like (under a blazer to save her own feelings) a couple of times, scrunching it up properly. 'By that stage, my beloved never looks for that tie again. It works every time.'

She also has managed to discover what makes ties splay. 'There's a thread down the middle of the back of the tie, where it joins. You just tug the thread and it starts to butterfly. Men hate that.'

You might try moving clothes you don't like out of sight to begin with, and into little-used drawers. After he's forgotten where they've gone, they can just fade right out of the equation. In this way, you can just retire the garments you can't stand. They disappear. It's his wardrobe, so how can it possibly have anything to do with you? This is the reason why you never finger any particular piece of clothing as one you can't stand.

While I am writing this, I am thinking of a pair of vintage board shorts, so old they must have been manufactured the same year King Kameamehawhooise won the all-Hawaii surfing championship. Threadbare, purplish, with a frightful pattern in chartreuse not fading fast enough into the background, these shorts have figured in my life for some years. Seen teamed with any of a wide range of brutal Mambo shirts, they have pushed me to the end of my rope. But I have never, not once, ever indicated that these boardies are anything apart from fabulous.

The man who owns them thinks they're brilliant, even though they make him look like a colour-challenged ibis when he wears them. He would be sad for a while if he discovered they had a small rip in the seat, and had to go into the mending basket for rehabilitation. They could be there for about — oh, I don't know — two seasons maybe, waiting for a stitch, but you know how busy modern life can be. I'll tell him I'll get to it. Soon, he'll forget all about them, and they'll move from the sewing room to the old clothes bin at the local shops without a single cross word. I can wait.

Rule 3 — Don't aim too high

You should be reasonable. If you've got a guy who looks like Daffy Duck on a good day, you are never going to be able to remake him into Debonair Duck. But working within limits — on just the basics — can be fun. Start with the simplest external — the hair. Take him to your own hairdresser (having primed the hairdresser beforehand) and then the cutter can suggest a change from that George Harrison cut into the very snappiest George Clooney look. Your guy will never know you were the force behind the change.

If your loved one is bald, get the hairdresser to shave what's left off immediately. You have a real problem, of course, if your bald testosterone package is a comb-over sort of guy. You could pray for an industrial accident to lop off the floppy bit (but this is a possibility as remote as it is dangerous), or pretend to sleepwalk and cut it off during the night. This is getting tricky. It's probably easier not to fall in love with a bald guy in the first place. If one goes bald on you, then that's just the luck of the game.

Change that aftershave. If his mother/ex-wife put him on to Drakkar Noir, it's time to move him into another scent age. You can get rid of the old aftershave by using it as bathroom spray or, by degrees, slowly tipping it down the drain. Surprise him with his new smell almost as soon as the old one disappears, and before he hustles himself off to the chemist for a replacement. Be careful at first with your replacement fragrance; you might not keep this guy too long and you certainly won't want to be reminded of him every time you smell Vetiver on your new man.

Remember, you must keep quiet about all you have done and are doing for this man: silence is the price you have to pay. You must never tell him, his friends, his family (though all your girlfriends and your family should know) that he is your finest piece of renovation work.

It might save you from a terrible blunder. Picture this. There you are, having afternoon tea with his mother/sister/nanna and suddenly for some reason, you unthinkingly blurt out what a complete dag Harry was before you found him. That purple body shirt (Nanna sucks on her false teeth, but you press on), the shocking pair of white Stubbies (sister's gone strange and you wonder why). Then, the *coup de grâce*, you start on the short-sleeved polyester work shirts that riddle his wardrobe. His mother remarks icily that's what she gives him every year for Christmas — two short-sleeved no-iron shirts for work. And that is why you never talk about his clothes to anyone with a vested interest in him — not even his ex-wife/lover.

Rule 4 — Finish the project

A lot of renovators like a piece of work in progress. They're the ones for whom the journey has the value, not the destination. What else can explain houses which are being fixed for years, but which are never really completed? This is complete rubbish.

You need to get your project finished and out of the way so you can admire it properly — and decide if you need to start again on any aspect of it.

However, understand that every time you increase your man's attractiveness, you increase his value in the market. And that means you never have to stop taking care that some maverick woman doesn't just appear one night out of a dance club and waltz off with your bloke. Which brings us to…

Rule 5 — The worst possible light

Sometimes, circumstances dictate a negative plan. For instance your guy, fresh with newfound confidence and all dressed up, courtesy of you, might find himself suddenly the object of unwanted female attention in the office. Men hate this sort of thing. Being adored by strange women makes them uncomfortable, poor little loves (this is irony).

So you will have to help save him. Begin by taking up his trousers by about half an inch. That should start to give him an oddly gormless Gomer Pyle look. Borrow his reading glasses, and have stronger, Coke-bottle lenses put into them. No one on God's wide earth has ever found this look — think Jerry Lewis — at all attractive. Or else reduce the prescription a little; he'll start to squint through his glasses and a lot of his peripheral vision will go.

Move his collar buttons slightly inwards. This really works in summer, cutting off circulation to the brain slightly. He'll sweat, obsess about his health and never look at a woman except you, as you come to press a cold cloth against his temples. Buy him a larger size in underwear and convince him he's lost weight and is not looking too whoops. With him a little chubbier, his sex appeal might be slightly muffled. Be careful about this: you don't want him worrying on a heart attack he hasn't really earned.

Let him shop for himself. You should express such confidence in his taste and his ability that the little darling takes himself off to David Jones and Myer/Grace Bros and starts to build-up his own wardrobe again. Which is really where we came in to this DIY renovation.

21
God is in the detail

Good grooming is a wonderful thing in a man, and the User is always very grateful for it. But it's pretty much underestimated by blokes before, during, and after the courtship period. It goes way beyond showering twice a day, shaving, understanding the benefits of a deodorant and passing the toothbrush across the teeth regularly. Though, of course, all these things are essential.

As a man gets past twenty-five, the challenges of good grooming increase. (Who are we kidding? This is not an age or gender specific issue. It also takes Users a lot more care to look carelessly glam after that age.)

Personal grooming never stays personal for very long. And the people we care most about are generally the ones in the best position to expose us to their own codes — and equally, we them. Therefore it is important that the pristine condition of the User is never in doubt. For her, this is a case of 'do as I do.'

> *Chère Joséphine,*
> *Stay out of the water!*
> NAPOLÉON BONAPARTE, 1769–1821

One remarkable deviation from the standards of even the most minimal personal hygiene is, according to historians, one Joséphine Beauharnais. The entrancing Joséphine, Napoleon's empress, occasionally received missives from her husband in the field telling her when to expect him home — and not to bathe until after his return. Given that the levels of plumbing available in France during the early years of the nineteenth century — not high — meant that most people would have been on the nose, it's impossible to try to imagine the results of Joséphine restricting even these rudimentary efforts and not feel a certain amazement at the request.

The follicular challenge

For men, there is always the problem of hair. Not enough of it on the head, sometimes, too much of it elsewhere. Men start growing hair wherever — around and in the ears, up the nose, across the top of the cheekbones, and then the eyebrows can go completely feral. At the same time, the body hair is taking off in all directions. Eventually it's everywhere *except* on their heads!

It seems incredible that men don't actually notice these changes. (It seems equally incredible that they don't notice the soap stuck in their ears in the aftermath of a quick morning shave.) It is obvious they do not have the faintest clue about the rampant nature of this stray hair. It can be wilder than a choko vine on a suburban back fence in summer and they still remain blithely unaware!

> *A hairy body, and arms stiff with bristles, give promise of a manly soul.*
> JUVENAL, 40–125

This oblivion might be caught up in a general idea many men have about themselves; they think they are pretty well perfect. That conviction explains why so many of them can hit the beach in their Speedos and appear to think they look the Apollo Belvedere, and not at all like the Michelin Man. (All that might be changing, though. Increasingly, men — and they can't all by gay — are trapped in gymnasia in pursuit of the body beautiful myth, which is both good news and bad news. The bad news is that men are being seduced into the cult of youthful perfection, foisted on women for the last five thousand years at least. The good news is that there will be an increasing pool of men who will look like Michelangelo's David.)

So, is his oddly dispersed hair the User's problem? Unfortunately, it can be, at least at the start. And if it is, what can be done about it? The User will once more have the vision thing, and see past the predatory eyebrows to the other gifts a man might have. (Women are *so* forgiving: which man would look past such things in a woman?)

While yours should be the vision thing, you might just give him an indicator of what that vision means by standing between him and a bathroom mirror quite early on in your relationship, and pointing out the problems. This should happen after trust has been established, because he will certainly need to trust you. At some time, you might be required to approach his face and head with sharp metal instruments, namely tweezers and scissors. Once you have trimmed the eyebrows, the cheekbone furze and the ears, you will need to cautiously move on with tweezers to the nasal hair. This is something you should really do only once. Then, you need to hand him over to the professionals to keep the undergrowth under control in the future. However, if you enjoy inflicting a little pain, this might be the way to do it. You can always pass the torture off as being for his own good.

Hair, apparently

The User generally considers herself lucky if the object of her desire and affection has his own and is not threatening to lose it in the next ten years. (Should we blame the hormones in battery hens for the reason that so many men don't have much upstairs these days?) This fact was rammed home once when I was standing in a pharmacy waiting to plonk down the dough for a new roll-on deodorant, the previous new deodorant having failed to live up to its dual function of no sweat and definitely no odour, making me one of the people I might previously have been a little sniffy about.

This pharmacy was in deepest Tuscany and the shutters were about to come rattling down on the wheels of commerce for some four hours and turn the place into Chianti's version of Brigadoon. The locals, fearing a medical emergency during the time the shop was battened shut, were busy trying to fill prescriptions enough to stock a field hospital during a shortish war. In the haphazard queue, I had time to consider a question posed by some point-of-sale material ranged around the shop. '*Cellulite?*' one asked. '*No, grazie!*' ('Cellulite? No thanks!')

After about half an hour, the wonder of the variety of cellulite remedies had palled, so my attention drifted to my fellow shoppers. Another amazing sight met my eyes — of the five men in the shop, four were affecting rather baroque comb-overs. The amazing thing was that most didn't appear to be much older than forty.

These hairstyles require not only skill on the part of the wearers, but a certain complicity (one of the consorts was carrying a comb for her husband) from the wives and a conspiracy of silence from loved ones at home. There, obviously, no one says: 'What's the story with the hair, fella?' No one asks the obvious question, and so the comb-over merchant clearly thinks his ruse is not only subtle but is also actually working.

It's multi-cultural, this comb-over blindness. You can see them from France to French's Forest. Everywhere are hairdos, wrapped and draped with a precarious precision, which would start to flap in the updraft created by a lighted match.

You'd never catch a woman with a comb-over. A comb-up, maybe, particularly since designer Donatella Versace seems bent on bringing the beehive back into style. Women are too smart for comb-overs. Users know that there is just so much time you can devote to pointless grooming.

> *It's very hard for a man with a wig to keep order.*
> EVELYN WAUGH, 1903–1966

Men in toupees are brothers in deception to the comb-over merchants. They obviously think no one notices the difference between real and fake fur, not even when natural hair of a completely different colour and texture peeps out from under the synthetic fault line. Honestly, those little hair carpets sit on top of those heads as convincingly as false fingernails sit on the ends of women's fingers.

How should the User remove the toupee? By stealth, if she must. Lose it under the bed and vacuum it up the next morning; shrink it in the hot cycle of the washing machine; take its owner out constantly in high winds or topless cars; encourage the cat to think of it as prey. Make it into a coat for your grandmother's cockatoo. Do anything, but get rid of that nasty little lump of hair.

> *While Darwinian Man, though well-behaved,*
> *At best is only a monkey shaved.*
>
> W. S. GILBERT, 1836–1911

Close shaves

Have you ever wondered about how shaving started? At some stage, primitive man, having fashioned a sharp edge out of a flint, made the leap from scraping it across a woolly mammoth carcass to skin it, to turning the blade on himself for a little self-shearing. Would he have ever started if he had known that in doing so, he had committed generations of Man to the daily tyranny of shaving?

It's hard to imagine any woman was ever in favour of handing over that sharpened stone and recommending a clean shave — what bloke would have paid any attention to her? Though in fact, that is probably exactly what happened. The prehistoric User decided she was tired of beard rash, so she encouraged her loved one to shave. He did it once, she liked the effect, and he discovered he got more sex when he shaved than when he didn't. Thus, perhaps, began the daily shave. Many of us have reason to be grateful for whatever accident of history started it. (Not so grateful, though, for the moment when that cave man turned to his User, pointed at her legs and suggested she, too, might have a go at depilation.)

> *A beard signifies lice, not brains.*
>
> GREEK PROVERB

It's difficult these days to get most men, even if already culturally inclined to the smooth cheek, to shave on the weekends, but that's growth in the Anthony LaPaglia sense rather than the more extreme arrangements favoured by creatives such as artist Salvador Dali and Christian Dior's designer John Galliano. Now, there are two examples of beards making a man look not manly, but rather like a deranged pimp (the former) or as though he's just about to rustle a flock of sheep on some wind-blasted Cappodocian peak (the latter).

Perhaps a short reminder from Shakespeare might be timely for men contemplating a shave-free Sunday. In *Much Ado About Nothing*, the hard-to-please (and, it becomes evident, true User) Beatrice tells Leonato, 'Lord, I could not endure a husband with a beard on his face; I had rather lie in the woollen.' (Actually, she wasn't too sold on a beardless youth for a husband either: 'What would I do with him? Dress him up in my apparel and make him my waiting gentlewoman?'.)

Face furniture has been in and out of fashion in Western civilisation over the centuries, with some remarkable results. Men have been etching their facial hair, with a view to display, for generations: Henry VIII sported a full, red beard; courtiers of Charles II cultivated nifty Van Dykes; Queen Victoria's father, the Duke of Kent, had a pair of formidable mutton-chop whiskers and her consort Albert teamed his with a matching moustache, and in doing so effectively created a lasting image for the Victorian *paterfamilias*.

> *Being kissed by a man who didn't wax his moustache was — like eating an egg without salt.*
> RUDYARD KIPLING, 1865–1936

Albert had a bit of help with that. Soldiers returning to England after the Crimean War in the 1850s wore their beards like badges of courage, but those whiskers soon became an indicator of a certain Philistinism. Some forty years later, aesthetes such as Oscar Wilde, W. B. Yeats and the beardless Aubrey Beardsley could go clean-shaven as an act of cultural rebellion against the prevailing middle-class, middlebrow mind-set.

Those Victorians have such a lot to answer for, not the least of which is that they managed in just 100 years, through an increasing preoccupation with propriety and morals, to turn eighteenth-century fops and Regency dandies (generally clean-shaven) into soberly attired Prince Alberts, equipped with decorative facial hair. Once fashion moved away from whiskers in the early twentieth century, however, men were left as plain as un-iced sponges, barefaced as well as uniformly dressed.

But now, you can see the most intriguing facial hair arrangements all over the shop — indeed, from the checkout counter of the nearest Woollies to the dance floor at the local rave. Even a quick glance will tell you that there are a lot of men aged eighteen to their late twenties who clearly spend hours in front of the mirror and are pretty pleased with the result. There's the head shaving (Mussolini's Mini-me's), the gel/mousse applications (should someone tell them that the smell of Fudge swamps any glamour cologne?) and then the careful sculpting of the whiskers.

It's all about trends, still, of course, and the fact that fashion, once the domain of the cockscomb and the sexually ambiguous, is an area men are approaching in a determined fashion, reclaiming it for their own. Not for them a subscription to the warning from Carlyle that 'the first spiritual want of a barbarous man is Decoration'.

The sobriety of the past is being overturned by men armed with Gillettes intent on creating their own images on their own visages. And why not? That bearded look works on Santa, TV environmentalists, explorers and one-earringed pirates (best worn without the peg leg and the parrot). Maybe men are once more transfixed by facial hair because it's still about sexual display and they're doing it for us. At the very least, they give the User something to wonder about.

Reading his hair

Completely shaven
In reality, he's bald, and he's shaved to make the most of a bad deal. He thinks it makes him look macho, but if that were the case, why don't newborn babies look tough? This look is great on men with well-shaped heads. Best ever example was Yul Brynner. Users give this look the thumbs up when it is just razored and three cheers if the shoulders and backs are treated similarly.

Is that a toupee or a guinea pig on your head?
He's sensitive, he's balding. You know the bit underneath is real because it is a completely different colour from the syrup (of figs = wig). Often seen on men desperately trying to retain their youth, and their youthful girlfriends. One Hollywood mogul was reputed to have a wardrobe of some twenty-eight

toupees, each a little longer than the last, so it looked as though his hair was growing for a month, and then had a cut. Users recognise that a man in a toupee has values, which are just as skewiff as the fake hair can be.

No one will notice this is a comb-over, will they?
He's trying to tell the world that he still has hair, or maybe he simply doesn't have the money for a wig. The rest of the world is supposed not to notice the subterfuge. Tell him he's dreaming!

Dreadies
This is a look that went out when Bob Marley was popped into the box. The dreadlocked guy is trying to say he's cool and in touch with his atavistic past, while his hair just says it hasn't been combed for a while. When he's unconscious from too much *ganja*, start to pull out the knots.

The 'Greed is Good' Gordon Gekko look
Seen on Michael Douglas in Wall Street, this look was hot in the eighties. This head said, 'Look at me, I'm a master of the Universe'. Now it says, 'Look at me, I'm a sorry leftover'. Users will have already confiscated every last bit of the hair product in question. Too much of it can addle a man's brain. (Though interestingly, rarely a woman's. Years of desensitisation, probably.)

The buzz cut
Great on the following: early astronauts and test pilots (like Buzz Aldrin). (They're complete shockers on women, unless you're a lesbian and want to be taken for one. Or by one.) Hair can range in length from just out of the scalp to standing up all over head. This look says any man can be made blokey by the right haircut. Users have no feelings on this one way or another, unless they make the wearer look completely neck-less. Then the User will start encouraging hair growth for definition.

The flopsy bunny
Hugh Grant was the greatest living example of this hairstyle, which dropped like a schoolgirl's fringe over the eyebrows. He cruelled his own patch, though, when he had it cut off after *Bridget Jones's Diary* was released. He wasn't so

pleased with the change; he said his new hairstyle made him look like a female golfer and he was growing it back. Users know that if they want to feel like they are dating schoolboys, this is the haircut to pick for the love object.

A full beard
Is he a member of a fundamentalist sect? If he is, then he's probably not for you, dear User. Though he could be trying to say he's really a *man*. Or maybe that he had a thing about Grizzly Adams when he was a small boy and still hasn't got over the fixation. Users know that if they want that much fur in their mouths, they'll kiss the bear.

Goatee
Nothing says aspiring intellectual quite like one of these. They looked good in the fifties on poets of the Beat Generation and appropriately silly on magicians and astrologers, but these days they are so Terry Try-Hard. Users will avoid pretentious men at the outset, but if yours grows one on you, you'll just have to Nair it off in the middle of the night. (Do an allergy patch test on his forearm first otherwise you might leave a scar in exactly the same shape as the missing hair.)

A moustache
Which one of the Village People is your choice? Or perhaps you are seeing John Newcombe? Moustaches can be so tricky; they can make the wearer look like a Colombian drug lord or an old-style professional cricketer in the way of Merv Hughes or Dennis Lillee. Either way, you have to be careful. Also, he has to be careful. A crumb trap like that under the nose needs attention and the User is not the curator. However, you might give him a moustache cup, to keep the whiskers out of the cappuccino froth.

Remedial barbering — how to fix his head

He's got a piecrust haircut gelled up across the front
Wait until he's asleep. Every week, trim the sticking up spikes a little. Steal his hair gel. Soon, he won't have a fringe to gunk up and won't even notice.

He's got a ponytail
Again, wait until he is asleep and cut if off. Keep hold of the scissors and the hair. Pretend to be asleep yourself, but then wake up brandishing both and shouting that you have just had a terrible dream in which he was Samson to your Delilah.

He's got a mullet
Time to give him the hook! No one looks good in a mullet, modified or otherwise.

He's got a Mohawk
He's either in a very avant-garde band, or he's left over from the Sex Pistols. The first possibility is good, so leave it. The second one is bad, and so claim loads of experience with hair and offer to give him a home trim and get rid of the ridge.

His hair looks just like David Beckham's
If the rest of him does too, you have no problem except getting to the mirror. Just hope he goes along with Beckham's many hair moments.

He's got a number two clip on a head that should be always covered
Buy him a beanie, a hooded sweater, a tea cosy, anything to keep phrenologists away from his skull and its bumps.

He's only twenty-seven and he's heading for a serious comb-over
Honesty is a wonderful thing in a relationship. But ridicule has its place too and this is it. Send his grandpa up rotten, and say how much you admire your loved one because he is too smart to fall for that nonsense. And encourage him to get a Brutus cut — all short and brushed forward, so he can't weave it strand by strand across his pate.

22
Care and maintenance (on-going)

Giving a man a wardrobe makeover can have many benefits. For a start, he will no longer have a tendency to look like one of the homeless or a superannuated homeboy, the loser in a fight, a jail escapee, one of the sartorially confused or even an unbuttoned leather sofa in the style of Shane Warne in mufti. It is both amusing in the short-term and rewarding: you will be able to take him out in public without fear of humiliation.

There can, of course, be considerable drawbacks. The principal problem is that the now-spruce object of your desire might somehow think that you are now responsible not only for his new image, but its on-going care. Every little thing that goes awry with his wardrobe will be down to you. Buttons, for instance. Broken zips. Trouser hems which are coming adrift or need to be taken up. (This is tricky. No man likes anyone to know he's too short for his pants. It's something best left between a man and his tailor, not admitted to the relationship between a man and his girlfriend, lover or wife.)

> *If it be our clothes alone which fit us for society, how highly we should esteem those who make them.*
> MARIE EBNER VON ESCHENBACH, 1830–1916

The User never allows herself to be turned into a needlewoman. In times past, to be accomplished, an unmarried gel had to sew a fine seam, play the pianoforte, speak a second language and be competent in the art of watercolours. But those days are gone and these days, his stuff is his stuff. If your bra goes mental thanks to a twisted piece of underwire, or needs to have the hook or the eye stitched back in shape, do you hand it over to him with a helpless expression on your face, in the hopeful expectation that he will somehow mend the bend?

Do you, like him, shove an offending garment in the mending basket to remain not so much an article of clothing as an article of faith, until some miracle somehow, sometime, resurrects it? I should say not. So what makes him think you have the skills of an Edwardian housekeeper, or any inclination to get out Granny's wooden darning egg and start running repairs?

> *Through tattered clothes, small vices do appear;*
> *Robes and furred gowns hide all.*
> KING LEAR, WILLIAM SHAKESPEARE, 1564–1616

Let's consider my second fiancé. The relationship was going along nicely until, after a sleepover, I found him in the hallway outside my bathroom. Wearing a mystified expression and not much else, he was closely studying a shirt. I recognised it immediately, since this was the very same cream shirt I had picked out for him on our last trip to Men's Heaven clothing shop. I had washed it (by hand!) the night before and ironed (!) it so he could go to work and not look like something the cat had coughed up or as if he had been out on the prowl all night.

I was feeling particularly pleased with myself, but he was almost shaking with rage as he brandished the slaved-over shirt in my face. He was shouting that there was a ring around the collar. His ring, his collar, it so had nothing to do with me, I reasoned in the split second before I laughed. Too late, I knew he was serious. That was the ruination of a day that had started very well indeed.

Pop quiz: so what would a smart User have done?
1 Apologised and promised such a laundry lapse would never happen again.
2 Removed the offending shirt and magically produced another in pristine condition.

3   Given him the address of the nearest one-hour dry cleaner.
4   Thanked him for coming, and ushered him out the door.

In the relationship with fiancé number two, I was in serious danger of being used, not the User. I might just as well have had 'doormat' tattooed across my forehead. In choosing both a and b, I was effectively at the beginning of the end of this relationship — unfortunately not before I got a really bad case of housework hands from all that hand-washing and scrubbing.

The correct answer, of course, is 3. The ongoing care of a man's wardrobe is a matter between him and the professionals. That might also include his mother or his granny (who might very well see a thirty year old leaving his dirty clothes in a trail from the front door to the back as a clear and caring invitation to express their love for him), the local dry cleaner, or even the neighbourhood hire-a-wife agency.

> *Women's styles may change,*
> *but their designs remain the same.*
>   ANON.

But apart from helping to choose and then superintending the survival of the fittest, and the things that fit best, his clothes should have little to do with you. Nothing kills sexual passion faster than becoming involved with a man's socks. (And sometimes, even his toes. Though occasionally the glimpse of white, hairy foreleg between sock and trouser bottom can do it as well.)

In fact, wardrobe can make or break a relationship. In the beginning, you tend to see a man dressed for work, at dinner — or naked. The suits are fabulous, he looks great when he's trying to impress you over dinner and you really like the look of him when he's undressed and ready for bed. But what if you don't like the look of him when he's off-duty and dressed? Does he spend time after-hours in the land of ghastly leisurewear?

Sometimes, time and circumstance mean that you might not actually see a single man in his less-than-well-dressed moments until it's too late. You're hooked, and he's as happy as a clam without the smallest idea that anything is wrong at all.

Will, one of Kira's boyfriends, was in the military, and that uniform kept her interested for months longer than the relationship fundamentally deserved.

'When we met at drinks, he was wore a suit and he looked really, really nice. We were going to the theatre with mutual friends, and we just clicked,' said Kira. 'I thought he was sweet, but wasn't really over the moon about him.'

A couple of days later, Will asked Kira out for dinner. 'We were to meet at the restaurant, because he was working late and was going to change in the barracks and come straight to see me. As it turned out, he had to work later than he'd planned, and didn't have time to change.' Was it luck or good judgment? Will isn't a calculating man, so it probably was a happy accident. 'I couldn't believe it when he walked in, five minutes late, apologising. He looked incredible.'

Sucked in! Kira was captivated by the oldest trick in a man's arsenal, the seducer's sure fire outfit, the uniform. (It works for women, too. Nurses' uniforms and schoolgirls in gym tunics are staples of soft porn. I know this because I looked — though I don't know if those white lace, stay-up stockings that those 'nurses' wore to minister to the sick and help doctors with quite odd bedside manners are quite regulation issue.)

Kira's on-going problem was that Will was always in a rush and never found time to change from his uniform. When she wasn't with him, she had some difficulty tearing her imagination away from even the thought of him in his khakis, or out of them. Just when Kira thought she was over both him and his everyday khakis, Will moved the temperature up a notch and appeared in front of her in his dress tunic. Then, it was the formal mess kit. That escalation of battle dress, his major's pips, and the fact that Will spent a lot of time interstate, was good for another six months of romance.

Then two things happened. She saw him in his off-duty clothes for the first time. 'I don't know where Will shopped, or what he was thinking when he did, but I have never seen so many polyester shirts of so many colours and designs in my life,' she recalled. 'They were beyond awful. A cab driver in Rangoon might have pulled off this look, but anyone else would only manage to appear as though he should be admitted to an institution devoted to the correction of terminally bad taste.'

Here's the thing: you have to see them out of their normal camouflage and in their play clothes quick smart. Then you might be able to make some sort of considered decision about whether you just want to spend six hours on a sweaty mattress with them, or if there is the possibility of something rather more long term. You can save time and problems later if you cast a quite hard eye over any new prospects right from the start.

And there's a footnote: be very careful if you meet a man wearing a dinner jacket (this goes double if he's a waiter), white tie and tails or a tuxedo. These outfits are complete traps, designed to render women senseless for hours. (This does not include dinner jackets in any colour apart from black, or worn with any accessory that's in the same colour. The full effect of the Technicolour dinner suit, cummerbund and tie with matching ruffled shirt is the territory of sad club singers.) If you find yourself being carried away by a man wearing formal wear, retire gracefully to the ladies room and have a little lie down until the mood passes. If he's wearing evening clobber he actually owns himself, you might need to have a little brandy.

If the man you have your eye on went to a boarding school or was in the armed services, you really have your work cut out for you. Somehow, in large groups of men in uniforms, the gene for knowing which clothes work and which should be in the ragbag is never developed. (No woman around to impress, perhaps, and no one who might flinch when they turn out in their oldest, grottiest duds.) All I can say to you is — good luck, *mon brave*!

23
Tattoo, you?

Let's move on the funk. Some men smell. First, there is the problem with halitosis. That's generally easily fixed but if it's not, his bad breath is probably the sign of some serious internal problem, and he would be glad if you mentioned it and didn't allow him to live in blissful ignorance of his disorder right up until the time he died in terrible pain of something major like a strangled bowel. (Or is that only horses? They've got shocking breath too, though it's not as bad as camels. But we're a little off the path. You'll never be puckering up for a camel. And not, with any luck, for a camel driver, either.)

Solution? A battery of chemicals in the bathroom — toothpaste, floss, mouthwash, Tic Tacs, breath fresheners — anything to make sure the ring of confidence extends past the teeth and to the gums themselves.

> *Tobacco is the tomb of love.*
> BENJAMIN DISRAELI, 1804–1881

Then there are the pits. Sometimes, your relationship can just be them. Other times, it can founder in them — his armpits. (It can be particularly bad if the man you have chosen has not stuck to the straight and narrow and kitted himself out in natural fibres. Synthetic fabrics trap body odour fast and keep on delivering it for months.) It is extremely unlikely that a User would be keen on a man who smells. The chemistry probably wouldn't allow a relationship to start — but it is possible.

There are still some men in the world who think that the smell of the male pheromone makes women swoon with desire. In Western Europe in the not-too-distant past, men stuffed hankies into their armpits so that the fabric could soak up the sweat and the stench. Then, once the kerchiefs were well primed, they would smack these supposed aphrodisiacs over the noses of unsuspecting girls, who would undoubtedly swoon but more from fear and the gut-wrenching odours than anything else, you'd think.

Solution? No synthetics in his clothes. And once worn, they're in the wash. Dry them in direct sunlight. Anti-perspirant deodorant. An anti-moisture powder to stop the problem at the source. Shave his armpits when he's not watching. (Not recommended.)

Tattooed fool?

There is nothing like a good tattoo — the kind in Edinburgh that incorporates blokes in kilts with brass bands. Tattoos, which require blokes with sharp instruments in tattoo parlours, are, however, beyond the pale on males and females unless you are a tribal Maori warrior celebrating the anniversary of the Treaty of Waitangi. If tattoos are not part of your warrior culture, leave them right out, particularly if you are hoping to make a romantic alliance of any consequence with someone. Besides, how would you explain this trend for body decoration to your mother, when she equates body graffiti with prostitutes, Yakuza gang members and repeat offenders?

Think about it: what kind of people do you see inside tattoo parlours? Moreover, why would anyone want to deface the covering of his or her temple? There are, however, some pretty impressive A-listers among the tattooed — junior media magnate Lachlan Murdoch, for instance, and his wife, supermodel-turned-actor and knicker-flogger Sarah O'Hare. Note they are grown-ups and can do as they please, even if what they please is pretty daft. They also have enough money to have those tattoos lasered off properly when they get tired of them. Some other celebrity tattoos are in the process of erasure — starting with Roseanne and moving on to Cher.

> *... Ever to be fashionable is ominous, since it afterwards must always be old-fashioned.*
> GEORGE SANTAYANA, 1863–1952

Body decoration is not new. And it *can* look extremely fetching. It was useful to the Picts, who were among the earliest recorded people who liked to paint their bodies, for frightening the enemy and recording life-changing moments. (Just to fill you in, the Picts' enemies, the ever-literal Romans, had started to refer to them by the end of the third century as the *Pictii*, from *picturare* meaning to paint. These Picts were the aboriginal inhabitants of what is now known as Scotland, and included several tribes in the area at the time: the *Caledonii*, the *Scotti* (paradoxically an Irish tribe), and the *Britanni*. After the seventh century the history of the Picts faded to black and they were not alone among Britannic tribes in painting themselves blue. It was woad from go to whoa for these colourful chaps. But all of that history is absolutely no excuse for tattooing these days.)

Who else looks good in a tatt outside a Polynesian and a tribesman from ancient Scotland. Mmmm. Let's think. Did Paula Yates? Does Chopper Read? Dennis Rodman? Okay, that would be no one. A really smart User is not going to have the loved one's name tattooed over any part of her skin. You never know when you might need to change the name to keep up with current trends, and it will be quite a struggle to change the name Dimitri to Jim, as many a nice Greek boy will tell you.

Solution? His mother should have stopped him early on. Now, you'll just have to make an appointment to have them lasered off — and that is not a cheap option. If he's talking about getting a tattoo, hang images of Angry Anderson around the place, or Ozzy Osbourne. Those two would be enough to put anyone off.

> *No self-made man ever did such a good job that some woman didn't want to make a few alterations.*
> F. MCKINNEY HUBBARD, 1868–1930

The same goes for body piercing. This is something the User restricts to her own ears and then only because earbobs are becoming quite expensive. Early in our relationship, my second fiancé asked what I wanted for Christmas. I thought aquamarines weren't very expensive, so I asked for them in a pair of earrings. Turns out they were both very expensive and difficult to find, so he bought me a pair of diamond ear studs instead. (Good boy! Very good boy!) But when I unwrapped them on Christmas morning, it was obvious these sparklers required a sacrifice. They were for pierced ears.

In short order, we went to a chemist somewhere in town, with him pushing me into having the piercings done. I heard him saying 'this won't hurt a bit', and then a tremendous bang next to my head and a shocking pain. Then the same thing happened on the other side. When I looked around, I was surprised to discover that, apart from the piercer, I was alone. Fiancé number two had fled, the sound of his footsteps muffled by the second explosion of the stud gun. (It was an insight into what might happen later. After that, every time we talked about having children, I could imagine myself alone in the delivery room while he was running down a hospital corridor, covering his ears and humming to himself.)

This brings us to jewellery on men. The User will see the presence of jewellery on a male as an indicator of how she has to manage him, with a view to future usage. The boring rule is that properly dressed men wear only a watch and cufflinks during the daylight (even a wedding ring is only grudgingly accepted in some quarters, though a signet with the family crest incised is always *comme il faut*). Having removed the watch, a man can add studs (gold, pearl or precious stones) to a pristine, starched white shirtfront for night. Full stop.

> *Kissing your hand may make you feel very very good but a diamond and safire bracelet lasts forever.*
> GENTLEMEN PREFER BLONDES, ANITA LOOS, 1891–1981

However, if the man you have in your sights for the moment wears chains and rings and earrings, you should consider the question: will any of these sparklers look good on you? If none would, you might need to consider whether you should be investing any more time in this guy. Men in jewellery all tend to look like members of rapper Ice T's bodyguard — not a good thing at all.

Solution? If he's wearing too much jewellery for you, borrow as much as you can as often as you can. It's a small sacrifice to make for a loved one. Pray for a break-in at home to make it disappear. Look downcast when he tells you the contents insurance had lapsed. If you 'misplace' it, wait some time before you have it reset and be prepared to have a good explanation about where your new bauble came from.

troubleshooting

24
Time out

Every so often, the accomplished User needs to get a man out of her sight — or even out of the house. (Can be a bit tricky if it's also his house. You might plead cramp and look like you might start to elaborate — that always makes men a trifle queasy and they start looking for the door.) Getting them out is not necessarily a malign event, or even an eviction (though sometimes that's necessary as well), but it can be essential, particularly if you want to maintain the creative tension in a relationship.

Remember, no one should ever see you doing the stuff you do when you hope that no one is around to see you. This might include, for example, giving yourself a beauty makeover, complete with oatmeal mask (something no sensitive creature should ever be exposed to the sight of, so close your own eyes while you do it) and olive oil treatment for the hair, or cleaning out your shoe cupboard. He could only be astonished and then horrified by the number of, what appear to him to be exactly the same, pairs of navy shoes that materialise.

(This lack of ability to discern subtle differences is often cited by scientists when they try to explain why men never seem to see the amount of housework which is waiting to be done, or why to them a sitting-room always looks pretty neat, when in fact to you it looks as though a marauding horde of Vandals has just swept through. This can, of course, sometimes come in very handy, because when he asks you if a particular shirt of yours is new, you can tell him he's seen it loads of times before and he'll believe you because he's apparently not genetically programmed to distinguish fine detail.)

The User knows it's also a good thing to spend one day apart regularly — for his sake, as well as for your own sanity. Absence truly does make the heart grow fonder so make sure you are absent as often as you can. It also means one day without his wondering if you know where his favourite sweater is (just one second: since it's *his* favourite sweater, why should you be tracking it?), or making you feel like you are the gatekeeper of all knowledge. It will be one day in which you can be secure that if you put something down, it will be there when you return to it. Tell him none of this though; insist it's for his health, that it will keep your relationship fresh and then send him out to play. A day apart can also mean that your relationship might actually survive the pressures that are naturally, in the course of everyday life, heaped upon it.

> *The right way to fight a woman is with your hat — grab it and run.*
> JOHN BARRYMORE, 1882–1942

This is a lesson Anastasia took some time to learn. She resented the time her friend Mr T (for Terrible, not Terrific, as it turned out) used to spend on sport at the weekend. 'He thought of himself as an all-round sporting hero,' she said. 'And he was — if there was something active to do, he would do it. The morning after my twenty-seventh birthday, when to say I wasn't feeling well would be a profound understatement, he dragged me out of bed after two hours sleep and had me on the golf course by 8 am. Not funny. It should have been a sign that he was verging on the sadistic, but I was too hung over to recognise it as one.

'I can't tell you the number of times I caddied while he knocked balls around in the rough. And not only did he play sport, he watched sport. He'd arrive at my place to take me out, and the next thing, he'd be on the sofa with a drink in his hand watching whatever sporting program was on. He'd settle in for hours. The only good thing about it was that at least the cricket seemed to keep him sedated. As a result, though, the sex life was nil.'

After what felt to her like the dating equivalent of the 100 Years War (but was, in fact, probably only three) the relationship came to an end. Now however, in retrospect, Anastasia came to understand a thing or two about men and sport. 'Now, if a man says to me he's going to the beach for a surf, go for a sail or to play eighteen holes of golf, I think yippee, that'll give me at least a whole morning to myself. When he wants to take me, and I don't want to go, I just make some excuse and cry off.'

> *Seek home for rest,*
> *For home is best*
> GEORGE TUSSER, 1524–1580

Anastasia had finally discovered the advantage of dating a man with outside interests. She had gone past the point when she couldn't bear to have the loved one out of arm's length for more than a moment, and was in the stage when a woman recognises that sometimes a man has to do what a man has to do, and that's got nothing to do with her. Users know that while he's out doing that secret men's stuff, she can be suiting herself completely, away from being monitored!

And that's where the shed comes in. John Gray in his Mars and Venus books talks about the tendency of men to retreat metaphorically to their caves. Like cavemen of old, he argues, they find these spaces reassuring, defensible, warm and their own. The modern-day Australian equivalent of a cave is the shed. And failing a stand-alone shed in the garden, a space under the house or away from the daily domesticity in which a man can have his own things and do exactly what he pleases.

Once you've seen the power of the shed in action, you long for one for your Everyman. My Dad, for instance, would retreat to his workshop downstairs. You have never seen such a collection of tools, but then he was an engineer and happiness to him was a vice attached to a strong bench. He would reappear some time later, having made something. A cedar bedstead? No problem. A turned sidetable? Ditto. (He had a seemingly endless stockpile of cedar and was excited whenever more fell into his hands. Didn't mind a bit of silky oak, either.) He even built a dinghy and then laid the keel for a half-cabin cruiser down there.

When he wasn't downstairs in the workshop, he was in the garage, stripping the car, giving it a service, fixing anything that needed fixing. The only problem with having such an accomplished handyman in the family is that it quite spoils you for anything less, and I find men who don't come equipped with their own full toolboxes very hard to take seriously.

The shed offers the User various benefits apart from the goods and services that emanate from it. For instance, if you install a TV in there, you might never have to listen to the football again. Equally, you will never be expected to clean up in there — you might accidentally put something in the wrong place. Also, if you are the mother of sons, you can send them into the shed as well, for a little male imprinting and father-son bonding. If you have a literary mate, you can send him off to the shed to write a classic — that's where Roald Dahl created his.

The shed, however, has some competition when it comes to an object that provides a man with loads of quiet fun and pleasure. The other object is one every User learns to admire and never to clean — the barbecue. It can keep them busy and happy for hours. Suddenly, under the benign influence of a barbecue, a man who has hitherto never demonstrated the slightest interest in cooking anything becomes the Escoffier of the spit. It is a modern marvel; so bless Barbecues Galore and their mighty Beefeaters for their efforts on the User's behalf.

There are also, the mobile forms of amusement — the car and the boat. Blokes and their machines can be a complete bafflement to even the most savvy User. There is a profound and complex relationship between man and machine which need actually never trouble you — unless you accidentally scrape the side of the car, or worse, involve it in a bingle. That's going to take some pretty fancy footwork and may involve sending yourself to remedial driving school.

Users never underestimate the value of the shed, the barbecue, the car and the tinny in a man's life. They are not rivals for his affection, but focal points for his attention. No need to be jealous, as the clever User knows. There are just so many things a jack and an anchor can do.

(And, as a footnote, you might like to make sure that the shed can be secured from the outside. That way, you always have the possibility of keeping him under lock and key and well out of harm's way. Make sure, though, that it remains only a possibility. The deprivation of someone's liberty is a crime.)

25
Love gone wrong

It's over. Can you tell? Some women seem to think that days, even weeks of silence, have no meaning in terms of the relationship. Here's a bit of a hint: to see what a man loves, see what he does. If he's keen on you, you'll know. He'll call, he'll take you out, he'll keep you in bed for days.

You might be able to seduce, trick or bully a man into a relationship just by always being there (few men seem able to resist propinquity,) but you are going to have to turn your back sometime. Ask yourself: if you are making the entire running, what's wrong with the picture? If you can't trust him, what is the point?

Cut these out and keep them on your fridge as an *aide memoire*:

- It's not happening if he's not calling you.
- It's not happening if he doesn't return your calls.
- It's not happening if you see him only at odd times and inside your house.
- It's not happening if you haven't met his family.
- It's not happening if he has a big work function and he doesn't ask you.
- It's not happening if you have had a sexual relationship, and it's now more suited to a couple after forty-three years of marriage than people who have only recently met and are yet to reach for the Vaseline.
- It's not happening if he is having a sexual relationship with someone else.
- It's not happening if he is remote and/or uncaring, distant, abusive, always in a bad mood and can never be bothered doing a single thing to please you.

Think how useful it would be, before any of the above happened, if men came with use-by dates. You could just check a barcode artfully hidden behind their ears to see if things were about to not happen. Think of the fun you could have reading it. There you will find the exact time when your loved one will no longer be good as a boyfriend (not serious), as part of a longer-term relationship (more serious) or as possible husband material — which should, of course, be a much longer period but, as anyone who has been married for only a matter of days knows, there are no guarantees in life.

For instance, Example A might be a sensational boyfriend for the first six months, but turn into a misery who could take a further six months of your time before you actually managed to extricate yourself. If you knew six months was going to be the prime time of your relationship, you could decide at the outset if you wanted to take this guy on for that period and then, as soon as he goes off, you could wave a fond farewell. Better than spending more months trying to shed, or an even more horrible thought, fix him.

> *Love is not love*
> *Which alters when it alteration finds,*
> *Or bends with the remover to remove,*
> *O no, it is an ever fixed mark*
> *That looks on tempests and is never shaken.*
>
> SONNET NO 116, WILLIAM SHAKESPEARE, 1564–1616

A use-by date could save so many dark and desperate nights as you tried to figure out what had gone wrong. There is simply no fixing a man past his use-by date — and you wouldn't have to feel guilty at all about saying, '*Hasta la vista*, baby!'

Men don't come with use-by dates because the technology doesn't exist which can tell you when a relationship with an otherwise great boyfriend, lover or husband is going to curdle. And can you imagine the fuss if you tried to get one of those barcodes on to a bloke when he was conscious? (Or even one of those little chips inserted into his ear, perhaps?)

That is a simple question to answer, but there are others in the same mode which are rather trickier — like the grenade lobbed into the conversation during a recent weekend at the beach. One of that gang of ruffians who pass for my godchildren asked me exactly where love went when it was over. I think she meant Love, with a capital L.

Wrapped around a good bottle of red and a series of sofa cushions, I was trapped. No studio audience, no lifeline, no dropping out of two of those choices, thanks Eddie. There we were with a relentless ten-year-old, and the opportunity to shape a young life forever. And it came down to one of Life's imponderables. Silence all round. 'Come on … tell her … Where does Love go to?' the on-lookers cried, and neither they nor the kid were about to settle for a 'Haven't got a clue. Sorry.' Or even: 'Why the Hell are you asking me?'.

Here's the only answer that was possible at the time: 'Back where it came from, I suppose.' It silenced the child, although the adults looked a little sceptical. I think that's right though. Love comes out of nowhere, and sometimes it disappears to the same place. It's about as easy a question for the User to answer as why some things last longer than others in the fridge and some men make better loved ones.

Running out of time?

In Italian, the word for the use-by date is *la decadenza*, which translates as 'decline'. Appropriately, it sounds like what happens in a relationship when a man goes past his use-by date. Here's the User's handy guide to the most durable fruit, vegetables — and men.

Is he a peach? Then look forward to a short season, once a year. Good through Christmas and summer, then nothing. Bruises easily. Goes wrinkly when chilled and kept too long. Men like this are young, seasonal and delightful as far as they go. Which is a couple of months. Enjoy while fresh.

Mango? Here is the first of three proofs of a living god. (The others are champagne and tuberoses.) He smells divine. Wonderful through the early summer. If left out in the sun too long after Christmas, can tend to become spotty and over ripe and then go off like the holiday turkey through January. Men like mangoes are heady and intoxicating and can be relied upon for an annual fling. If you like the taste, though, you can have it all year round. Just treat him right. (To enjoy the pulp throughout the year, freeze it into an ice-cube tray and drag it out whenever you feel the need for a mango daiquiri coming on.)

Apple? The apple guy can be deceptive. Can look perfect on the outside and be floury and yukky inside. The green ones can be immature and not worth biting into. Some are not really suited to fridge life — it can make them cold *and* bitter. However, those luscious new Japanese varieties hold up over time. Men like these are great to cuddle up with during the chill of winter. Maybe share an apple cobbler with one on a nippy evening. To keep them fresh all year around, keep them in a cool place and get them out whenever you feel the need to sink a fang into one.

Orange? Navels. Valencias. Mmmm … sunshine in a skin. Can last for weeks on the shelf without much trouble, but then suddenly come over all mouldy. Watch out — some can be more pith than flesh.

Pineapple? Can tend to be over-tart, rather like some men who stray into the 'too gay' part of the continuum from 'not gay enough' to 'just gay enough' then sheer foppery. Will keep for a while, but needs to be watched carefully so can be consumed at exactly the right moment.

Bananas? The perfect fruit, comes in its own ziplock bag. Let's avoid the sexual overtones but agree that a case can be made for either the Lady Finger (or Sugar) banana or the Cavendish. The first is sweet and a bit thick, the second long, thin, curved and tends to develop nasty black spots with age. Both are very good for you and should be taken regularly in season. Loads of potassium in here.

Zucchini? They win the award for the worst ever in the fridge. These vegetables can look for weeks as though they are doing really well, and then suddenly, when you decide it's their turn to jump into the pot, you go to pick one up and get a handful of slimy stuff. Erk. Same can go for squash, lettuce, celery. Men like these might look good for ages, but the rot set in some time ago.

Carrots? The hardiest of the vegetables in the fridge. Only problem is that they can be sooooo dull. Men who are like carrots — durable, non-limp — can also tend a bit to dullness. However, you can scrape bits off them, and they will be as good as new.

Time to say goodbye?

How you get out of a relationship depends on how long you have been in it, and whether or not you want to stay in touch, which really is a necessity if you have children in common.

Six weeks. If you are single, and have been seeing him for anything up to six weeks, you are still in the non-serious zone. You do not have to answer his calls, or reply to his text messages. And you don't really have to explain anything, though it would be neater and more polite if you did. You can use the phone.

Up to six months. You really do have to say something. You could identify differences in your approaches to the relationship, and say that you think a separation now will be better in the long run. You can do this by phone, but that's pathetic — do it in person.

Up to a year, but you are not living together. Go *Seinfeld* on this. Tell him it's not him, it's you, he deserves someone more committed to him, and you'll always have a special place in your heart for him. You could do this by snail mail or email, but if he would like a face-to-face meeting, you should probably say yes. He deserves this, at least. If you have doubts about how he will take it, ask a family member along to help mop up afterwards.

More than a year, or you are living together. It is not acceptable to leave the shared home without notice and take all the stuff with you (unless it's your stuff.) Except, and it is a pretty big except, if you think that he might be violent or abusive. If so, take a couple of burly friends as you move out and leave no forwarding address. Use of the fax machine is not acceptable: musician Phil Collins gained a worldwide reputation as a dudder when he dumped his former wife and the mother of his children via fax.

You are engaged. Apologise for having taken up his time (you will look gracious), and wish him well in the future.

You are married or living together with children. This is a life event that affects many people and needs to be addressed with care and understanding to get the best possible outcome. There are many examples of really bad behaviour in these circumstances, but among the saddest I heard of was the husband who came back from a business trip to find his house empty except for a single bed with linen, a portable TV, a cup, a plate, a spoon, a knife and a fork. He called his neighbours to find out what had happened and was told that she had moved the previous day. It turned out that his then-wife had discovered that he, a pillar of society, had been cheating on her. Humiliated, she planned over months to leave him. She said nothing, organised the move, told the children at the last possible moment, and abandoned him and their fifteen-year marriage. It was a pity about the kids, but she argued he should have thought about that earlier and not tomcatted around.

Better to leave an established marriage calmly and rationally, though that is not always possible. Let the lawyers talk about the money and debate the detail, while you carry on concentrating on the important thing — the family and how it manages its way through.

Want to drive a man away?

Follow this simple fourteen-point plan and blow him off!

1. Ambiguous and ambivalent — that's the way to go! Never say what you mean, except when you are certain he is not listening.
2. Sad or happy? Cry! Make sure you never tell him why.
3. Focus on the past, his or yours, with other lovers.
4. Make him apologise for everything, all the time.
5. Do what Anna Kournikova did to Mark Phillipousis — demand to be reassured about your looks twenty times a day.
6. Question everything. Don't forget to nag.
7. Be late — always — but complain when he is.
8. Make him guess what you want for your birthday. Get cranky when he fails to mind read.
9. Stand backward in front of the mirror. Inspect your bum. Announce you are fat. See how he gets out of this. Dislike all possible responses.
10. Criticise the way he dresses, the music he likes, and his friends. And then say you won't even start on his mother…
11. When asked, 'What's wrong?' tell him that if he doesn't know, then you're not going to tell him.
12. Tell him that if he loved you, he'd dance with you.

13 Blame everything on pre-menstrual tension, cramps, post-menstrual depression. Talk a lot about menstrual flow.
14 Ask him what he's thinking frequently. Particularly in the middle of the football. Men do so not love this.

26
The other woman

No, sorry, you cannot even begin to think about permanently eliminating the bitch. This is the sort of behaviour that could earn you a short moment of happiness and quite a long term in jail if you're successful. (The crime of passion is no defence in at all — with the possible exception of Sicily where it is almost compulsory. No matter what side of the man she is on, the betrayed User should appear completely insouciant about infidelity, while all the time planning her revenge. (For those who need a white board and a diagram to help deal with these complexities, that would be a diagram of the cuckolded partner looking at the mistress, or the mistress looking squintily back at the cuckolded partner.)

Alert the double-dealing husband/lover/partner to the fact that you are planning to even the score and that he should just expect it (whatever *it* is) when he least expects it. You need then do nothing more — although a slightly acid reference every now and then to his offence could help. He will spend the rest of your life together with the sword of Damocles hanging over his head, waiting for the moment when it finally crashes into his skull.

Both the betrayed partner and the mistress probably think that the other has the prime position, but they're both wrong. The person in a love triangle who benefits the most from it is — guess who? The man. Again. And the User should understand that she can never win. To stay in either of those positions, you'll need some pretty compelling reasons — which we will try to arrive at a little later.

> *A man should be upright, not be kept upright.*
> MARCUS AURELIUS, 121–180

However, first let's say that there are some women who become mistresses unconsciously. They can be going along merrily in life when they suddenly develop an interesting new boyfriend — or in Anastasia's case, a boyfriend who reappeared after more than five years apart. That's what happened when Anastasia met Joe again. He was still sort of handsome, he had most of his hair, he said he was single (never found a woman to equal her, is what he actually said, never stopped loving her), and he was keen to pick up where they left off. No matter that where they left off was her sobbing for a week over bottles of cherry brandy and old Dire Straits CDs. Anastasia was certainly ready to fall in love with him again. 'He was so familiar, we had a shared history, and I really felt that we had unfinished business,' she said.

There were a couple of hints that perhaps their relationship was not as straightforward as it might have seemed. There was the question of his home telephone number. 'He lived out of town,' said Anastasia. 'In the country. And he told he didn't have a home telephone. I didn't worry too much — I could always get him at work or on his mobile.'

> *Traditionally, sex has been a very private, secret activity. Herein perhaps lies its powerful force for uniting people in a strong bond. As we make sex less secretive, we may rob it of the power to hold men and women together.*
> THOMAS SZASZ, 1920–

There were other clues that might have indicated to Anastasia, had she been thinking properly, that Joe was leading a life which would have done credit to an ASIS double agent. Like his hours. 'He used to come to see me after work. And we hardly ever went out. We just had dinner, watched videos, then we used to go to bed. First, I thought it was a huge compliment that he wanted me to himself, but then I started to wonder why it was that we were always ordering food in and never actually appearing in public together.'

> *The chain of wedlock is so heavy that it takes two to carry it, sometimes three.*
> ALEXANDRE DUMAS, 1803–1870

Anastasia blames youth and inexperience for her incredible naïveté, which is why Joe was able to pull this off for so long. 'And then I started to wonder why it was that he never spent the whole night with me, that he always had to get up and go at 4 am on a Saturday morning. He said he had to go trout fishing with his father, but I never had a single fillet of fish out of him.'

It was fishy though and the warning bells should have been sounding loud and clear. (Any User with a fisherman for a lover will almost inevitably have a freezer stuffed with frozen fish and half-used packets of bait.) When Anastasia complained, Joe would take her out to early dinners — in remote, darkly lit restaurants where they never ran into anyone they knew.

You can guess the reason, of course. During those five missing years Joe had married, but he omitted to tell our Anastasia about the little woman and the two little children under four who were waiting at home for him. He had made her into the other woman without her knowledge or assent. 'When I found out, I freaked,' she said. 'I had left a bad marriage because my husband became involved with another woman. So when Joe cast me as the other woman in his own little love triangle, I took to that bottle of cherry brandy and kept playing soppy love songs over and over to myself for a week. It took about four weeks before I snapped out of the pathetic stage, turned off Dire Straits and started to get angry.'

> *False face must hide what the false heart doth know.*
> MACBETH, WILLIAM SHAKESPEARE, 1564–1616

When Joe eventually owned up to Anastasia, he said he would work things out. 'He told me that he had only done it because loved me and that he hadn't told me he was married because he knew I wouldn't have seen him. Finally, Joe and his wife separated. She blamed me, I know, for ruining her marriage. I had no idea. But she should have been pleased that no one was happy — things were never the same again for Joe and me. He had betrayed me once and I knew I would spend the rest of my life waiting for that to happen again. And I knew I could never allow a man who was so dishonest to be the father of my children.'

> *A liar is worse than a thief.*
> PROVERBS

The relationship eventually just fizzled out. 'I have to say that I am still amazed that I was so gullible, but I had never experienced that level of duplicity in my life, so why would I expect to have it from a man I loved and had planned to spend the rest of my life with?' And now? 'I still think he's weak and a sneak. I really feel sorry for him. He's probably the only one of my old lovers I can't speak to now.'

Anastasia had a lucky escape: she could have ended up spending a lifetime waiting for what had happened to Joe's first wife to happen to her. As British financier and arch *roué* the late Sir James Goldsmith once famously said, 'When a man marries his mistress, he creates a job opening.'

> *A mistress should be like a little country retreat near the town; not to dwell in constantly, but only for a night and away.*
> WILLIAM WYCHERLEY, 1640–1716

The role of the Other Woman has never had much kudos attached to it, unless she was the official *maitresse en titre* to a king. By necessity, less elevated mistresses are part of a secret life, an addition to a domestic arrangement that is rarely acknowledged in public. 'Other women' never get their lovers on the major holidays; they rarely spend holidays away with their lovers (unless those lovers are mega-rich and have their own planes), although they can have their birthdays with their lovers if the birthdays don't fall on important family dates. It seems a complete bore and yet some women not only go along with the plan, they embrace it. Some access to their loved one obviously seems better than none at all.

If you have a look at some of these men who are alleged to have 'mistresses', you will be amazed that they have managed to pull even one woman, let alone two. There's Prince Charles, of course, who famously betrayed Diana with

Camilla Parker Bowles (when she found out, years later, Di put the cuckold's horns on Charles apparently, with Major James Hewitt), but Charles's appeal might have something to do with the Crown Jewels.

> *But love is blind and lovers cannot see
> The petty follies that they themselves commit.*
> THE MERCHANT OF VENICE, WILLIAM SHAKESPEARE, 1564–1616

Have a look at a couple of other cheats. Famously, French president François Mitterand's mistress and youngest daughter were an open secret in Paris for years, but they were never publicly acknowledged, and they made their first 'official' appearance over his catafalque with his legitimate family — very Gallic. And President Bill Clinton regularly exposed his wife Hillary to embarrassment when his womanising ways were revealed in the press through a range of big-haired, air-headed bimbos from Gennifer Flowers to Monica Lewinsky.

But back to Anastasia, who is familiar with both sides of the story. Before she started to see Joe again, she had been married to a man who had cheated on her. So which position is easier? 'Neither, they both have bad outcomes,' she said. 'It's all about betrayal, and I always thought that was unforgivable. My husband wanted us to have therapy and work on the relationship, but I could not continue to be involved with a man who was a liar.' (Instead, she started work on her selection skills.)

Some women — not generally, it must be said, intelligent Users — continue in relationships with married men. Some wives come to terms with their husbands' extra-curricular activities. Those women are either saints, who have managed to work through their own hurt and anger and have found the truth in the old saw that sex is a very bad reason to go into a relationship and one of the worst to get out of one, or perhaps they stay for the sake of their children. Then again, maybe they are just stupid.

There are some notable exceptions to the rule, of course.

Famously, Edwina Mountbatten, wife of the last Viceroy of India, Lord Mountbatten of Burma, conducted an open marriage. (Among her reputed suitors was the first Indian Prime Minister Nehru, which must have made negotiations for the sub-continent's independence between the two men piquant to say the least.)

And equally, married women in France and Italy can take a pretty broad view of a husband who has mistresses. There seem to be benefits all round for them. They hold the position as wife and mother, and while they might be betrayed sexually, they retain their positions within the family and social units. (It might also sometimes suit them to be relieved of their husbands' sexual attentions, too.) The husbands have their little *cinq-à-septs* (five to sevens — named after the period in the afternoons between work and home), in which they entertain their lovers. It's not at all a modern phenomenon: the Latins can apparently distinguish between love and sex and have acted accordingly for years.

The other, willing, woman

Sometimes, this is the easy position to find yourself in. You're busy with a career, you're working hard. Things on the relationship front are not going so well. You work with someone who is attractive, kind, interesting. You go for lunch with him, a drink. He's a mate, he understands. You start a flirtation.

> *Merely innocent flirtation,*
> *Not quite adultery, but adulteration.*
> DON JUAN, LORD BYRON, 1788–1824

And that's the start of an affair. That's what happened to Madeleine. She had been married for a few years to a man who was consumed with his job. 'There were obvious advantages for us. We loved to travel, we had a lovely house. The down side was that Rob travelled a lot and he wasn't home that often,' says Madeleine now. 'Our sex life was irregular at best and non-existent most of the time.'

Madeleine worked at a television station, in a busy on-air unit. 'Tom was the head of the department. He was really kind and very funny. It seems like such a cliché, but after a farewell at the pub for one of the staff, he offered me a lift home. We'd been having a flirt, but I thought there was nothing to it because Tom was married, with three children.'

When he drove her home, Tom asked to come in for a coffee. 'Rob was away, but it didn't worry me. Of course, I asked him in. I was making the coffee in the kitchen and Tom followed me. I'll never forget, I was standing in front of the sink and he came up behind me.' In that moment, Madeleine wasn't thinking about her husband, his wife, just the fact that a man she fancied obviously fancied her too. 'It was so unexpected. And so sexy. I felt right for the first time in a long time.'

The next day at work, Tom behaved as though nothing had happened, and Madeleine decided that it had been a moment of madness that would never happen again. She was wrong. Soon, they settled into a twice a week routine, more often if they both stayed back after work and could find an empty edit suite. 'I loved it. I loved having sex with him in his car. It was a little dangerous, but it was thrilling too.

> *A man in love is incomplete until he is married. And then he is finished.*
> ZSA ZSA GABOR, 1916–

'I knew Tom wouldn't leave his wife. And I still loved Rob. But there was something so exciting — the possibility of being caught, the secrecy of it — about having an affair with him. Tom and I talked about it, and he was happy for it to remain an office romance. But I was worried about his wife finding out. I knew I could keep it away from Rob, but Tom was hard to predict. If his wife had accused him of seeing someone, he probably would have confessed.'

Madeleine broke off the affair after seven months and has never told Rob. 'I suppose I have always thought that owning up was selfish, that it was my decision to sleep with Tom and I had to live with it. I couldn't see any good come out of a confession, so it's just a shared piece of romantic history for me and Tom.'

Would she do it again? 'No, never. It happened, and that was that. I'm not proud of it. I regret it. But equally I'm not going to torture myself forever because I was stupid. Some people might think I got away with it, but in a way I didn't. I know that I am capable of deception and that doesn't make me feel comfortable.'

And she thinks the price she would pay for honesty would be too high. 'I can't ask him to forgive me just to make me feel better about my choice to sleep with Tom.'

What if someone told Rob about the affair? 'I would just deny everything.' Would he believe her? 'He would decide to, I think. Rob and I are good together.' And what if he decided to have an affair? 'I'd live with that but I still wouldn't throw what I did in his face as some sort of revenge.'

Why be the other woman?

You are a simple fool like Anastasia and you have no idea that the man you are dating is married.

You are a lonely and a little bored, like Madeleine. And he's there and willing.

You are a masochist. You love spending all the major holidays alone. You enjoy trying to explain to your family that your boyfriend is, unfortunately, away again, visiting his family in Brunei/Brisbane/Brussels.

You need therapy, not a boyfriend as you really believe his wife doesn't understand him.

You are in love and the tragedy is that it's with such an unworthy individual — a man who deceived the wife he promised to love, honour and cherish, presumably in front of family and friends. What makes you think he won't do the same to you? He told you he loves you? Right…

You're frightened of being alone. You think he's the only boyfriend you will ever be able to find and have no idea that sometimes none at all is miles better than a bad one.

He pays all your bills. He's as rich as Croesus, takes you on overseas holidays a couple of times a year and gives you lavish gifts. Would you prefer to be called a gold-digger, a courtesan, or a mistress? Remember, hearts are expected to be loyal, while money is not.

What should you do about the other woman?

Nothing. Even though you might want to strangle her with your bare hands for the heartbreak you're suffering, and the harm done to your family, she's not the one who broke the terms of your relationship. Your partner did. Place the blame at the feet of the man who earned it. Or throw it at his head.

What should you do about your cheating boyfriend, lover or husband?

Kill him, metaphorically speaking. He should be as someone dead to you. Make sure you get him out of your arrangements very smartly, though not before you give the rat a full character reading. Feel free to continue these assessments whenever you see him. (But not in front of any children. You wouldn't want to ruin their relationship with their father when he's perfectly capable of doing that himself.)

If you decide to forgive him, think very hard about what you want from life and wonder how does a man who can betray you fit into your revised plans. And if you do forgive him, you can never throw the aberration in his face again.

If you think that it is worthwhile, then try to preserve the marriage. It's not necessarily the smartest User option, but it might just be yours — particularly if you have children.

strategies

27
Say a little prayer for him?

So, you've been trying to use your man for fun and profit, you've read the histories of women who were successful Users and those who needed to go to remedial classes, and it's still not going so well?

What can you do? First, don't panic. As they say, Rome wasn't built in a day (actually it was built in about 2,755 years, give or take) and a great User isn't made in a day either, although you might like to see your conversion to prime User happen sometime before you have to start going blonde to cover the grey.

However, when the User's skills seems to be delayed in developing (if not materialising at all), you could turn to the metaphysical for a little assistance and ask yourself the question: if all else fails, is it time for the big guns — a little divine intervention?

If the answer is yes, then your first stop could be Mary, the Mother of God. It's in the interest of the BVM (Blessed Virgin Mary) to help out. She is, after all, the patron saint of women, the family and all those other fundamental elements of society. (She's also an equal opportunity sort of woman and would be sympathetic to the pleas of anyone — Muslim, Hindu, Jew — in extreme need.)

You will have to be careful what you are praying to the BVM for, since it is hardly likely she would intercede on behalf of anyone who just wanted a one-night stand. She's the port of call for the User who has heard the biological clock, whose intentions are honourable, and who is aiming at the procreation of children within the safety and the sanctity of marriage (and there's the rub). If it's a night of unbridled passion and meaningless sex you are after, then don't rely on the BVM.

If your search is for someone to help you in your quest to become the complete User, however, try to find a more broad-based blessed bod. Finding one might not be not easy, since most of the female saints celebrated in the calendar died virgins. However, here are some suggestions.

Agnes. In the early fourth century, Agnes declared she would have Christ for her heavenly bridegroom, and no one else. Despite her wealth and beauty, she was murdered at the age of thirteen when she declined to renounce her faith and marry an earthier sort of fellow. Here's a saint who knows about suffering.

Agatha. If you think you've had bad boyfriends, spare a thought for poor St Agatha. Young and beautiful like Agnes, she was installed in a brothel by a thwarted suitor, then had her breasts cut off before she was racked and thrown on to burning coals. Also someone who appreciates suffering.

Barbara. She refused to marry her father's choice and was sentenced to death by her bloodthirsty old man. Just as the fatal blow was about to be struck, a bolt of lightning crackled out of the sky and smote (appropriately Biblical) her bad dad on the scone. That was the end of him. Saint Barbara is, not surprisingly, the patron saint of the infantry.

Cecilia. Eventually the patron saint of music, she vowed herself to chastity, which must have come as something of a surprise to her Roman husband, Valerianus. Ever accommodating, he said he would respect her wish if an angel confirmed it to him. Valerianus wasn't a Christian, so at first he wasn't allowed to see this angel bearing tidings of no great joy. Instead, he had to go to Rome and be baptised by Pope Urban I. When he got home, the angel of the Lord was waiting and presented him with a wreath of flowers — probably in remembrance of the death of his hopes.

Monica. In the fourth century, Monica was married to Patricius, who turned out to be a rather unsatisfactory husband. When she was forty, the deadbeat had the grace to die, leaving Monica free. The pious Monica, however, was more distressed by the dissolute life of her son Augustine (he was taking after his father, obviously) and cried rivers of tears over his sins. This same Augustine (the perfect illustration of Aphra Benn's aphorism that 'there is no sinner like a young saint') eventually converted to Christianity and turned into St Augustine. Not a bad result for Monica and the Church. Since she had such a breadth of understanding of life, St Monica might make a sympathetic intercessor for the modern User.

> *The only difference between the saint and the sinner is that every saint has a past and every sinner has a future.*
> OSCAR WILDE, 1854–1900

Margaret of Cortona. Here's the woman for today's Users, a saint who knew her way around a man. She was the live-in lover of a young nobleman who lived in Montepulciano (famous for its wines even then) for nine years, and bore his child. Disaster struck when he was murdered. Distraught, she was forced to return home to Cortona. After her father refused her assistance, the Franciscans took her in. She founded a community for women and a hospital for the poor. Margaret would be an understanding go-between for a woman keen on developing her skills as a successful User.

Jude. If you've prayed to the female saints to no avail, you could try your luck with the chaps. St Jude, the patron saint of lost causes, would surely lend a sympathetic ear to the desperate and dateless.

Anthony. Or speak to this very helpful saint from Padua who operates the celestial location service. I'm always on to him about anything from lost glasses to lost mobiles and remotes and he always comes through. So he might be good at finding a lost love, as well.

If the saints of the Christian pantheon leave you a little cold, go *wicca* and try the pagan deities. What about the ancient pagan goddesses who protected women? Try **Hathor,** the cow-headed Egyptian deity who was the goddess of joy and love (always a good start when you set out to use a man); and **Ishtar,** goddess of war and love (a recognition that sometimes it's hard to pull the two apart?) in Assyro-Babylonian mythology. If you fancy a Celtic interpretation, try the triple goddess, **Danu, Anu and Brigit,** a one-stop shop for aid. They are all deities of plenty, and also have a place in the Celtic fertility cult. Brigit, who managed to survive into the modern saints calendar as Saint Brigid, is also a deity of learning culture and skills. She is said to now share her grave with St Patrick at Downpatrick in Northern Ireland.

The smart User should also be in touch with her Classical World goddess within. But which one? Would you pick **Hera**, the queen of Mt Olympus, constantly betrayed wife of her brother/husband Zeus, who is the goddess in charge of marriage and maternity? Or the mighty **Aphrodite**, the goddess of sexual love? Or **Artemis**, the goddess of the moon, childbirth, and (less endearingly) sudden death, particularly among women? **Hestia** might also be good, if you are inclined to the domestic, since she is the goddess of the hearth.

I was hoping to find a little Athena, warrior-goddess, in me at the end of a www.iVillage.com quiz I found on the Web. Athena Nike is in charge of victory (without her, those up-market runner manufacturers would have had to hitch their marketing campaigns to another deity), intelligence, peace, and spinners and weavers. As you can see, this is a full-service goddess who busied herself across quite a diverse portfolio of interests.

The iVillage quiz was impossible to resist — after all, it offered the opportunity to attain quasi divinity in thirty days. First step, you must find out which of the seven — Athena, Artemis, Aphrodite, Hera, Demeter, Hestia or Persephone (daughter of the earth goddess Demeter and Zeus, though the details of the conception are mysterious) — you favour most.

The twelve questions are designed to quickly work out if you are obsessed with sex, status, or the interior life, or are bookish, home-oriented or self-sacrificing. The quiz stresses that your aim should be to achieve as much of a balance as possible — which means some of us might have to have several shots at the quiz to actually achieve some sort of equilibrium. But after three goes, I still missed two of the goddesses altogether: out for a duck regarding both Demeter and Hestia and that means zero points for the goddesses of the earth and hearth.

No need to worry though; it's possible to sign up for the Web course in how to work on those missing aspects, for example: 'Become a love goddess in thirty days'. Week one, reveal your inner beauty with Aphrodite (and there you were thinking sexual love was all about surface): week two, be more independent with Artemis. (Any more independence, and a lot of women I know will be going solo on expeditions to the South Pole, so perhaps you might need to be careful with this one.) So, I found my hidden goddesses: Persephone, Hera, Artemis, Aphrodite and the goddess of wisdom herself, Athena. Now, if only I could get more in touch with Athena, I could leave poor St Anthony alone.

Put a spell on him?

When it comes to managing men, no plan can be discarded as too way out. In the past, I have spent quite some time in the dark with a book of incantations, a pink candle and a small snap of the object of my desire, trying to work the mojo on him. The method was simple. I had to repeat his name over and over and assert that he would be in love with me by the end of the year, while singeing the edges of the picture. Since the photo was tiny to begin with, I ended up with a small, blackened square, burnt fingers and the firm belief that I would win his heart.

It didn't actually work, however, and I am lucky to have escaped. The dashing young man is a lawyer now. He's married with 2.3 children and not that long ago stood for a conservative political party in a local election. I just would not have had the nerve to cope with the requirements of his job as well as the demands of his dark and brooding personality. If you imagine TV's supervampire Angel without the laughs, you've got him.

However, if you are intent on dabbling with the dark arts, you could do worse than start with a fetish. These amulets and love charms, which can contain material as diverse as hair (pubic is best), nail clippings, bone, skin or sweat can be worn, slipped into drinks or even burned. (Just by the way, if you are close enough to a bloke have him by his pubic hair, then you would seem to have a walk-up start to using him.)

The blood of a man, taken from the little finger of his right hand and dropped into a woman's glass, is thought to make her fall head over heels in love with him. But in these days of sexually transmitted diseases, starting with Hep B and moving on to AIDS, you might want to think twice about allowing any man with a pin free access to your wine goblet.

Urine is also considered a potent love force. If you urinate into a man's shoe, according to a European folk tradition retold in Pamela Allardice's

Love Potions, he will be unable to resist you. If he finds out it was you who went in his shoes, though, it is more likely he'll be unable to resist giving you a piece of his mind.

Animal sacrifices are definitely out, but you could cook a little saffron into a cake (the saffron indicates that it's a sacrifice to whichever goddess you choose) and bolt it down.

20/11/2014

*Two lives,
two hearts
joined together
in friendship
united forever
in love.*

elegraph classifieds is your local source.

594-6555 · ClassifiedsNH.com

PETERS KIA of NASHUA

The Lowest Prices. Period.

200 CASH

November 30th.

2012 KIA SEDONA LX POWER PACK
- $27,200 MSRP
- -$2500 CUSTOMER REBATE
- -$1500 COMPETITIVE BONUS
- -$660 PETERS KIA INSTANT SAVINGS

28
The smart User's rules

1. Men are not women with penises, so never treat your man as you would a girlfriend.
2. If you want to share your life with someone you can talk to and tell your innermost thoughts to, make sure you maintain a good relationship with your mother and your female friends. A man is absolutely useless in this area. You might as well try to explain the compelling shades of white to them for all the effect you'll have. Equally, if you want unquestioning love and fidelity, get a dog. You'll never hear of your pooch dumping you for another woman.
3. If you want a man to be your soulmate, make sure a lot of the communication is non-verbal. You'll get into tremendous trouble if you try to articulate the bond.
4. Don't tell a man too much. It will just confuse him. Tell him things on a need-to-know basis, and then tell him again closer to the time. If you want to keep things secret, and he finds out you are keeping things from him, tell him you have already told him. Since men rarely listen to women, the chances are he will think you did and at that particular time he had turned on the white noise in his brain to filter out all in-coming intelligence from people with higher-pitched voices.
5. Don't tell a man something too often. He will think you are nagging. Tell him once as a preliminary then remind him. Twice is okay,

three times is once too often. If he's ignoring you after two attempts at communication, get used to it. It's obviously your problem, not his.

6 Sex is a very bad reason to go into a relationship for a woman, and one of the worst to get out of one. Make sure he's interesting enough to have a conversation with before you commit to having sex with him. If you discover after you've had sex with him for the first time that he could bore for Australia, just cut your losses and run. Sometimes, a one-night stand can just be a mercy fuck for you both.

7 Don't take him home to your place on the first date. Or the second. Or the third. Take a long hard look at him before you decide what you want. Make him wait. This is, of course, the basis of the Unified (Treat 'Em Mean to Keep 'Em Keen) Theory.

8 If the sex is lukewarm, and that's how you feel about him, get out while you can. What on earth are you doing spending any time with him? A kind User will put him back in the ocean for some other, more suitable woman to find. And he should be very grateful for this, and not turn into a stalker.

9 Smart Users know that good men are hard, but not impossible, to find. Consequently, they never do that hideous whining about how all the good ones are taken or gay. It's not true. You only need one at a time, and how hard is it to find one good man? You will have to be patient, and discriminating, while you are looking. Remember, you're in the market for a brand new Ferrari or a classic Rolls Royce, not a resprayed and second-hand Holden Kingswood.

10 Here is the best rule I ever heard, and it's one my mother told me when I was an adolescent and asking her about what to look for in a husband. This is what she said: you should look for four things with a potential life partner. First, you have to like him. Then, you have to love him, which is quite a different thing altogether. Next, you have to respect him — and that means he in return should respect you. And finally, the most difficult of the four — you have to admire him. If you've got that combination going, you've got the basis of a relationship that should be able to withstand whatever life brings to it. It also means that you become very, very picky about men — and the pickier you are, the more likely you are to find a man who is decent,

kind, caring, loving, respectful, intelligent and who really could be the smart User's Mr Right.

Some final instructions for Users in the new millennium

- If great love always involves great risk, you can minimise those risks by listening to your instincts.
- Where there's love, there's the risk of loss. Better to use than lose! But remember that not getting the man you want can sometimes be a wonderful piece of luck.
- Never forget the three Fs: flirtation, flattery and faking it (when necessary).
- Know the rules. Break them when appropriate.
- Do not let a little fight break up a good relationship. You could regret it forever. Sometimes that means you have to say sorry, even when you are not at fault.
- When you realise you have chosen the wrong man, take immediate steps. Either correct him or say goodbye — fast.
- While silence is sometimes the best answer to a man, muttering can also work.
- In a discussion with your loved one, live in the present. Do not bring up the past unless you have to.
- Be gentle with the earth ... the air, the fire, and the water signs. You never know where in the zodiac you will find a soulmate.
- In a healthy relationship, love exceeds need.
- Love and cooking both require recklessness. Try not to spill too much, because you'll probably be the one doing the mopping up.